UNSENT LETTERS

Also by Malcolm Bradbury

Fiction

Eating People is Wrong

Stepping Westward

The History Man

Who Do You Think You Are?

The After Dinner Game (television plays)

Rates of Exchange

Cuts: A Very Short Novel

Mensonge

Criticism

Evelyn Waugh

What is a Novel?

The Social Context of Modern English Literature

Possibilities

Saul Bellow

The Modern American Novel

No, Not Bloomsbury

The Modern World: Ten Great Writers

UNSENT LETTERS

Irreverent Notes From a Literary Life

by
Malcolm Bradbury

VIKING

VIKING
Published by the Penguin Group
Viking Penguin Inc., 40 West 23rd Street,
New York, New York 10010, U.S.A.
Penguin Books Ltd, 27 Wrights Lane,
London W8 5TZ, England
Penguin Books Australia Ltd, Ringwood,
Victoria, Australia
Penguin Books Canada Ltd, 2801 John Street,
Markham, Ontario, Canada L3R 1B4
Penguin Books (N. Z.) Ltd, 182–190 Wairau Road,
Auckland 10, New Zealand

Penguin Books Ltd, Registered Offices:
Harmondsworth, Middlesex, England

First American Edition
Published in 1988 by Viking Penguin Inc.

LIBRARY OF CONGRESS CATALOGING IN PUBLICATION DATA
Bradbury, Malcolm, 1932–
Unsent letters.
1. Imaginary letters.   2. Literature—Anecdotes,
facetiae, satire, etc.   3. Criticism—Anecdotes,
facetiae, satire, etc.   4. Authors—Anecdotes, facetiae,
satire, etc.   5. Authorship—Anecdotes, facetiae, satire,
etc.   I. Title.
PR6052.R246U57   1988   826'.914   87-40466
ISBN 0-670-82070-9

Printed in the United States of America by
Arcata Graphics, Fairfield, Pennsylvania
Set in Plantin and Bembo

To
Chris and Pam Bigsby

Acknowledgements

Some of the material in this book draws on pieces published in a number of magazines, including *Punch, The New Yorker, Mademoiselle, Spectator, The Times Educational Supplement, Sunday Times, Magazine,* and *Atlantic Monthly.* I have also drawn on my introduction to Laurie Taylor, *Professor Lapping Sends His Apologies: The Best of Laurie Taylor* (Trentham Books, 1986).

Contents

UNSENT LETTERS

Introduction

All through my writing life there have been many letters I have wanted to write. Friends who know me well will testify – in fact they frequently do – that I am not exactly a good correspondent, comparing badly, in this respect at least, with Lord Chesterfield, John Keats, Ezra Pound, Franz Kafka and indeed almost anyone else. This does not mean I never write letters. I do it all the time, but the trouble is I never write them *down*. The truth is that my head is full of letters – letters to go off here and there, about this and that, replies to my many correspondents, whether friendly or aggressive, political letters, philosophical letters, begging letters, fan letters, love letters, poetic letters, letters proposing remarkable financial or diplomatic transactions, state letters, letters to the living and letters – like those of Saul Bellow's admirable Moses Herzog ('Dear Nietzsche') – to the famous dead, letters to my dearest friends, and letters to people who have never existed at all (but are also, often, my dearest friends). What these letters mostly have in common is that they are unsent. They stay in my head, in their abstract, transcendental condition, for days, months or years, constantly being revised and improved over time. Admittedly, you cannot see them, but you cannot see the good or the true either, and it doesn't prove it's not there.

As I say, these letters are about a variety of topics, but quite a lot of them are literary letters. They are about art and creativity, research and scholarship, publishing and editing, earning a living and making a crust, writing for the market, writing for art, writing for television, writing for posterity. They are about writers' lives, and writers' wives, about great books projected and even greater books lost or fled. Some of them I have not written down because I could never send them, since they would cause upset and pain, and in reality I am a very polite and civil person, despite my failings in dealing with the correspondence. Some of them I have written down but still failed to send, such being my Yeatsian ideas of perfection and my belief that if they could just be put away in a drawer for a couple of months the style could be improved enormously. Some represent the mulish defiance, if not terror, of the author who confronts a large pile of post, along with the cornflakes, every morning, and realizes that a writer can either answer his letters or write his books, but probably not do both.

But why, now, should I suddenly sit down and start answering some of them? Perhaps it is out of respect for my postperson, who brings the sackful every morning, and whose load might be lightened if I can provide some answers, therefore meaning that people will ask me fewer questions. But I doubt it; I suspect letters simply breed letters. Perhaps, then, it is due to the onset of my middle years, which some unkind people might consider my later ones, and the need to get things a little straight. Or perhaps it is the acquisition of this very pretty word-processor, which – apart from the now permanent backache and the rapidly failing sight – has generally improved life no end, and certainly makes writing very much easier, except when it goes wrong. Possibly – though this explanation I greatly doubt – it is because I have realized that, thanks to my neglect in the past, there is precious little, if anything, to go into the great volume of my collected letters that will one day be conceived by some opportunist scholar and literary executor, after I have passed on, probably to Yorkshire.

Whatever the reason, here are my unsent letters, my literary letters. They may be less good than Keats's, less psycho-analytical than Freud's, less philosophical than Nietzsche's, less aggressive than Hitler's, less sensitive and aesthetic than Virginia Woolf's. But at least they are real letters, all written down on paper and properly addressed; and anyone who says I never write any at all will now have egg on his or her faces. Naturally, for the sake of understanding, I have tried to make them quite extensive; equally, for the sake of economy, I have tried to make them collective, representative and all-purpose. I think you will find they answer most if not all the queries you might possibly have of me, should you ever be thinking of dropping me a line. After all, I have tried to cover all the main areas – literary reminiscence and literary advice, some wisdom for literary neophytes and aspirants, who love a bit of wisdom if you call it creative writing, some sage academic reflections, a piece of amazing Nabokovian scholarship, and some broader glimpses of the academic world, in which I do happen to spend quite a portion of my so-called existence. You will also find advice on how to write plays for television, what linguistics actually means for all of us today, how to run a successful conference, and whether if you do I might or might not come and speak at it – all of those things, in fact, that you might have thought of asking me in a letter, and also some of the things I might have thought about asking other people. I'm sure it will prove, for one and all, an invaluable volume. To be frank, I do believe it will deal with everything, and at the same time spare me the trouble of ever having to do an autobiography. And, with a bit of luck, I may never have to write another letter again.

The Wissenschaft File

One of the letters I regularly receive in my large daily post is something I have come to call the Wissenschaft letter. It comes with a foreign stamp, and can be from Germany, France, Italy, Spain, Denmark or Greece – certainly one of the European countries where they study contemporary literature in a decidedly energetic and theoretical sort of way. The impressively headed stationery declares it comes from an academic institution. The often spidery handwriting suggests it comes from a student. There are a lot of letters in my Wissenschaft file, but most of them, excusing a pardonable exaggeration or two, tend to run something like this:

> Seminar für Englische Sprache und Kultur,
> Liebfraumilch Universität,
> Gewurztraminerstrasse,
> Rheingau 13,
> West Germany.

Dear Herr Doktor Professor Bradburg,

Excuse please that I address you so, but I think in your country you do not mind such informality. My name is Hans-Joachim Wissenschaft, and I am advanced student in Anglisten-Studien at Liebfraumilch University, with nice manners, rimless glasses and a small moustache. I have already passed the examens for my Arbeitsnachtrichen, my Fernspreche and my Hinauslehnen mit Pradikat, and I also have good competences in Philologik, Linguistik, Pedagogik, Psycho-Analytik

1

and Aerobik. Now I must write my thesis for my Habitat. Always I love very much your Englisch litteraturs, ever since as a boy I made holiday in Grimsby, and came to relish the distinct flavours of your country. My favourite authors are E. Waugh, A. Huxley and M. Python, and always I hoped to·make a thesis of their works. Unfortunately, this is not possible, because my famous professor, Frau Doktor Professor Brunehilde Zwischenprüfung (who tells you know her very well), likes it better that I write rather on the 'campus-novel', called also the 'university-novel', which is much studied in my country. I do not find this so easy because the subject does not interest me very much. But of course I take her advices, because as you know she is a very big lady and one day she likes to write a very big book on this subject. Also there are not so many jobs now, even in Germany, and I like to take a little care for my future. So now I am very pleased to make my thesis on this 'campus-novel', and I write for your helps. I think you will please to know I intend to make a special concentrate of your works!

What I like is to take your 'campus-novels' *Forbidden to Eat People, Step to the West* and *Der Geschichtsmensch*, and compare them with the works of your better competitors – as, Thom. Hardy, Max Beerbohm, J. I. M. Stewart, Thom. Sharpe, King. Amis, Howard Jacobson and David Lodge. Perhaps you know a lot more authors whose works compare very well with yours. If so, please quickly send their names, as I am an efficient person and like to write a very complete thesis. In fact I like your helps with my work as much as possible. I write to you with the urgence of Professor Zwischenprüfung, who tells that once you met together in Hamburg in a very exciting congress, which was greatly enjoyed by all present. Now she sends you her very best greeting, likes to remind you what a small world it is, and also that she lended you a small black folded umbrella that she now likes very much to have back, as it is raining here. She tells also that you are a good critic, but even so a very nice person who likes much to answer big questions. This is good because I have very many.

Please give all the helps you can, for certain things of your writings cause here a confusion. Perhaps you do not know it yet, but this type 'the campus-novel' does not really exist in Germany, I think because all our professors are very great scholars who write only very serious books, and have no need of such strange publications. For us 'campus-novel' is a very peculiar praxis, found only in Britain and small bits of the United States. Explain me this please. I know your professors are not so well paid – I have met some once and seen their very worn clothes – and must find other ways to survive. Yet this does not explain the representations of universities in these novels, which seem always wicked and dishonest. Does perhaps your government pay you to write these books to stop students attending your universities now with economic crisis you have no more places for them? I have also been told that many of these novels are in the tradition of humoristic satire, but I do not think it is so. I do not understand how it is possible to make humour about a university.

Please give me a very full answer to these questions so I can write an excellent thesis. I would like an explanation of the history, ontology and aesthetik of the 'campus-novel', also full bibliography. I like you to interpret the representation of university life in these novels from the standpoint of *Landeskunde*, and explain me, from the standpoint of *Reception-theorie*, who likes to read them, and why so. If your books are funny, please tell me where, and send me your ontology of the comedic and your theoretiks of the humoristic, and how you like to compare yourself with Aristotle, Nietzsche, Bergson and Freud. Only one more question now! My professor hints me that you and David Lodge are the same person. Perhaps you are also T. Hardy, M. Beerbohm, T. Sharpe and H. Jacobson. If so please tell me in your letter, and give me a full bibliography of your writings, under all your names. Also please send a cassette of Supertramp, *Breakfast in America*, which is not so easy here to obtain. I hope you reply to this letter very quickly, as in my country we like an efficience in our correspondences. I thank you in expectation of your good helps, yours fidelistically,

Hans-Joachim Wissenschaft

Naturally, since I get so many letters of that kind, I have worked out a reply which is rather of this kind:

My dear Herr Wissenschaft,

Thank you so much for your letter. What a pleasure it is to hear again of Professor Z., all of whom I remember with vivid clarity. Please give her my warmest and most affectionate good wishes. It does not surprise me that, as her student, you are such a diligent asker of questions. I recall she herself was famous for her proficiency in the extended theoretical question, and indeed in Hamburg I urged her to collect hers together and publish them as a book. This doubtless explains why she thinks I enjoy extended interrogation, and why she has been so kind as to point you at me. Naturally I am delighted to help, to the best of my abilities – though I well know my answers can never reach anything like the standard of your teacher's questions. However, you will be happy to learn that, owing to the sudden cancellation of a ten-part television series I was writing, I do suddenly have several weeks to spare. So, out of my great attachment to your excellent mentor, I shall try to confront the many cogent points raised in your missive, or missile, as best I can. After all, even though I have supervised many theses myself and know the consequences, I am naturally delighted to hear that someone – indeed, anyone – is writing yet another dissertation on my work. I feel even more privileged to be invited to write the bulk of it for you. I fancy between the two of us we shall, for once, be able to get it more or less right.

Nonetheless I fear I could prove a dreadful disappointment to you. You ask me about the ontology, palaeontology, teleology and neurology of this mysterious and unusual literary genre some of us practise in my benighted country, and has been called the 'university' or 'campus novel'. I do not want to seem discouraging to someone as evidently diligent as yourself, but I have to tell you the phrase causes me some anxiety, and has even brought me out in large red blemishes. It is said, I think, that Thomas Mann had similar problems when people described his *Der Zauberberg,* or *The Magic Flute,* as we call it here, as a 'hospital novel' – and that Franz Kafka turned into something totally different from his so-called normal self when he was asked to compare his work in the field of the 'castle novel' with that of P.G. Wodehouse. Of course no one is more in favour of theories of genre than myself, so I will explain my antipathy with a personal anecdote. I know that answering a philosophical question with an anecdotal answer bears all the shameful marks of British empiricism, but I suggest you pour yourself a health-giving draught of the local product and hear my reasons.

My difficulties with the term 'university novel' began in early life, when I published my first book, which I like to call *Eating People Is Wrong*, though this clearly is up for argument. It so happened I published the book, took my first academic job, and married my first and only wife, all in the same week; but we all have difficult weeks from time to time. No sooner was the book out than my publisher, Frederick Warburg, summoned me to London to discuss my future, and, drunk with expectations of literary fame, I and my new wife hastened to satisfy him. We lived in the North, and my wife had never been knowingly south of the River Trent in her life. Nonetheless she made a week's supply of sandwiches, in case they did not have food in London, and we took the train to the great metropolis. We arrived at St Pancras Station, where my wife, mistaking it for St Paul's Cathedral, knelt in the left-luggage office and gave prayers for our safe return. There was another small fracas when I tried to lead her down into the underground, and she refused, calling me a lunatic for supposing that trains could run underneath cities in small round holes. She made me hire the most expensive taxi I could find, and has persisted with the practice ever since – though she has now been to London frequently, and can find her way blindfolded from any part of it straight to Harrods' food hall.

Warburg's office was at the very top of one of those charming Georgian houses in Bloomsbury without which the British publishing industry could not exist. And he made an impressive figure as he stood, infinitely tall and in a white suit, at the top of the stairs and ushered us into the lavatory, perhaps thinking this was what we had come to London for. 'This is your *author*, come to see you,' said my wife. Warburg bent graciously, kissed her hand, and led us into a vast white room with a great white desk. It had one chair opposite, and in this he seated my wife, gesturing me to a stool in a far distant corner. For an hour or so, my wife and publisher had an extended, warm conversation, she blushing prettily when he rose now and then to kiss her hand again

5

or make her more comfortable in her chair. From time to time they waved at me. Then Warburg rose suddenly, and we were out in the street again. 'What did he want to say to me?' I asked my wife anxiously. 'Oh, well,' she said, stopping a passing Rolls-Royce and telling it to take us to the station, 'he just wanted to make absolutely sure you didn't write any more university novels'.

Frankly it was only now that I learned my book *was* a university novel – and that getting a place to write one was even harder than getting a place in university itself. Admittedly my book was set in the academic groves, but since I had spent my entire life in educational institutions, from kindergarten to graduate school (I fancy you will know the feeling, Herr Wissenschaft), I naturally assumed that trotting off to class or the library every day was normality itself. Everyone gave lectures to everyone else; life was books, and books were life. To me the true passports to being were readers' tickets for the world's great libraries – the London Library, the Senate House Library, the Sterling Memorial and the Widener, the Borg and the British Museum (about whose falling down I wrote my famous novel). I imagined the whole of life was the same – that plumbers spent their pipeless hours writing Ph.D's on joints, that the friendly local barmaid took postgraduate courses in pumping, that everyone everywhere kept large shoeboxes filled with file cards and footnotes. I had not written a university novel; I had written a universal novel.

So Warburg's warning came to me as a terrible shock. What was worse, I was already on the last lap of another novel – set on the, well, campus of an American, well, university. Back home again, I picked up the unfortunate manuscript and assaulted it desperately, trying all I could to alter the location – to a factory, a prison, the forecourt of a garage, anywhere but where it was. But despite all the grime, hard labour and street brutality I tried to smear over my characters, I simply could not prevent them from discussing things like epistemology and the liberal dilemma. I laboured for years to hide my crime, until one day the manuscript suddenly disappeared, along with my wife. For days I wondered where it had gone, and sometimes I missed her too. Happily it, or rather she, returned some days later, to say that she had delivered the very first draft to Warburg, who had been delighted to see her, and for that matter the book. In fact, if she was to be believed, it was just what he had always wanted. Apparently I had now acquired some reputation for that sort of thing, and he now wanted me to write yet *another* university novel. 'I knew you'd be pleased', said my wife, taking out her cheque book and riffling through all the torn-off stubs.

I was not. Taking my publisher's warnings to heart, I had already set my next book entirely at the bottom of a mineshaft – which, incidentally, is quite different from a *Gemeinschaft*. Indeed, if you have a course in colliery fiction I might be able to dredge it up from the lake where I threw it when I had this news. But, always one to follow the whims of a wise publisher's advice, I now sat down and invented a fiction partly set in a new university during the student revolts of the 1960s (you may remember you had them too, Herr Wissenschaft, though I doubt if you took part), the book called, as you rightly said, *Der Geschichtsmensch*. One day, when I suddenly looked up and discovered it had somehow become 1975, my wife, once more exhausted by my interminable revisions of this remarkable and meticulous manuscript, grabbed it from my feeble hands, rushed for the train, and went to London. She was gone this time for two weeks, and naturally I began to worry. However, her explanation, when she came back, glowing, was quite convincing. Apparently my publisher had changed. Warburg had left, and been replaced by a man in a grey suit called Tom Rosenthal. The whole difficult relation between the author's wife and the author's publisher had had to be reconstructed from scratch. 'How does he feel about university novels?' I asked. But apparently the expensive London restaurants in which they had been forced to chat had proved so noisy that my wife had not really been able to find out.

Naturally I was on tenterhooks for days, until Rosenthal rang up, thanked me warmly for the wife I had submitted to him, and said he quite liked the book too. It was published, and indeed became quite a success. However, by this time I had grown in cunning and deviousness. I set my next novel, *Wechsel*, in an imaginary Eastern European country called Slaka. That, too, appeared to generally warm reviews. However, several of them suggested that my imaginary country was not utterly like Eastern Europe, but remarkably like a university. I suffer through these harrowing experiences again because from them I learned a few lessons. One is that publishers, and the publics they speak for, like genres or sub-genres even more than we critics do, so they know what they are marketing or buying. Another is that, therefore, once a writer is known for one thing, it is almost impossible to do anything else, even if you do. It is with genres as with sports cars; once inside one, you will never get out of it again – except perhaps by death or the taking of a pseudonym, whichever is easier. Another is that, however fictional you say your books are (and all sensible authors say that), people insist that they describe some reality or other – even though reality was abolished in the 1890s, and if an imaginary country is the same as a university or vice versa we do have a problem of, as we academics say, separating our signifiers from our signifieds. Another is that it may not be such a good idea to let your wife keep going off to London, especially since the advent of the credit card; but perhaps you do not have that particular problem, Herr Wissenschaft.

I hope all this will explain why, as a writer, I am not always enthusiastic about being called a 'university' or 'campus' novelist. At the same time, as a literary critic, I do have to admit there is some truth in it here and there. I must also acknowledge that the 'university novel' does show some signs of being a commonplace form, especially in Britain – perhaps because the British novel has always been about places that are rather difficult to get into. We can even trace back a history of sorts, back to the sentimental Oxbridge romances of the nineteenth century, which you can, and doubtless will, compare with *Wilhelm Meister* and the *Bildungsroman*. These are tales about young men's education in pastoral surroundings, part of an Oxbridge myth that grows a mite more ironic in the twentieth-century novels of Forster, Waugh and Aldous Huxley. Perhaps what made the story more interesting was when it crossed over with the fiction of the academically excluded, like Hardy's *Jude the Obscure* and the novels of D. H. Lawrence. Certainly it was after the Butler Education Act of 1944, which admitted cartloads of pimply social refugees to various academic destinations, that the whole affair took on pace. Many of the new books were set not in glowing Oxbridge but in 'redbrick' universities, which are frequently converted lunatic asylums or extended public lavatories, and in time the 'new' universities, 1960s architectural

8

wonders built in green fields by Finnish architects driven mad by the remarkable plastic properties of concrete. You may possibly find some trace of all this in my own works.

Since then, the university novel, like universities themselves, appeared to undergo a period of expansion. In fact the books began to acquire what you and I would call 'intertextuality', which of course is quite different from plagiarism. For example, a newish book by this young man Howard Jacobson, whose cognomen somehow seems to have come your way, refers I suppose very comically to an institution called 'Bradbury Lodge' – where, he implies, most British novels that are not about India are set. And I suppose that in theory one would have to say that where there is intertextuality, there is very probably a genre – or so my old professor told me, before he discarded Structuralism entirely, and took up hang-gliding instead.

But, as you rightly ask, why *should* this very peculiar practice have grown to such proportions? In the many boxes of scholarly apparatus I am shipping to you by separate sea-container, you will find various scholarly attempts to answer just this question. Study, for example, the article by P.R. Elkin, a fine scholar who sees the university novel as a kind of campus epidemic, rather like glandular fever or genital herpes. Throughout the Anglo-Saxon world 'Every kind of person connected with universities appears to have tried his hand at writing them', be they college don or campus porter. The main reason, he seems to suspect, is that people in academic life have an excess of leisure time, and no doubt get paper at discount prices as well. Alas, this creative spectacle does not exactly make him excited. Indeed he complains that all these books 'have much the same caste [*sic*, as we say] of characters, and much the same preoccupations – which is no doubt another way of saying that universities these days, wherever they may be, are in significant respects strikingly similar' – and also, I suppose, another way of saying he doesn't like them. If only at the time of writing Professor Elkin had, like ourselves, access to the word 'intertextuality' – that might have changed his attitude completely.

But perhaps not. For I notice everywhere throughout the many articles on the subject – when you collect the sea-container from Hamburg docks, which I take it are convenient to the Rheingau, you

9

will see what I mean – a rather grudging note. Professor Elkin, for example, speaks of my own *Der Geschichtsmensch* as 'a step forward in the genre', thus showing himself a man of fine critical acumen. But then he complains: 'Like Zola, Malcolm Bradbury seems unable to leave a room without describing everything in it'. I will not try to speak for Zola, who has his own lawyer, but I should point out that in fact I am famous for not being able to leave a room at all, or certainly not until they have removed the drink and furniture, whether I have described it or not. I would also add that, just as Anthony Powell once observed that good books do furnish a room, so I believe that good rooms do furnish a book, or even a good room a good book.

What does seem clear is that critics who, when confronted with other kinds of fiction – books about Japan, for instance – will insist on their 'purely lexical existence', critics who will indeed passionately assault the entire concept of realism, and prove that it is dead, will become oddly different when they encounter the university novel. Thus I commend you, when you unpack the truck, to look up the two fine articles on the matter by George Watson and Professor J. P. Kenyon – whose recent study of historians was, I note with the interest of a dedicated intertextualist, called *The History Men*. Mr Watson's piece will provide you with an excellent short history of our genre, good, I'd say, for at least ten footnotes. But he then comments that 'he has several reasons, all partly selfish, for hoping that Anglo-American campus fiction will fade away and die', not a view he takes, I believe, of epic poetry, for example. However he does explain, a little surprisingly, that he thinks it hard for universities to have to do their excellent work in what he calls 'the blaze of glamorizing publicity'. Professor Kenyon's is also a thoughtful piece, offering many useful social observations on the matter. He is generous in acknowledging that the university novel 'fills a remarkable gap', though in what he does not quite say. Yet he, too, concludes that 'we have had too much of a good thing', and suggests that it is time for British novelists to start looking elsewhere, to social problems and business life – or, presumably, anywhere else but a university.

I will leave it to you, Herr Wissenschaft, to judge just why it is that university critics do not always like university novels, and even sometimes upset their entire critical theories when they discuss them. Actually I suspect I know the answer, which may have something to do with another word you use in your capacious enquiry, the word 'satire'. And now I fear I am going to disappoint you severely, Herr Wissenschaft. Yes, of course, my novels are complex textual monads, philosophical reflections, tales of human tragedy, novels of pain. But to be frank they are quite heavily infested with satirical intentions, humoristic practices, and the like. In fact, to be entirely open with you – not something I do often when there are critics about – they *are* comic novels, and certain pages here and there are intended to produce a physiological comic reflex, which in Britain we call laughter. I fully understand entirely why this should produce anxiety, not least among my academic colleagues. For it is true that if universities – communities of largely good, decent, brilliant, enlightened people, committed to the best of ends, such as the survival of humanism and the differentiation between B + and B + + – can be subjected to satire, then what cannot be done to all the rest of life, which is so very much worse?

So it is very proper of you to ask me about my ontology of the comic and my theoretic of the humanistic, and I wish I could answer you. Unfortunately this is a matter I usually leave others to discuss, while I sit in the bar with a few close friends. My relationship with Aristotle, Nietzsche, Freud and Bergson has been for some time a vexed question, and my lawyer advises me it could well be subject to litigation. So I will comment only briefly. As I understand it, Aristotle never completed his work on comedy, being overcome with a paroxysm of something. He did, however, argue that comedy is an inverted tragedy, or a tragedy written upside down, and this is exactly the way I have always tried to write my books. On the matter of Nietzsche, I have, to be frank, tried to avoid him as much as possible, and I believe he has taken the same attitude towards me. As I understand it, Nietzsche's theory, while admirable, applies effectively only to Wagner's *Ring* cycle, which only King Ludwig of Bavaria seems to have found a load of laughs. I have learned a good deal from Freud on many matters, but perhaps least in the realm of wit and the comic, which he sees as a manifestation of the unconscious, something we do not have in my country. Bergson on comedy is certainly enlightening, proposing that the comic occurs when the human is turned to the mechanical. As you know, he gives the example that we all laugh when a man slips on a banana skin, and no doubt in France they do; in Britain we always try to help such people. But I am most inclined to set my own work in the tradition of the modern British comic novel, which as we all know started with James Joyce's *Ulysses*, but has improved since. In my experience the best thing is just to mention the comedy briefly, and then get on to something more substantial as quickly as possible.

I hope all this puts you straight about university and campus fiction. Happily there are some writers who transcend or transform the genre in which they write, and I congratulate you on having chosen one. I trust all I have said will prove useful material for your thesis. I advise you to incorporate as much of it as possible, if only for what George Watson calls 'several reasons, all partly selfish'. For that would give me the chance to acquire yet another pseudonym, not something I reject lightly, as you – or more probably Prófessor Z. herself, never one to halt at the obvious in matters of literary study – have so cunningly surmised. It was clever of you both to work out that in fact I am several if not all of the authors you mention. To be frank, this is something I have been trying to conceal for many years, not wanting to overcrowd the market. But – strictly on the condition that this information is divulged to no one whatsoever, but is safely buried in your thesis, which will, I take it, shortly be locked up in an obscure university library and be securely protected by the unbreakable code of academic language – I am prepared to acknowledge to you, and you alone, the versatility and complexity of my literary achievement, as well as the fact that, although my wife and family believe me to be quite young, I have indeed been writing steadfastly and productively ever since the mid-nineteenth century. Over that period, as I have indicated, things with the university and campus novel have changed very greatly, as I am told they have in life itself, which for obvious reasons I never have the time to check. It is this that explains the inordinate variety of my styles, my rather swerving approach to my theme, and the fact that I look very tired these days, with so many books to write. In all honesty, it has been a difficult business, especially the episode of being married to Mrs

Thomas Hardy. But now theses like your own are being written and all the pieces being put together it has all been worth it.

Just one of these matters is rather complicated, and that is the question of whether David Lodge and myself are the same person – the vexed issue of the well-known writer 'Bodge'. A great many people ask each of us if we are the other, and this has grown extremely confusing to the one or both of us. In fact there are distinctive differences, but also close similarities. He is small and I am tall, but he is dark and I am dark. He professes to be a rather sceptical sort of Catholic while I profess to be a rather sceptical sort of humanist, but he is a university professor of literature, and so as it happens am I. He professes his literature at the so-called Birmingham University, while I profess mine at the far better-known University of East Anglia, but both of us write critical works on the practice of fiction which deal with many of the same subjects. Hence quite often we find ourselves together at conferences, lecturing side by side or in consecutive spots, often he on my topic and I on his. His wife is said to be called Mary, and mine Elizabeth, but they are constantly confused, though more often by other people than the two of us. Some people claim that we both fell in love with a Polish girl in a shower in Warsaw, but this is vehemently denied by all three, or possibly two, parties concerned. He gets my telephone calls, and I get his telephone bills. Thus it goes on, leaving each of us with the conviction that one or both of us is the other, and if you were able to settle this matter definitively in your thesis it would solve a lot of problems, and the whole thing would have been very worthwhile. Again, please give your excellent professor my good wishes, and tell her it was not I but David Lodge that went off with her umbrella. Also say that either or both of us remember our solemn undertaking never to include her in any work of fiction; we will continue to respect it. And very good luck with the Habitat.

Yours sincerely,
Max Beerbohm

Orders from Editresses, and Other Fantasies

Of all the literary letters I have ever wanted to write, I recalled just the other day the most touching. The reason for drafting it mentally, which is what I always do with letters, perhaps needs a little explanation. It arises from one of the several roles I perform in the course of a very busy and tumultuous life, a life so demanding that it causes me to rise very early of a morning, almost as soon as my wife has left for work, and keeps me at it, typing, editing, researching and thinking away until the late hours, when the evening chatter of the blackbirds and the ice-bucket summon me away. I write, I edit, I teach. And one of the more mysterious things I teach is a course in creative writing, where I take brilliant writers, subject them to rigorous pain for a year, and then bask in the glow of their subsequent achievements. I teach them many things – how to withstand misery and deprivation, how to deal with fame or more commonly the absence of it, how to be interviewed by Melvyn Bragg, how to maintain a point of view, whether in a novel or at a publishers' party. I teach them not just to write novels, but to rewrite them, a fascinating enterprise I have always been rather good at myself, and has delayed my writing career by at least ten years. I teach them about narrative lines and plot muscles, and how to imagine that one is of a quite different sex, or in another period of history. Quite a lot of it is good fun, as you see.

But I do realize that in the advancement of human creativity I do not work alone. In fact one of my responsibilities is receiving from time to time the various brochures and alluring packages sent out by

14

the many writing schools who abound now in this country, trying to fill it up with writers. No doubt they feel my own brilliant protégés could do with more knowledge of the harsh commercial realities of their art, and they are certainly full of wise saws. 'Journalism and Short Story Writing produces returns more speedily than does any other profession', they say, for example, and I for one can confirm it is true. Nonetheless, as these attractive brochures make very, very clear, the record of success they produce is quite remarkable, and in their pages the alumni and alumnae of these establishments positively fall over in their enthusiastic testimony to this fact. 'My earnings have enabled me to modernize entirely our country cottage', cries Mr X. 'I now want a country house with an orchard and paddock'. From this it seems clear that the School in question not only brings people to profitability but conveys something more intangible, the correct or only way to live as a well-known writer in this country. And so they go on: Mr A and Ms B, Mr X and Miss Y. 'It's an excellent testimony to your methods that after the third lesson I was swamped with orders from Editresses', wrote Miss Y. Miss Y, Miss Y . . . What was it about her that made this presumably young lady stay in my mind? What was it that made me want to address to her, of the many successful thousands who can testify, this literary letter?

Dear Miss Y,

You are probably all too used to receiving fan letters like this, but I always believe if you have been stirred by someone's writing you should at once write and tell them so (I know I would like it to happen to me). So I have to tell you how much I was touched the other day by reading one of your most recent publications; you will probably never guess what. It was not one of those which appear in the usual amazing outlets ('$88 from New York for a 2,400-word story!') with which by this point in your writing course you must be growing wonderfully familiar, but somewhere else – in the well-produced and finely proof-read little pamphlet that was sent to me in response to an enquiry to the Hotshot School of Writing, to whose excellent methods your latest 'appearance in print' gives testimony. Or is it to whose methods your latest 'appearance in print' gives excellent testimony? One thing I know about writing; you have to be very careful with words, or they will never trust you. As Thomas Carlyle said in a Writer's Guide I was reading only the other day, 'Giving a name is, indeed, a poetic art'. Your comments seemed so warm and heartfelt that I knew I had to pick up my typewriter, put in a sheet of clean A4, and write to you at once in a double-spaced format. So here, using a fresh ribbon, I am.

First to tell you all about me. (You will know, or if you do not yet you will soon find out, that all letters to writers are really about the writers of the letters and not about the writer to whom the letters are written.) I am a very interesting young man with what I have been told is a quite extraordinary gift of the literary gab. In fact I have been writing important books ever since I was three, when I conceived a novel of memory which I would have written on the spot had someone not warned me in the kindergarten playground about the prior existence of *A la recherche du temps perdu*, which, being only a tot, he thought was about a typing agency. No discouragement (I was beaten severely at the age of seven by a teacher who had read a small volume of poems by me and found them sexually over-explicit) has put me off, and we know that not being put off by discouragement is one of the greatest signs of a good writer. I wrote and wrote and wrote, and then wrote again. If I was not writing I was rewriting, either my own work or someone else's. Since the age of twelve I have been pestering publishers and editors with the contents of the massive pile of manuscripts which by that date I had accumulated, and for the past decade I have been in an unending correspondence with many of them which has produced another pile of paper of roughly equivalent proportions. I am told the University of Texas is now interested.

My range of interests as a writer is, as it happens, prodigiously wide. Believe me, I write everything. I write novels and short stories and plays and playlets, interspersed with novellas and two-hander sketches. I write histories and biographies and introductions to the difficulties of modern science and cook books and books about the Loch Ness monster and travel books, mostly about East Grinstead, where I live and do not often leave, since my typewriter is old and very heavy. I write children's books and school textbooks and works of abstruse philosophy in the Kierkegaardian mode and scholarly articles on the Etruscans and works of sociology and anthropology. I write articles for the women's page and send in stories about the most unforgettable characters I have ever met to *Reader's Digest* and informative pieces for Do-It-Yourself journals and I have been trying to get into part-works. I write romantic novels under a female pseudonym and detective stories and I have pretended to be Indian and written several novels of the Booker Prize type. I write film-scripts and television-scripts and comedy serials and one-liners for comics both stand-up and sit-down and abridgements and adaptations for radio, television and now compact disc, and I write instructions for detergent packets and eye-catching advertisements and promos I try to sell to the advertising agencies. I write publicity material and handouts for free news-sheets and political parties and I write traffic signs for the AA and 'This side up' instructions for cardboard boxes. I believe I am really a writer.

The only trouble is, I have not been doing very well. You will not, I am afraid, have seen my byline very much, because even the newspapers to whom I have offered it for nothing will not use it, with or without the accompanying article. I have been starving in a garret for five years with only a cat for company, and now that she has got an agent and is miaowing regularly for the TV cat food ads even she has left me. My shoes are paper-thin and heavily written over. From time to time I begin to feel a little discouraged, though of course adversity is the lot of most writers. There is a lot of material in it, especially for elderly reminiscence, once one has become an amazing success and is sitting there with one's big house and paddock, talking to Melvyn Bragg. Sometimes I can already see myself coming back here with the camera team and walking through these rooms where I suffered when young in Tricker's bench-made shoes. I remember Oscar Wilde said somewhere that a writer is not the sort of chap to complain when things go wrong for a bit, as they always do. So I wrote him a letter too and have tried to emulate him in several but not in all ways ever since. So I hope you will not think this letter is a young writer's failure to accept the reverses of our profession. It is simply an appeal for your advice.

To tell the truth, I have never done the 'obvious', not being an

17

'obvious' sort of person, and so I have never actually taken a course with a writing school, like yourself. I have written to many but my letters have always been returned, sometimes without even a rejection slip. 'Your Success as a Writer could be as simple as Posting this Enrolment Form . . .', it always says on the brochures. These brochures are always wonderfully heartwarming about the kind of people they seek. They are people 'out of the ordinary', usually young women 'who have never written a word before!' But now all over the Cotswolds they sit in small cottages, always rising early ('as early as 4.30 in the morning'), because then the house is quiet and the baby has not started to puke, and writing away. Soon they are selling serial rights in America for a million, having the bush and kangaroo epic they wrote in Dorset filmed in sixty episodes by Australian TV, or winning the Betty Trash Literary Prize for lush romantic fiction.

What I do not understand is how these schools will take absolute beginners ('Once she had never written a word! A year later she was the toast of mystery writers!') and yet seem unable to find a chair in the corner for someone like myself. I hope I am not snobbish but I do not regard these people as real writers and their background of adversity is nowhere near as strong as mine. I realize I may have said the wrong thing in writing to them when I told them that my passionate integrity and my Lawrentian blood-gut view of inspiration made me find their proposed writing schedule – write a story with a setting in the first week, write one with a character in the second, and 'put them together!' in the third – a mite mechanistic and utilitarian for a natural genius like myself, bursting with divine guidance. Perhaps you could give me the benefit of your experience and say whether I have been approaching them in the wrong way, and possibly even draft out the format for a letter that might produce one of those 'sudden realizations that here is a real writer' that they talk about so often.

Of course you will imagine that I have not been totally defeated by rebuttal – as they say, 'a good writer is someone who understands the experience of rejection'. My own impression is that these schools ('£1,000 earned in the first two months of your course!') can tell I know too much already and that they realize they have nothing they can teach me. It is true that for months now I have been, as it were, extra-

muralling on my own – studying in the privacy of my own garret the
various useful writers' handbooks that abound in the literary market-
place, doubtless producing for their authors what I see is called 'a speedy
return'. Through careful study I think I have mastered most of the
eternal verities of writing already, and the only thing that is missing
from my portfolio is the consequential money and fame. For instance,
I know already, as you see from this letter, that a true writer is one who
uses only A4, types only on one side of the paper, double-spaces, leaves
wide margins, and also always sends a stamped self-addressed envelope
when submitting an unsolicited manuscript (to think, oh God, of the
errors I made once!!). I know, as every real author knows, that offcuts
of scrap paper are usually available cheaply at the local printers, or the
newspaper office. I know that 'he, or more often she' has a style as
unique as a fingerprint, keeps corrections to a minimum, and that 'writing is not easy'.

I think I probably do have already, then, 'the extraordinary skills
required, but can with effort be mastered'. I know that 'every word is
a risky business'. 'To be able to control syntax exactly within a tight
verse-form is an achievement equivalent to crossing the Niagara Falls on
a tight rope, without a safety net, and stopping half way to do up one's
bootlace. For these gymnastics our gold medal goes to Alexander Pope',
is one wise saw that has stuck firmly in my head and is pinned to my
wall. But that was actually in a book about writing poetry, and I have
on the advice of the brochure of another School of Writing given up the
form ('Poetry has not been included in the Course simply because verse
is difficult to sell'), though presumably Pope went to a different school
and got contrary advice. I know that 'the best way to find out how to
write novels is to read one', and I will. I even know that some people
despise these books and these courses, and, as our Poet Laureate says in
one of them, are 'negative towards any deliberate cultivation of excellence, negative towards the methodological release of creative energy,
negative towards enthusiasm, negative towards the future'. I know
exactly what that means. I too have submitted work to those people.

I know all these things, but I really am willing to go on learning. As
it says in the brochures: 'Perhaps now the time has come for you to take
steps to Learn the Art, as so many Famous Writers did before you?' I

am all set to take steps, and if there is, dear Miss Y, anything you can do to help I would be grateful. For the truth is, you are selling, and I am not, and any old notes you are not using could make all the difference. You on your course are getting 'individual personal tuition' and 'a supply of paper for your first exercise' – indeed clearly you are way past all that now and are doubtless the recipient of the fifteen exclusive copyright blueprints and individualized marketing information that come towards the end of your studies. No doubt it is against college rules to pass such things onto a stranger, especially if they are individualized as they say, but just a few small hints would come far from amiss. And you are, I see, 'keeping company with Writers of Quality, and getting their experienced advice'. Wouldn't it be possible for you perhaps just to slip a word to one of these Writers of Quality – I imagine you all go round to the pub afterwards for a quick noggin and a chat – and see whether they could see their way to slipping me into the odd lecture? I would sit very quietly on the back row, and they could have my 'first month's earnings from any profits I subsequently made'.

I realize that all this sounds grotesquely impertinent of me, but I am desperate. For there you are, Miss Y, getting Orders from Editresses, and I, well, I never get any Orders at all. Orders from Editresses . . . I think it was that phrase, forged in the smithy of your imagination, that first attracted me to your writing, perhaps because somehow, like all the greatest ideas in writing, as it says in some book I have just put down, it calls up the world of all our dreams and desires. I did meet someone who called herself an Editress once, on the train to Worthing. I fear she could keep neither her three squalling children nor the family Alsatian under any kind of control, and certainly when I opened my bulging briefcase and showed her what I had written at 4.30 that morning, before even the milkman was up, namely seven short stories and three uncommissioned and random obituaries intended for the London *Times*, she showed little interest. Indeed she shifted bag and baggage to another compartment, and I last saw her leaving the train with all her brood before it had even come to a complete halt. On subsequent reflection I think she was lying and was not even an Editress at all.

And this is why I wonder whether you could just pick up your pen and describe to me, in less than three hundred words, just what 'the actual experience is like'. What do the Editresses actually order, and how? Where do you meet and what do they say? How does one define their appearance? (I imagine them like the women in *Dynasty*, with designer dresses in silk with black lapels, and big like queens.) What do they commission you for: romance? or cookery? Do they ask you back to their Hanover Square flats, as I imagine, for dinner by candlelight, and so give you the flavour of both and a whiff of interior design as well? If you have taken the course I am sure you will know exactly what I am asking, for as Henry James said the task of a writer is to *constater*. Whatever you say you know I will read with pleasure.

Well, as it says in the brochures, you have read this far because you are interested in writing. I now should explain that I am not really who – whom – I say I am! Yes, my dear, I have been forced by circumstances to conceal myself, and really I have been testing you all the time! In my real life I am a very famous novelist, lately divorced and with a very laid-back life-style. My hair is just beginning to grey a little and I like the swinging scene and classical music in moderation. I am witty, very even-tempered, and politically a mite to the left. I have a well-set jaw and twinkling eyes. My work has been selling very well lately and now the orchard is full of apples and there is a prancing pony in the paddock! From the moment our paths intertwined through what some dull and sublunary soul would call coincidence, I was struck by your prose-style and the photograph that accompanied it. Surely we must meet and try to make good and marketable fiction together! I am bold, I know, but no no, do not reject my importunity out of hand! You must feel as I do there is something vital there between us, that more than simple fate has brought us together! The message is in the air, the sign is in the stars!! Do not hesitate or delay, for this is one of those once-in-a-lifetime moments that if lost now is or are lost for all time!! Surely it is obvious to us both that what we already have are two extremely well-defined and interesting characters and all that is necessary is to put them into a plot of the uplifting romantic type! And there is something about this instant that tells me that what I feel you feel, in your deepest heart of hearts, also and too!!!

I enclose a small passport photograph, a full list of my many writing credits – and, of course, a brown paper envelope stamped with sufficient return postage for your reply.

Yours in anticipation of a speedy return,
'Mr X'

Getting Started

Like, I suppose, every writer in that rather anxious category that is sometimes called 'established', I receive a great many letters in a rather heartbreaking genre. They come from the vast number of would-be authors in our society who are trying, as we say, to 'get started'. The description is inaccurate, the truth of the matter being that most of them have been started for many years. There is an old saw that says that every one of us has one novel in us, and I can personally attest that this is true – since what they do when they have written it is pack it in a parcel and send it to me. No, they are started, all right. And what we are talking about is something rather different, the task of getting started on getting published, an activity not at all like that of writing itself. For the truth is that most of the books that are written are never published, just as most of the books that are published are never written, but rapidly concocted on the back of an envelope in the bar of the Groucho, and then illustrated by David Hockney.

It is not surprising that in this situation a folklore has developed about how to get a book from the state of rejection it has suffered at the hands of all the crass publishers to the state of acceptance which, as a matter of course, leads to bestselling sales, meetings with accountants, and eventual tax exile. The means that has been devised for this, it would seem, is to get a so-called established writer to read it. He or she will then put in a magic word of recommendation, the publisher will bang his head on the desk and cry out in shame at his own folly, and all things and all manner of things shall be well. And it is unquestionably this folkloristic belief that explains why I, and, I understand, many of my writing contemporaries, constantly receive variants on, along with bulky enclosures with, the following letter:

Dear Markham Bradberry,

Do not put down this letter. It contains very important information that could entirely change your life.

I am a very famous writer, and I have been writing for forty years. I have written thirty-five remarkable novels on every aspect of human experience known to man, and even more to woman. Each one of these novels I have sent to thirty-five publishers, making a total of 1,225 postal packets in all. Every one of these publishers has turned down every one of my books, sometimes within hours of it being posted, usually with just a rejection slip, if that. Now I always ask in my covering letter for them to do me the courtesy of sending me a few scribbled words of critical abuse. Once I did receive a letter from a famous publisher saying that he was wild about my book and wanted to publish it. However, I realized something was wrong and looked at the envelope. I then saw it was addressed to Mr John Fowles; and I sometimes wonder what letter he received, and whether this could have anything to do with his long silence after *Daniel Martin*.

Naturally I am not discouraged by this, because I know I am a neglected genius. None of this has put me off, and to tell the truth I rather thrive on it. The fact is I was born to be a great writer. All my relatives think so too, though possibly I am more convincing at being a writer in the flesh, so to speak, than actually on the page, where you can't see me as well. However, it is possible I may be doing something wrong. All my relatives think so, though they have never understood me at all, as happens with great geniuses. And now you know why I have chosen to write to you, and even ask for your advice!

You will be pleased to know I have just completed seven more novels, and I enclose them with this letter. All I want you to do is to read them and suggest how they can be made more publishable. I know in my heart the books are right already, but publishers are fools, and it is very

24

hard to understand what they are 'into' these days. So perhaps you can suggest a few small changes – perhaps I was wrong to set *The Fire and the Chariot* in tenth-century Bessarabia, so do tell me if you think it would 'go down better' if it were set in nineteenth-century France, something I could easily do by altering the names of trees, etc – that would make them vulgarly publishable, since you seem to be expert at that sort of thing. I realize my handwriting is, due to disability, rather difficult, but please ring me here in Northumberland if there is any word you cannot read. I am afraid these are the sort of books where you cannot skip a single pronoun or adjective, but that is how it is with works of genius.

I know you will enjoy and admire my work and I will call you in three days to find out. If you are not in, I could come and sit on your doorstep. A few words of passionate support from you would, I believe, make all the difference, and you should not miss the opportunity. Maybe if you just rang all the publishers and gave them the roasting they richly deserve we could get these forty-two books out at once without changing a thing! But you might as well send me your advice on any improvements you can work out, and I will see what I think of it. Also send me the name and home telephone number of your literary agent, and any used typewriters you do not want.

Remember! Do not ignore this letter! Or Posterity would never forgive you!

Yours expectantly,
P. S. Bricktop (Miss)

I am, to be honest, a good-hearted soul, and I would like to be helpful. But in most of these cases the letter I would like to write would go pretty much like this:

Dear Miss Bricktop,

Thank you so much for your letter and its massive enclosures. As you do so rightly assume, there is nothing we writers love more than giving our aid to the authors of the next generation who are all set to supersede us. And certainly I for one have always believed in doing everything I can on behalf of the up-and-coming young – or as it seems in your own case, unless you write inordinately quickly, here-and-going middle-aged – writer. Believe me, I should not wish to do anything to add to your sense of rejection, which I can see must by now be considerable – though, be reassured, a masochistic and paranoid temperament is a well-known sign of a great writer. If then I feel compelled to return these bulky and prodigious manuscripts to you at once, without actually read ing them, you will understand it is for the very best of reasons.

The fact is, dear Miss Bricktop, you just happen to catch me at the most unfortunate of moments. Just the other day I strained my back, carrying about some royalty statements. My doctor, who is visiting me regularly, advises that on no account should I lift manuscripts of very great weight – especially any that begin 'In the beginning was the Word', as I see all of yours do. My oculist, who has just gone, has warned me that if I spend long hours over crabbed and ill-formed hand-writing I shall not be word-processing for very much longer. And, even worse, the Tax Inspector has just been with the warning that I am now faced with a very stark choice. I can choose to spend all my time reading unpublished novels by other people, in which case he will provide me with comfortable circumstances to complete the task, such as a cell in Parkhurst; or else I must get some writing done at once and clear off my contribution to the National Debt, since the Chancellor has till only next April to balance his budget. I am sure you will agree that the only thing for me to do in the circumstances is to switch from reading to writing mode at once.

Or perhaps you will not; re-reading your letter I can see I could well be wrong. So please understand that there are yet more important reasons why I return your packet unperused. To be utterly frank with you, I am a terrible literary magpie. I should hate this information to get out, and I tell it to you in total confidence; but no sooner do I read the brilliant words written by some other author than I feel a vile temptation to appropriate them for my very own. This has become a profound dilemma for me, and I have discussed it with my priest, who serves fine counsel and an excellent Chablis. He, I fear, recommends that for a period, until my moral equilibrium is restored, I try to avoid reading anything not yet published by anyone else whatsoever. I know plagiarism is very fashionable indeed these days, but I am ethically opposed to it, except in the case of James Joyce's *Ulysses*. Thus I am trying my very best to do you a favour and ensure that when your books are published, as one day, if you keep up this kind of correspondence, they might be, they get an absolutely fresh, fair hearing, and are not confused, as say David Lodge's are, with my own.

So, dear Miss Bricktop, I say again that I have decided with all regret to avoid reading your actual manuscripts, but of course this does not preclude me from offering you some sage literary advice. And I do have a few general thoughts on what makes a good and publishable writer that I tend to offer on all possible occasions. Briefly, a good and successful writer is to be distinguished by several qualities I would recommend you cultivate. A good writer, in my experience, is a good rewriter, who does not write a very large number of books but works back over the first one and gets it more or less right. A good writer is also someone who possesses a good typewriter, and knows how to use it; some of the most successful are effective with the Tippex as well. A good writer is usually a good reader, especially of the works of contemporaries (there are certain special exceptions to this, such as those who for medical, tax, or ethical reasons must refrain from reading for a while, but this is generally true). A good writer is someone with a mind so fine that no idea can violate it, someone on whom no impression is lost, and someone who also has a relative, friend, or lover who happens to work in the editorial department of one of our leading publishing houses. And, above all, if I may say so, a good writer is almost never called P. S. Bricktop. May I recommend a pseudonym – something like John le Carré, though not too much like it, to avoid confusion – and I think you may well find your chances are quite considerably improved.

But if all this fails, may I make a broader observation. I believe that in the literary life of this country we face a very severe social problem which is almost beyond our wits to solve. It is akin to the problem we have faced in industry, where there were far too many producers and not enough consumers. In Britain today, as is evident from my own postbag, everyone is writing, in your own case in quite inordinate quantity. On the other hand, perhaps because of this intensive creative industry, the number of readers appears to be dropping very dramatically. Is it not time, in a period when everyone has to think about alternative employment, to think of taking some of these writers, and retraining them as readers? This is a situation in which we are all responsible, and I rather wonder if you might feel inclined to take a pioneering role, Miss Bricktop? No, looking at your letter again, Miss Bricktop, I rather doubt it will find favour; please forgive the suggestion, brought on only by the arrival of a new postbag containing several rather bulky packages. No, I have a better idea. Why not pack up your parcel yet again, as you undoubtedly will, and send it to G. K. Chesterton? I know he loves to hear from people.

Yours sincerely,
Markemstein Braddlebonny

The Man with the
Grey Flannel Head

In the literary circles in which I twist and turn, there is – and some people would say not surprisingly – a good deal of anxiety expressed about how a writer can make a reasonable living these days. By a writer, you will understand what we mean in our circles is a *real* writer, a *serious* writer, a *major* writer, not just someone who plugs into a Mills and Boon or Harlequin romance instruction tape and delivers the goods as requested. For the fact is that, even in our age of entrepreneurialism and arbitraging, when everyone you meet is not a person but a small business, the true writer still has problems in keeping him, her, or itself in the paper, Chinese food and designer clothing needed over the time it takes to produce, say, a really great novel – the kind of novel that will displace *Ulysses* once and for all and leave D. H. Lawrence on the sidelines, jaundiced with envy. Naturally this kind of thing can take a lifetime; James Joyce, after all, took seventeen years with *Finnegans Wake*. But in those days there were real patrons, people who guaranteed the restaurant tabs at the bank and brought round fresh croissants in the morning. The breed, I fear, has scarcely survived, and one of the dilemmas of the modern world is just how to solve this problem.

Of course various solutions have been mooted. One is that any sensible government should realize that great art is a great national investment, and therefore they should invest all the profits gained from the sale of all the public assets now on the market in a well-chosen group of writers. Suggestions to this effect have been made to Mrs Thatcher, President Reagan and indeed all the major world leaders, but so far none of them has got round to sending an answer. Other people, more philistine in disposition, take the view that authors themselves should take responsibility for ensuring their own survival, by gearing their work to the market place and appealing to the reading public. Alas, any great artist knows that the reading public he is appealing to is posterity, which, by definition, has not arrived yet, causing cash-flow problems. Yet others say that, if this is the case, writers should get on their bikes and go and find some gainful employment to finance their work, and various forms of suitable work have been recommended – from that of working after hours in a nightclub (not always easy; one of my friends lost her Bunny Girl status totally when she was found offering an even more indigent fellow writer a free drink) to other vocations often thought to go with authorship, like begging in the streets.

But in the circles where these matters are discussed, one form of employment for authors comes up more than the others. I get quite a few letters about the matter, and here is a sample reply I am brooding at this moment:

Dear Mr Rushdie,

Many thanks for your letter; I do see the problem. The book you describe is substantial indeed, and you are going to have to do an awful lot of writing to complete it. No wonder, then, that you are looking around for a well-salaried position, and are now considering becoming an advertising copywriter. You will not mind me saying I have heard it all before. At various times I have had similar enquiries from other fine writers – Peter Porter and Gavin Ewart, Fay Weldon and Clive Sinclair are some of the names I seem to remember – who had the notion of reconciling art and commerce in this particular way. And indeed I believe that for most of them matters worked out quite well. Certainly advertising has benefited, and there are suggestions that Fay Weldon's 'Go to work on an egg' slogan will be studied in universities long after her more extended projects have dropped from the canon, though I am sure they never will. Of course I am thought to take a rather hard line on these matters, though not as hard as some scholars, who would claim that in the interests of creative integrity you would do far better to accept malnutrition and early death. My own feelings on the matter are a little more ambiguous. To explain this, it is necessary to recount the following small narrative.

The time it takes us back to is the 1950s, an era when the world was a good deal younger than it now is, and so was I. It was a time of alienation and anguish, of outsiders and angries; it was also a time when everyone who was anyone rode a little Vespa motor-scooter, often in a bowler hat, but such is the ambiguity of culture. And it was one day in this complex, creative season of things that Henry Clubb, doorman at Saul and Protheroe, a very well-known accredited advertising agency set opulently just off Berkeley Square, was interrupted in his duties of burnishing the brass carriage lamps that decorated the Georgian entrance by an unusual sight. A thin youth of strange countenance, wearing plum-coloured trousers far too small for him and apparently carrying all his possessions in a moth-eaten briefcase, was hovering uncertainly outside the establishment. His manner suggested something provincial; the return half of a day-return ticket stuck up from the top pocket of his jacket, and he scratched one red ear with a finger trembling with trepidation. Coming a little closer, he stared at the brass plaque outside the offices and began mouthing each syllable to himself, as if otherwise they might disappear at any moment.

Clubb was just about to frogmarch the youth off the pavement and right out of Mayfair when he stumbled yet nearer, blushed an extra-ordinary red, and asked if he might be allowed to speak to a Mr Fazackerley, who, he believed, worked for the agency. Mr Fazackerley worked for it indeed; he was nothing less than the personnel officer, and no man to be trifled with. Clubb was therefore just mouthing up a few words of the harshest discouragement when the young man produced from the interstices of his worn and outdated clothing a letter written on company stationery, and signed by Fazackerley himself. It was an invitation for an interview. Clubb therefore took the young man into the lobby and sat him down, under the Kneller portraits, on leather. 'Who shall I say is calling, sir?' he asked, picking up the telephone. 'Say it's, er, Malcolm Bradbury', said the red-eared youth, and so, indeed, I believe it was.

31

For, insofar as anything is constant in this relativistic, post-Einsteinian world, this young fellow was an early or Mark 1 version of my own self. I was twenty-one or so, and just in the process of graduating from the provincial redbrick university in the sock-making Midlands in which I had pursued my literary studies; I was, I suppose, a rather strange youth, who affected strange types of trouser and clip-on bow ties that kept falling off, rather embarrassingly, into cups of coffee. For three years I had been lying on Midlands golfcourses, reading Proust, Lawrence and Kafka, supported by a minuscule grant from a grateful government. As students go, I was quite frankly something of a bargain, my wants being minimal if almost non-existent. All I asked was a bob or two to buy a few paperback books, a groat or so to mail home my laundry, and a half-crown every other term to buy a gin-and-tonic for some girl I had fallen hopelessly in love with. Even in those days I was unusual, though perhaps rather more usual than I thought. For I had no doubt at all of the vocation to which the universe had summoned me. I was going to write a great novel. A significant part of it existed already, typed on a small typing machine that had been built even before they had settled on the full alphabet. It was set, not surprisingly, in the only world I knew anything of, the world of a redbrick provincial university. I kept it in shoeboxes, honed and polished it daily, and I knew, simply knew, that when it was finished it would knock posterity sideways.

It was Mr Bobbs who warned me one day that clouds were gathering on my horizon. Mr Bobbs was a rather dour, uncooperative man who cycled in from time to time out of the dense countryside thereabouts to act as the university careers officer, and double as coach for the cross-country running team as well. In my third year of study he asked to see me, to discuss what he called my career plans. They were simple, I told him. The great novel was almost done. Now I was sketching out a 4,000-line epic that would be compared with *Beowulf*, and a couple of stage plays that would upset the entire tradition of modern theatre. Mr Bobbs took his bicycle clips off and looked at me. 'But what do you intend to do to make a living?' he asked after a while. 'Isn't there some kind of grant?' I asked. 'Grant for what?' asked Mr Bobbs. 'Well, for writing,' I said, 'and, well, for being me'. Mr Bobbs stared at me for a while with red-veined eyes. 'I should think it very unlikely', he said. 'In many places they'd probably charge you for it. Now isn't it time you stopped being silly, started thinking about getting on with life, and turned your mind to finding worthwhile employment?'

It was my first encounter with the crass world, and it grew worse as Mr Bobbs got out some forms and questionnaires that had been prepared by some firm of industrial psychologists, and began asking me questions designed to elicit my various aims and abilities. After I had answered his queries as well as I could, Mr Bobbs sat and stared at the form for a moment. He opened up a few small primers on human psychology, and grew even more despondent than usual. 'According to this you're absolutely not suited to life at all,' he said. 'You appear to have absolutely no aptitudes, your potential quotient is minus, and the textbooks offer no solution to your problem, though we could call the Euthanasia Society.' 'I see,' I said, 'so there's nothing.' 'I wouldn't say that,' said Mr Bobbs, 'one does not like to give up. No, in these circumstances I usually recommend advertising.' 'For what?' I asked. 'I mean as a career,' said Mr Bobbs. 'I know a man called Fazackerley whose life I saved during the war. He owes me one. I'd like you to go and see him.' For an hour or so I sat in Bobbs's office, expostulating, pointing out that art and commerce did not mix, and most great writers would rather die than prostitute their talents. 'That is the course I'd recommend,' said Mr Bobbs. 'But if you do decide otherwise, I'm arranging an appointment with Fazackerley. If you go, do get rid of that ridiculous bow-tie, spruce yourself up a bit. And don't – under any circumstances short of extreme torture – admit that you're writing a novel.'

I did think matters over for a couple of days, but you will have already gathered that prudence won out. A day or two later I purchased a day-return ticket to London, and set off for Saul and Protheroe, which is indeed where you found me a few moments ago, this narrative having a modernist time-scheme. Moments later I was ascending an Adam staircase to the navel of the building, where Mr Fazackerley was closeted. He proved an affable-enough fellow, seated behind a tubular desk, natty, charming and Turnbull-and-Asser shirted, a red carnation glowing like a cigar end in his lapel. 'Take a pew, dear boy,' he said, rising to greet me. 'So you wish to enter the world of power and influence?' 'I suppose I do,' I said. 'Then why didn't you go to Oxford?' he asked. 'I couldn't afford it,' I said. 'The train-fare was too expensive'. 'I see,' said Fazackerley. 'So this means you don't know anyone, anyone at all?' 'I know quite a lot of people,' I said. 'I didn't think there were any, in your part of the world,' said Fazackerley. 'I talked to Bobbs and he said you didn't really know anyone at all.' 'Well, I don't then,' I said.

Mr Fazackerley leaned back in his chair, hands folded behind his head. 'Young man,' he said, 'we are in an age of daring social experiment. The world's changing, the network's growing wider. Oxbridge has dominated this country for far too long.' 'Golly, you're right,' I said. 'Meritocracy is the name of the game now,' said Fazackerley, growing warmer on the matter. 'The new men are ready to take charge. I'd like to take a risk with you, a redbrick lout, a total unknown. You're in touch with forces we here in advertising haven't even begun to master. You've got dirt under your nails, snot in your nose. You're just what we're looking for. So long as . . .' he looked at me suspiciously, '. . . so long as you've got no literary ambitions.' 'None at all,' I said. 'I hate books.' 'Of course you do,' he said. 'I don't suppose they have any where you come from. Yes, I'll take the risk. I'm going to plunge you straight into washing-up liquids. Now come and I'll introduce you to Stella darling.'

Stella darling was eating caviar on cheese crackers and was in charge of Ideas. She briefly briefed me on the accounts the agency held – airlines, breakfast food manufacturers, brassière manufacturers by the score, and innumerable world-famous conglomerates of whom I had, to be frank, never heard. She told me about the great new excitement that was thrilling the world of marketing: boffins somewhere in the North had invented something called detergent, which would shortly be removing all the dirt in which life up to then had been encased. Then she led me to a small Danish desk in a dark corner under the Adam staircase, which she promised would be mine. I looked at the desk and saw a vision of the future. There I would sit, in a pin-striped suit, my Vespa parked in front of the brass carriage lamps outside. There would be a little mews house for me, somewhere round the corner, with a rubber plant in the window and bath salts for the bath. I would sit at the desk, touting universal cleanliness, and writing about the straps of brassières, until it became time to take clients out to lunch at Claridge's, talking to them about the American musicals we had all lately seen. In the desk, in a secret drawer which only I could open, there would be the novel, the great novel, to the provincial splendours of which would be added a wise urban knowingness.

With great excitement I bounded out of the building, said goodbye to Henry Clubb, who pointed wordlessly to my untied shoelaces, and I took the steam-train back to the provinces, thinking the while of all the well-connected people I would soon be so well-connected with. Next day I went to see Mr Bobbs, who sat in his office, his face set in its usual despondency. 'They offered me the job,' I said. 'My God,' he said, 'then take it. Nothing like this will ever happen to you again.' 'I think I will,' I said. 'The time has come to reconcile art and commerce, artificial enemies at the best.' 'You don't mean you intend to go on with the novel?' he said. 'Young man, there's no future in that, none at all. People do not want books about the kind of life you lead. There's no point in depressing them unnecessarily. Now, take the job, smarten yourself up, find someone with a bit of professional training to cut your hair, and get rid of those old trousers in the incinerator. I should put the novel in as well, while you're at it.' 'I ought to thank you, Mr Bobbs,' I said. 'No need,' said Bobbs. 'When they hear I've managed to get you placed, I'll win prizes.'

I went out of his office, full of delight. After all, a lot of great writers had worked. Dickens had done a youth opportunities scheme in the blacking factory business. Rimbaud had been an executive with a gun-running consortium. Conrad had been a shipping magnate, Eliot was a merchant banker, and Henry Miller had been a telecommunications expert. It was a legal requirement in the United States that all aspiring writers should first work in canneries or the logging industry, and all the great Modernists had had to do a stint in Hollywood, writing or possibly driving vehicles for Myrna Loy. All had kept the wild side of their genius, and in fact their experience of employment had given them, or at least some of them, something to write about. And yet, and yet ... There was something Faustian about the compact I had signed.

Would Ezra Pound really have written about bra-straps for Saul and Protheroe, or Fyodor Dostoevsky accepted without nervous crisis the world of brass carriage lamps and parked Vespa motor-scooters? Would I indeed be able to go on being me as I understood me to be – a wild, unkempt, provincial child of the moors, mills and chimneys of the city spread below?

I returned to my lodgings, my mind moving towards doubt and dejection. And there, to my amazement, was a letter of formal aspect. It was my degree result, in an envelope, and it contained rare and unexpected news. Mr Bobbs had told me I would be lucky to get a Lower Second, and that something closer to an outright fail would show that the examiners were doing justice to their standards. Matters had gone otherwise. I had won a fortunate First, the best of results, and what is more along with it went a truly remarkable prize – the Elijah Penury Research Fellowship, which permitted the bearer to do three years of intensive research on a bestowed pittance. Life was not unfair after all. There was, for those totally unfitted to it, a solution. It was to do research. I knew salvation when I saw it, and I saw it then. I scribbled a note to the University of Whitechapel, accepting the Penury Fellowship. And then I wrote another to Mr Fazackerley, thanking him for his kindness, but saying that owing to genetic defects arising from my lowly background I did not think I was fully fit to engage in the violent commerce of advertising, and could I therefore be excused.

It was the great turning point of my life, and it set me on the path I still tread today. I started a thesis, and in its interstices I returned to my novel, which began to bloom like a provincial flower. I kept the plum-coloured trousers, and did not get my hair cut until the middle of the 1960s, when the rampant coiffeur became, alas, all too fashionable. And, during the rest of the 1950s, the world curiously came to favour odd provincial people like myself. The provinces came in, Kingsley Amis published *Lucky Jim*, and the meritocratic generation, the New Men, most of them women, became the flavour of the month, and the novel – even my kind of novel – boomed. Even academic life acquired a gamey flavour with the world, and I climbed its difficult mountain-side, as thesis led to antithesis, fellowship to lectureship, and so on up the incremental scale until I found myself sitting all by myself in a chair.

In some curious way, it had all the time been all right to be me after all.

Or was it? From time to time, as I sit in my office, marking essays and telling my students not to write novels, there being enough already, I have occasional doubts. I think, for instance, about the real world, and what sort of person I might have been if I had lived in it, rather than regarding it as a total fiction. Roughly speaking, when I brood on reality, and its strange epistemological meaning, I see a small Danish desk. It is in a corner under a staircase at Saul and Protheroe, just off Berkeley Square. A figure sits at it, in Turnbull and Asser, red braces adding a glow to the scene. Telephones are at his fingertips, and he deals in accounts worth millions. When elections come, he is consulted on the presentation of candidates. His club is the Garrick, his drink is Campari-and-soda, and he frequents the Hurlingham at weekends. Privileged traveller status entitles him to free slippers in executive class on the jumbos. Yes, Rushdie, it could be worth considering. But if you say yes, don't tell them you are writing a novel.

Yours sincerely,
Malcolm Bradbury

I Have Answered Six Questions and That Is Enough

Now that academic posts are disappearing everywhere, this is no time for anyone setting out on that path in life that we academics call 'research'. Even so, we frequently do get a good number of enquiries from prospective candidates for the Doctorate of Philosophy, most of them, as it happens, from the Indian subcontinent. They arrive plastered with stamps, and written on a special and peculiar paper that evidently has some important use at an Indian seat of learning. Usually it is an aspiring candidate who announces that he is about to gather up his evidently large family and come to Britain to do what he calls our 'Ph.D. pogrom'. Since I have spent a good deal of time being a research student myself, I have naturally a certain amount of advice to offer, and some special brands of discouragement to give. And thus I am usually tempted to answer these letters in something like this fashion:

Dear Mr Bannerji,

Thank you for your letter, and may I say how much I appreciated your affectionate good wishes, and your kind words about the books of mine you would certainly have read had you been able to get hold of them. My daughter loves the amulet, and the thoughtful message from your soothsayer about the intentions of the Transcendental Mind I have passed on to the Vice-Chancellor so he can act on it without a moment's delay. How generous of you to say how much you would like to sit at my feet and thus acquire my wisdom. However, before you leap hotfoot onto the plane and head for this institution, there are a number of matters worth clarifying. I should first like to explain that a supervisor does not, as you suppose, write the thesis for you, and then invite you to put your name to it. In my experience matters are quite the reverse. Then there is this 'Ph.D. pogrom' you mention. In Britain we do not, to be honest, have such things, or not in the arts, preferring to assume that the desire to do research is unfortunate proof of the fact that one has simply not worked hard enough as an undergraduate, and is now trying desperately to catch up. In fact when you ask me to consider your prospects, compare research in Britain and the United States, and judge the future accordingly, you ask – as a prospective research student should – a very wise question. I will try to answer it, with my usual deviousness, in the following fashion.

The other day, scuffling through the accumulated detritus on my desk (I am not a tidy person), I suddenly uncovered a small, mouldering pile of magazines that had presumably once mattered to me, in a past and now forgotten stage of my existence. Why I was not sure, for they were copies, dating from the 1950s, of a journal called *College English* – an American academic trade paper targeted at teachers who work on the very front line of English language and literature education, where the artillery fire is always greatest. In an idle way I riffled through the bookwormed pages, wondering whether I had kept them for some important article – a handy two-page explanation of Structuralism, for instance. Then I suddenly noticed that some lunatic hand had been at work, inscribing over and defacing some of the essays. The obscure annotator had been busy, marking up articles with massive under-linings, heartfelt cries of 'Baloney!!' and wild shouts of 'N.B!!!!' Naturally, Mr Bannerji, as any good scholar would have been, I was at once totally fascinated.

I zoomed in closer, scholarly hackles alert. I then discovered, with the detective-like cunning that marks our trade, that these strange hiero-glyphs were all attached to a single series of articles called 'Teaching College English: Five Dialogues', which ran across five issues! What is more, there were only five copies of the magazine, an important clue, I felt. However, when inspected, the essays seemed innocuous enough. I call them essays, but they were rather playlets – dramatized conversations between an elderly and highly experienced university academic, starkly but neatly called Old Man, and a beardless neophyte who was just entering the profession, and was simply known as Youth. The drama that brought them into conflict was an urgent matter – the problems of teaching one of the staple courses then to be found in the English Departments of most American state universities, and known formally as Freshman Composition, and more colloquially as Readin', Writin', Speakin' and List'nin'.

The time, as I say, was the Fifties, which was, as you will probably know, the very springtime of education, especially in the United States. The system was in growth, and on many American campuses the only qualification for admission was the ability actually to find the campus and then discover a parking space. Comp. was a way of solving the consequent problems, a course designed to educate these entering freshpersons in the simplest rudiments of academic life – how to underline and write in margins, what a comma is and where to put it, how to open a book without cracking the whole thing in two, how to find the library and where to leave your chewing gum when you get there, and suchlike. Briefly, it aimed to bring these young candidates to such a state of literacy that, having found their way into the campus, they would be able to read all the signs and get out again – probably into careers as doctors, lawyers, army generals and possibly even future Presidents of the United States.

The task was a very responsible one, as I knew well, because I had once taught the course myself, in a vast state university somewhere amid the hog-rearing steppelands of the American Middle West, when I was at much the stage of my life that you are now. Naturally I read on, fascinated. I cannot say it was the limpid prose of the articles that attracted me, for stylistic grace was not the forte of its author. No, what I was interested in was the scholarly question of what had driven this anonymous, mad annotator to such frenzies. But I delved my way through the five dialogues, and suddenly a strange thing happened. For, by one of those strange, involuntary processes of memory about which someone, preferably French, ought to write a novel one of these days, I found myself transported back in time, as if in some magic capsule, or one of those American youth movies. And all of a sudden the past was before me again, grinning like a clown, and I was once again there, in the middle of the Fifties, in the small wooden office I had once shared, with five other graduate students like myself, on that remote, hot, wide, frisbee-throwing campus.

There must have been a hundred of us. We were called teaching assistants, and we were whiz-kids with Ph.D.'s from California and Berkeley, leading experts on the liberal dilemma, irony, ambiguity, and Christian imagery in anything you could care to think of. Nothing was more natural than that we should therefore spend our time sitting behind office flyscreens marking student essays, or 'themes', as they were called, on such demanding topics as 'My Home Town' or 'Is My Education to Improve My Mind or Train Me For a Job?' which our thousands of composition students had written for us. To me, a visitor, these essays were invaluable sociological introductions to American culture, but it was not for that we read them. Our task was to hunt them for errors, above all for what were called the Gross Illiteracies – five crucial solecisms that included the Unjustifiable Sentence Fragment ('I came to college. Having graduated from high school'), the Unjustifiable Comma Splice ('He told me about it, I did not believe him') and, most terrible of all, the Dangling Modifier ('If thoroughly stewed the patients will enjoy our prunes'), all of which earned an automatic penalty of F, the failing grade.

The task was arduous, often involving teaching the freshman how to recognize the letter F in the first place. So it was very necessary that we, who taught, had in turn to *be* taught, taught how to teach. So, once a week, all hundred of us attended something called the 'Teaching Round Table', where we sat round a square table and learned the basic principles of our trade from a worn old scholar in a plaid tam-o'-shanter – remarkably like Old Man, in fact. He gave us the finest points of his immense experience: never smoke in old wooden buildings, never stand with your back to a class, avoid intellectual arrogance until you have earned it, do not take money from students in exchange for favours, always sit when you are not standing and stand when you are not sitting, and so on. Here I began my teaching career, and learned nearly all of what I know today, such as it is.

It was strange to be carried back to it all, and memory grew stronger.

41

Hadn't there been some set text or other for the course, some small bible we used to read and discuss? I looked again at the five dialogues, and realized that these were what they were. Then, in a sudden leap of scholarly insight, I suddenly realized the identity of the mad annotator who had scribbled so frenziedly in the margins. Mr Bannerji, I will not delay you further. It was, of course, myself, or rather some former, neophytic, transatlantic form of I. That was it! The magazines dropped uselessly from my hands to the desk, my thoughts whirled and, as unbidden as the raging sea itself, floods of memory and nostalgia began to wash through my fine scholarly mind.

Yes, I was once, in the middle Fifties, a teacher of Comp. For two years I had been a British research student, of much the kind you are now seeking to be, Mr Bannerji, though in those days research was not what it is now. In fact I well remember when, having won a fortunate fellowship that took me to London, I first talked to my own supervisor and went to sit at his feet. He was a strangely fat man who lived in a small den behind one of the lesser-known London colleges, and appeared in public only at night. I was full of intellectual excitement, and ideas for my thesis bubbled like French fries in the boiling fat of my mind. I recall his door opened but a tiny crack, and an eye inspected me before his hand reached out and dragged me inside. 'You didn't see any Indians out there on the warpath, did you?' he asked me. I looked at him mystified, and explained my journey down the corridor had passed in perfect safety. He then explained to me that he had a great many Indian postgraduate students – in those days they were called Chattergee – all writing theses on E. M. Forster. They hovered in the corridor, left bowls of rice outside his door, and then knocked on it, asking for wisdom. That, he said, was the problem. 'You see, young man,' he said, 'and one day you will remember these words, one man has only so much wisdom to offer. I have learned the hard way to be very sparing with mine.'

So indeed he had. In fact his spare way with wisdom is practically all I now remember about him, for I saw him very little after that. Research, he said, was a lonely business. And indeed, as he explained to me, it was the British way that I should see my supervisor only four times during my two years of study. In our first meeting, the one we were having, we would settle on a subject. (My own notions not being much to his taste, he proposed I took the topic 'The Influence of Anyone on Anything', which he just happened to have spare.) After a few weeks I should bring him a statement explaining what I intended to do with it. After a couple of years I should bring him a completed thesis, having done it. He would then lose it, and call me back for a second copy. Then we would have a chat about it, or something else if he found it difficult to understand. That was the sum of his duties as a supervisor, but he firmly believed that good research was easily spoiled by excessive interference by others.

Thus my life as a research student began. For two years I worked among the high stone pillars of the British Museum, daily taking the small red underground train that brought me in from the convenient digs I had found somewhere near Uxbridge. Every day I would walk through the grey heart of Bloomsbury, looking for the famous 'Group', though unfortunately it seemed to have dispersed, mostly to more comfortable circumstances on the Sussex Downs. Passing between the offices of publishers, infinitely mysterious then, and past the espresso bars, I would enter the high portals of the world's greatest seat of learning, show, if I had remembered to bring it, my Reader's Ticket, and enter the great forehead of the Reading Room, packed with solid green silence. It was warm, and a very pleasant place to spend one's time. In those days they even kept a writer, Angus Wilson, in a sort of cage in the centre of it, to show the kind of thing one ought to be studying. And soon I discovered I was part of a community of peers, who – rather like the peers in the House of Lords – proved to be as curious a bunch of eccentrics as one could hope to find out of confinement.

So I became what I longed to be, a true and committed scholar. I was always at my desk at nine, when the Museum opened; I was always the last one to be kicked out when it closed. I would sit, always, at desk D-4, and indeed for two years in the history of the august institution the symbol D-4 and the name Bradbury went symbiotically together. Here, amid the strong aromatic flavours of leather bindings and the even stronger flavours of the Middle European *émigrés* who used the establishment to write works of sedition, I would order unusual tomes, copy notes into notebooks, and generally follow my dedication. There were various pleasant relaxations. At ten I would go down to the lavatory, to watch the *émigrés* washing their top hats in the washbasins. The British Museum is, or then was, surrounded by teashops, and I would frequent these at lunch and teatime, usually in the company of bookish girls whom I met by leaning over their desks and murmuring, 'I say, those books look interesting, much more interesting than mine'. From time to time I caught a glimpse of my supervisor, who would wander into the Reading Room now and again, and on one occasion wrote a letter of introduction for me to T. S. Eliot, who in turn wrote back saying he had never heard of him.

And in these various intervals I began conducting a love affair with a large, flamboyant and rather rich girl from Sheffield, who was herself, naturally, engaged on a dissertation of her own. Since we were dedicated scholars with theses to write, we met rarely except for lunch and tea, and our relationship was largely conducted by a desk-top correspondence, as we passed notes, folded in books, to each other. 'I'm mad at you, you said you'd have lunch yesterday,' would come a message, tucked into Havelock Ellis's *Strange Genitals* or some such. 'Sorry, my supervisor came and I had to buy him a meal', the news would fly back, in Burton's *Anatomy of Melancholy*. 'How about today?' I duly completed my thesis on the influence of anyone on anything, and sent it to my supervisor, who indeed lost it, as he had promised to do. Happily there was another copy, which I took to a small bookbinder up Gower Street who hit the edges with a hammer and put a binding on it. Some long time thereafter, I was called for an oral examination.

When I arrived, my supervisor was there, this time as an examiner. He clearly had no recollection of me whatsoever, and when asked for his opinion said the topic was absurd and no supervisor in his right mind would supervise it. Fortunately the other examiner had read the papers, if not the dissertation, and was able to prove that he had supervised it himself; in the confusion that followed, I was awarded a degree. 'Research finished, got M. A.', I wrote one day to the girl from Sheffield. 'Going to America.' The return note came more quickly than usual. 'Why America? What about marriage?' it said. 'Ph.D. next', I wrote, 'then life'. 'Swine', she wrote. That night, unusually, we spent time together; I took her to dinner in Soho, then to see a play in Greek, and finally I saw her back to her hall of residence, somewhere in Chelsea, where her curfew tolled at midnight. But for a golden hour, as a sign saying HOVIS flashed randomly at us, we sat on a riverside bench. The seat was wet, and ants kept taking things back and forth along it, but we didn't mind; our hearts were anxious, and too full to speak. Alas, curfew hour duly came, and I handed her over to the chaperone at the girls' hostel; but not before I had given her a copy of T. S. Eliot's *The Cocktail Party*. It had, of course, a note in it. 'I won't forget you', it said. We kissed and wiped a tear or so from each of our eyes. And, as these recollections make evident, I have not overlooked the promise.

For this was the Fifties, when departures were momentous, and America very, very far away, indeed a ten-day sea passage on the old Cunarders, which still plied their trade. Thus the next day, in my clean socks, I stood at the docks at Southampton, looking up at the R.M.S. *Grand Cham*, a great wedding cake of a ship, sturdy yet pleasantly worn after years of yeoman service on the Henry James run. I was a wandering scholar at last, following my dedication to places afar. Various governmental minions opened my cases, knotting my suits together under the pretext of facilitating embarkation, and then, as a military band played, I picked up my hand-baggage, which consisted of a portable typewriter, a full-size X-ray photograph of my chest, and my mint thesis, and clambered up the rope-ladder to the vessel, my British Museum days over, the glories of study in what you so wisely call an American 'Ph.D. pogrom' ahead.

A moment later white-uniformed flunkies were welcoming me on board the *Grand Cham*, and directing me to my quarters, which proved to be down many mahogany corridors of diminishing size, and well below the waterline. The four-berth cabin was frankly scarcely bigger than a child's coffin, and my three cabin mates packed it already – three long-faced, dark-haired English youths who seemed to me to possess a curious resemblance to myself. Nor was that the end of the similarity. For, as I unpacked my travelling baggage, taking out the X-ray photograph and the mint thesis to put them out on the one convenient shelf, I found the space already occupied by three other X-ray photographs, and what is more by three more Master's theses. I turned to my cabin mates enquiringly, and they nodded. Evidently I was not the only one of my kind to set forth on this kind of scholarly quest, and so it was to prove.

For, after the ship had got under way, and we had wallowed off down Southampton Water, into a blood-red sunset, we repaired together, a comradely group, to dinner. We selected a table for four, and chatted among ourselves, as people naturally do, of Dryden's dramatic criticism, the later George Eliot, and F. R. Leavis's latest views of Milton. A pause fell, perhaps to allow us to eat something, and then we noticed another oddity. The people at the next table were also talking of Dryden, Eliot and Leavis. So were those at the next table beyond that, and the next beyond that. Indeed, as a curious, questioning silence fell over the entire dining room, it grew clear that virtually the entire complement of tourist class was drawn from the world of learning. We were nothing less than the Fulbright generation, the grant getters, the new foundation-sponsored intelligentsia, going on pilgrimages. There were American intellectuals returning from a year's stint Guggenheiming in Paris or Rome or London, sitting next to British intellectuals, mostly youthful like myself, just off for a year's stint at the Folger, or the Widener, or at various other desirable places of academic resort in the Middle West. There were English-Speaking Union Fellows, Commonwealth Fund Fellows, Jane Eliza Procter Visiting Fellows, and Henry Fellows, some of them girls. There were Gulbenkian and Ford Fellows, and even Rockefeller Fellers.

'What a blow for the human intelligence if this ship should sink,' someone suddenly said, and it was a truly sobering thought. Why, some-one else asked anxiously, had we not been split up among several vessels, so that some form of scholarship, however attenuated, could survive if the fate of the *Titanic* should be repeated? Someone else began to consider which fields of scholarship should be given priority in the lifeboats, and proposed that a small committee should be formed to rate projects in order. A sociologist on a Guggenheim noted that the statistical likeli-hood of any group like this gathering in any one context was rare indeed, though a historian of emigration recalled some nineteenth-century analogies. Several people agreed that nonetheless there was a thesis in it, if only the right person could be found; someone else remarked that with a passenger list of this proclivity, no thesis topic of any kind was likely to go begging for a moment. A man who was going to the States to visit relatives in California and had been seen carrying a copy of Nevil Shute asked the steward if he could move into first-class, and then general conversation resumed; but it was obvious this would be no ordinary voyage.

This grew more evident later that evening, when, as my room mates and I were sitting in our cabin, idly gossiping about chapter four of Erich Auerbach's *Mimesis*, there came a tap at the door. A young American we had met at dinner and who had given us offprints of some articles on Swinburne entered. 'Hi,' he said, sitting in the washbasin; we said 'Hi' back, and he went on to explain that a meeting had informally forgathered in the lounge after dinner, at which a resolution had been passed, with only six abstentions, calling for the discussions begun over the six-course repast to be put on a more regular basis. The notion was that, after bouillon in the morning, we should start some daily seminars, devoted to the topic of comparisons between European and American life and thought. (The abstentions had come from those supporting a rival project for lessons in Hittite.) This would prevent fine-honed minds from rusting in the sea air, and at the same time serve as orientation for those entering an unfamiliar land for the first time. 'There are some of the best people in the business on board,' he explained. 'They've got C.V.'s as long as your arm. We'd be crazy not to take advantage of them. There's only one problem; we're not authorized to give any formal credits. But some of those kids are so keen I guess nothing will stop them from attending. You know how it is with real scholars.' And he adjured us to be present at ten-thirty the next morning.

And an interesting session it was, with someone from King's, Cambridge, giving a very good paper on how to use the London Underground, followed by a Harvard scholar's possibly over-Kleinian analysis of how to get off a turnpike in the United States. It was searching stuff, well delivered, and it is not surprising that a groan went up when we were interrupted by the crew, who for some reason tied us all up in life-jackets and then briefly lowered us in lifeboats over the ship's side. At lunch afterwards everyone agreed the meetings had been very useful, though some people complained the reading lists were too short and there should be slides if possible. And so, for a couple of days, as we passed down the Channel and into the Atlantic, it went on, while the pool stayed empty and the shuffleboard facilities went unemployed.

It was on, I think, the third day – when a resolution was passed suggesting that the ship's newspaper, which up to that time had contained small quizzes, which were normally completed in about thirty seconds by the high-flying company of passengers, along with announcements of fancy-dress competitions too trivial for learned minds to bother with, be turned over entirely to scholarly articles printed according to the rules of the MLA stylesheet – that I began to feel the symptoms of a certain intellectual claustrophobia. When the Swinburne man, who somehow seemed to have taken charge, came by that evening after dinner and assigned me fifty pages of Benjamin Franklin's *Autobiography* to read by the morning, something, possibly the lobster pâté I had just eaten, made me feel strangely nauseous, and I was, to be frank, ready to take an Incomplete in the course. Happily my anxieties were relieved by a chance encounter at a dance that, despite the notices saying 'Silence' that had now appeared all over the vessel, took place that evening, with an elegantly proportioned American nurse, tanned brown as a berry by a two-month study tour of the beaches of Italy. Viewing this excellent specimen of contemporary American culture, who appeared curiously charming despite her low score on the Graduate Record Examination, and driven by my usual desire for knowledge, I resolved to find out more about her *Weltanschauung*.

I began my course of study the following day, cutting the Franklin session completely. Being a modest, provincial, British youth, I found I had much to learn. 'You're so polite I don't believe it,' said the nurse. 'You'll never snow an American girl that way.' Some hours later she was still telling me how to *really* snow an American girl when the Swinburne man appeared. 'Say,' he said, 'you missed class today.' I apologized for my absence, but said I needed time to do field-work. 'It was great, how to use an Automat,' he said, 'then one of the guys in your cabin told us how to put shillings in British gas meters. Those classes are really taking off.' 'I'm sure,' I said. 'I'm sorry I missed it.'

'You can pick up on the course in the morning,' he said, and by nine the next day he was hovering outside my cabin door when I came out. 'Not today,' I said, 'I have this very important project of my own to work on.' He left, a trifle dejected, and my project came along shortly afterwards from her cabin, where she had been putting on her swimsuit. We went to the pool, which we had totally to ourselves, and I learned a good deal about what to do on dates.

In fact the voyage became extremely amusing, until one day the Swinburne man came by and announced that on the following morning I was due to present the paper I had, he claimed, long ago promised to give. I went back to the cabin and remembered other unfulfilled promises — to the big girl from the British Museum, for one. Whether it was guilt, the prospect of unfolding my thoughts on the *Weltan-schauung* of the young American female to my scholarly peers, or the rising swell that was to blame, I do not know, but the following morning I felt remarkably queasy. The Swinburne man came by and proved unexpectedly sympathetic, promising to set the group a one-hour quick quiz in lieu, and guaranteeing me medical attention. Not long afterwards the ship's nurse, who was researching heart transplants, arrived, apparently on his summons, and thanks to various kinds of thoughtful ministration I improved by evening, when the skyline of Manhattan appeared and the classes were concluded. I went up on deck and stood next to the Swinburne man. 'I'll never forget this trip, it was better than MLA,' he said. 'I really learned a lot. I guess nothing ever like it happened before in history.' 'I learned a lot too,' I said, staring at the extraordinary apparition of New York, which looked like a European city, but tipped on its side. 'I think I'm going to like American education.'

And so it all began, my personal Brain Drain. Alas, little did I realize that the shipboard orientation I had received on the *Grand Cham* would bear little relation to the practicalities of life on the Great Campus that was my destination. For two more days I travelled, crossing the great American continent in a Pullman daycoach where moths flew out of the seating, watching the great American landscape turn from highrise city to unending prairie, where nothing blocked the view to the far-distant horizon but the odd red barn, bearing the legend CHEW MAIL POUCH

TOBACCO, TREAT YOURSELF TO THE BEST. Then on the third day I was there, and a cabbie deposited me and my luggage at Doolittle Hall, the graduate dormitory that was to be my home for the rest of the academic year. It lay on a great pastoral campus the size of a small town, with its own radio station, football stadium, 5,000-seater auditorium, and a library with a sign on it saying, rather sensibly, THIS IS NOT THE LIBRARY: THE LIBRARY IS INSIDE.

So began my second life as a research student, the life of the young annotator whose anxious scribbles provoked all this recollection. And now it all comes back to me, I well understand his note of frenzied anxiety. For the world I entered proved hard to understand and conquer. By day, the campus seemed a quiet, contemplative place, where the carillon trilled hourly for the change of classes and the students swarmed from session to session along the campus paths, the coeds in their blue, yellow and green slickers, the fellows in their shorn-off jeans. By night, though, it changed into something else, as loud whooping cries of oestrus and mating filled the glades and hollows, while the miles of telephonic wiring that linked the sororities and fraternities tingled with the endless hum of seductive sexual trans-actions. It was little wonder that these students appeared listless, if not decidedly sated, as they stumbled to class of a morning, to learn the mysteries of the Gross Illiteracy and the technique of creative underlining.

Indeed their lives seemed the reverse of my own, as by night I studied and wrote my thesis, and by day I tried, with frenzied energy, to teach them wisdom. I met my classes, for some reason, in an amphitheatre in the Chemistry Building, where the lecturer's desk had a sink and many gas-taps, which I used to turn on and off in sheer nervousness, while the beautiful girls in the front row turned pallid under their pancake make-up. For the students who sat before me in tiered rows were a formidable sight. There were acned youths in fraternity beanies, and seven foot-ballers all called Bukovsky, who dozed frequently and when awake proved to have arms that could reach all round the room. The rest of the group consisted of beautiful girls, all about eighteen, who sat in class in full *maquillage*, wearing jewellery, cashmere sweaters, and skirts with darts under the rump that made their bottoms stick out – a terrible distraction as I tried to interest them, moving from simple spelling to details of my scholarly activities, in which they pretended a polite interest. Mostly, though, they seemed remarkably inert, if not comatose. Only after a few weeks did I discover why. Finally a delectable girl in the front row, whom I had identified as Evangeline Winthrop Proops, ceased wriggling, crossing and uncrossing her fine legs, fluttering her notebook, uncapping and recapping her golden pen, and broke the silence, asking if I would speak more slowly. They were all having problems in understanding what I said, because I spoke English, like Churchill, with a foreign accent.

The bafflement proved mutual. In time the essays came in, and proved that even Evangeline Winthrop Proops, delectable as she was in life, was a dullard in print, and indeed, like most of her fellows, a high-wire artist in the Gross Illiteracy. 'If a couple loves one another they will realize many things about them. The couple knows if the other is love-able, selfish, rich or poor, good or bad, educated, can make a living, religious and many other things, but if they love each other. They will want to marry,' began her touching but imperfect first essay. And it was, as it were, par for the course. Only when the semester came towards its end, and it was time for the grades to be announced, did I discover that other ways of passing than actually writing literate essays were the local norm. The seven footballers called Bukovsky, who for months had not opened an eyelid in class, came in with the football coach and told me they expected A's; otherwise, they could guarantee, I would be ceremonially lynched in mid-field by the collective alumni at the game against Purdue. Essays began to arrive that seemed to have sources other than their accredited authors, and when one came in entitled 'One of Nature's Marvels: The Mighty Bee' ('The bee is one of the most all-round of nature's insects . . .'), even I, a British innocent, recalled glimpsing it in *Reader's Digest* a month before. Similarly a piece on 'The Function of Criticism at the Present Time' seemed vaguely familiar, especially since the copyist had been faithful enough even to transcribe the name Matthew Arnold at the very end.

But it was when Evangeline Winthrop Proops came by and told me that she would do anything, and she did mean anything, to get an A, which she needed for an upmarket career profile, that I finally realized

I was in a moral dilemma. My interest in the *Weltanschauung* of the American female had not diminished, but I did have a scholarly honour, bred in the bone in the vault of the British Museum. Cogent advice was clearly necessary, and I was not sure the Teaching Round Table was an ideal venue for discussing my crisis. And it was now I began delving with fury into the pages of 'Teaching College English: Five Dialogues', which no longer seemed a dry-as-dust drama, but high art confronting the deep dilemmas of existence itself. These playlets may have been a little stilted in tone, small in cast (you could have staged them in any handy broom-closet), and somewhat plain in exposition, when compared, say, with Ibsen, or anyone else for that matter. But they dealt with eternal themes – innocence and experience, youth and age, folly and wisdom – and the hard verities of life. In fact there was even an incursion into the drama of a mad student named Lowboy, whom I immediately recognized, and a good deal of consideration given to exactly the kind of problem posed by Evangeline Winthrop Proops. Indeed, Mr Bannerji, if you yourself decide to become a teaching assistant in America, I recommend these dialogues to you.

Basically they are a duet in the Socratic form. They are largely conducted by Old Man, deeply experienced in academic life and not lacking in self-assurance ('With age and experience one may become too full of wisdom,' he pronounces in an unusual moment of humility), and who has all the basic rules of teaching at his fingertips, as the following cogent comment makes apparent: 'The best tests are "A" and "B", the worst are "D" and "E", and the ones in between are "C"'. He talks with – or rather at – Youth, who is young, wet-eared, probably acned, and keenly pursuing the pathway towards academic success, even if it means being something of a toady in the process ('We have had another good conversation,' he is given to saying). The basically Wordsworthian relationship between the two is clearly set out in the opening exposition:

YOUTH: I have just arrived on your campus, fresh from graduate school, for my first full-time teaching assignment. The department head suggested that I talk with you.
OLD MAN: I think I understand ... You have your Ph.D.?

YOUTH: Well, practically. I still have to complete my dissertation and take my finals.

OLD MAN: In other words, you hold a master's degree and have fulfilled the residence requirements for the doctor's degree.

YOUTH: Yes, sir, and the course requirements.

Some may call this stark, but in me it evoked an immediate shock of recognition, and it is no wonder that I was hooked. Indeed, re-reading it all the other day, I felt myself completely involved again with these two realistic characters, especially when more flesh is put on their bones. For Youth, it turns out, is an engineer *manqué* ('When I was a boy I liked to tinker with motors and light sockets,' he explains), who has switched to the study of English, as if struck by some blinding light, as he might very well have been. Old Man is the voice of saddened experience, at times a little suspicious ('We sometimes have an instructor who doesn't see – or doesn't want to see – our problems,' he remarks, when Youth for once shows a little spunk), yet willing to acknowledge good qualities in others: 'You seem an extraordinarily perceptive young man,' he admits, whenever Youth is sensible enough to go along with his views.

Little wonder that, as the marginal notes make clear, I identified immediately with Youth and his troubles, even though his electrical history was a little different from my own. On the other hand, Old Man, the notes suggest, produced a more complicated reaction. Evidently I was at first inclined to distrust his pontificating manner, but firm underlinings show I recognized his high pedagogic insight:

YOUTH: I thought you might have some suggestions.

OLD MAN: It is a reasonable assumption. I have been teaching freshman composition on and off . . . since I was your age, and I have written some things for and about the course.

YOUTH: Yes, I know.

OLD MAN: It is slippery footing, however. What works for me may not work for you . . . By suggestions, do you mean such things as whether to stand up and lecture or sit down and discuss?

YOUTH: I didn't have that in mind, but I should like to hear your comments.

OLD MAN: Generally speaking, I should say sit down and discuss. On the other hand, with a large class or with inattentive students it may be more effective to stand.

But, good and liberal-minded as he proves himself on sitting and standing, Old Man offers yet more, indeed frequently getting to the places other Round Tables cannot reach. Youth has clearly had a bad time with a problem that had troubled me a good deal myself – what to do with those belligerent students who come demanding higher grades, and will not take F for an answer. When Youth puts the problem, Old Man is wise enough not to give a direct reply. Instead he offers to perform a specimen conference, telling Youth to conceal himself in the background and affect insouciance ('Why don't you sit back there and read a book?'). Luckily out in the corridor there stands a classic example of the student species, a youth named Joe Lowboy, one of those fellows whose knuckles clearly touch the floor before his feet do. He comes into the room, totally fails to notice Youth, who is effectively hiding behind the office copy of *Webster's Dictionary*, slouches down into a chair, and promptly complains about the D he has somehow gained on his last test. The mark's intrinsic generosity is soon made clear, Lowboy proving himself a consistently poor grammarian. 'I don't read very good,' he comments. 'I went to both the Writing Clinic and the Reading Clinic last year, but they don't seem to help me in this course very much.' Nonetheless he shows the student cunning typical of his kind, challenging the entire concept of applying marks to people such as himself: 'I still don't see how you can tell what grade to give a test. Do you grade on a curve?'

Oh, yes, Lowboy, I recognize you still, and all those techniques of illogical argument, like complaining that if you have low marks this only proves your teacher has not taught you properly, with which you attempt to raise a D to a passing C. Happily Old Man remains steadfast, resisting all arguments, abuse, and honeyed persuasion by feigning ignorance, uninterest, and at times total senility, and passing the buck when necessary: 'That is not for me to say. Your faculty adviser is the person to talk to,' he remarks cunningly at one point, in a deft sideways move. The scene and situation are classics of their kind, and inevitably

Lowboy retires deflated, Old Man's words ringing in his ears. 'I'm afraid you will have to accept my judgement about your grades. Assigning grades is one of the things I am paid to do,' he cries, adding as the door slams, 'come in again if I can help you in your work.' And when Youth reveals himself behind his tome, and wonders if Old Man has not been too lenient, he learns a saddened truth about the role of the scholar and intellectual in a crass culture. For now Old Man explains the grim social meaning of Lowboy:

> His values are not yours or mine, but they are very simple, and the product of a dominant element in our culture: get something out of the other fellow – inside information, unjustified grades, unearned money. In ten years, whether he graduates or not, he will be making more money than I make now, after a lifetime of teaching.

Indeed, hints Old Man, the lad may be crass, but one of these days he could be hiring and firing *you* – one of the darker truths of life that has rarely before been brought out in high literature.

But even this is not the greatest peak of intensity the drama reaches; that comes a little later, and undoubtedly it put my dealings, if you can call them that, with Evangeline Winthrop Proops in a clear light. For, as the relation between ephebe and master progresses, Youth comes out with a strange confession – nothing less than the fact that, while working with his freshman class on the hyphen one day, he has come to fall in love with one of his students, a comely coed who has batted her legs at him from the front row. Passion still rages, but a familiar and hideous barrier stands in the way of anything like consummation. As he explains quaveringly to Old Man: 'I couldn't do anything about it because of the ethics of the profession' – a comment that draws even from stoic Old Man an understanding 'Quite'. Nor is that the end of the matter: condemned to peer mutely at his temptress through the fanned leaves of the freshman anthology *Learning to Write Right*, Youth has adopted a desperate expedient, choosing instead to breathe down the neck of one of his fellow graduate students in the Milton class. 'We had a lot in common. I was lonely,' he explains in what may not be a total *non sequitur*.

And now the inevitable has happened. Though the flame of love for his freshperson student burns bright as ever, he has cautiously plought his troth to the fellow-Miltonist, beside the Coke machine during the ten-minute break. 'I suppose it was kind of calculated', he admits in shame. Old Man broods for a moment, and I have to admit I awaited his answer as keenly as Youth himself. But when it comes it shows him in finest fettle. Romantic love is all very well, Old Man remarks, but it is bad news when it comes to the choice of a faculty wife – who always needs, like a new faculty member himself, to be selected very carefully, and not just for her skill on the footnotes. There are other duties, like compromising the departmental head into incautious offers of tenure, that require sterling qualities:

OLD MAN: A wife can assist one in his career.
YOUTH: Oh yes. We read together and discuss our reactions.
OLD MAN: If a wife is attractive, a good hostess, subtly aggressive for her husband, and has money in her own right, she may be very helpful – if her husband is not a clod. Sometimes even then.

Once more Old Man comes through with flying colours, and I believe it was the very night I read this that I sent off a brief, abrasive note to Evangeline Winthrop Proops, returning the locket with her hair in it, and started hanging around Bergdorf-Goodman's, watching the talent go in and out.

But how, we might ask, are we to read these powerful playlets, and their message? Clearly they deal with one of art's most profound themes, that of disenchantment, or paradisial loss, and its role in human understanding. Youth is a creature of illusions, believing that in entering academic life he has entered a world of romance, not unlike literature itself. Hence he utters such sentiments as 'I would never marry a girl for her money', and harshly criticizes a colleague for his base, diurnal habit of slipping out of the office to go home and mow the lawn, or shop for groceries. Old Man, however, is the voice of saddened reality, the master of things as they are. 'He could do worse', he says of the lawn-mowing colleague, in a striking judgement. 'Almost anything he does will help him in his appreciation of literature' – assisting him in the reading of Marvell, perhaps. Life, he sees, is constructed in the realm of the practical, and arcadian dreams can no longer fill the groves of academe. As he puts it to Youth: 'The long-cherished conception that a college is a community of scholars, even including the lowly composition instructor. Would that it were true.' (Actually, the first sentence here would, at my own Midwestern university, have counted as an Unjustified Sentence Fragment, a major or Gross Illiteracy carrying the penalty of an automatic F, but, as Old Man wisely says, 'Every college has its own traditional way of doing things that is not like the way of any other college'.)

Like much great art, 'Teaching College English: Five Dialogues', takes us from illusion to reality. Desperately, Youth offers Old Man his fanciful dreams – of romantic love, of wise students, of the joys of endless footnoting, and finally, in one last saddened fling, of actual literary creativity itself. 'Have you ever known anyone who has become a writer?' he asks in desperation, evidently about to unpack some bulky manuscript from his briefcase. Old Man looks, and sorrowfully shakes his head. 'Only one,' he says, and for a moment the pain is terrible, as Youth – and no doubt myself, his youthful reader – contemplates the barren, uncreative ordinariness that is the campus scholar's life. But, pulling himself together, he accepts the truth, in a telling moment. 'I have been here for a year and a half, and am concerned about my prospects. You see, we're going to have a baby ...' he announces with stiff upper lip. Old Man rises in his usual way to the momentous occasion. 'That is the kind of question for the department head,' he says, and we watch Youth depart for the last time, off to beg the boss for tenure, so he can follow the path of the master at last. Then the lights go down, and we are left with Old Man, Tiresias himself, he of wrinkled dugs, who has seen it all, sitting, perhaps blinking a little, at his desk – and possibly awaiting the reappearance of Lowboy, ready at last to take him up on his generous offer of further help.

It was, I now realize, 'Teaching College English: Five Dialogues' that taught me that American academic life was not just a bed of roses. And, to be frank, I took the easy way out. At the end of the academic year, I posted the final grades, which happened to be mostly F's, hid in the bushes for a day or so until the baying students had given up hunting for me and gone home, and then planned my future. I packed my tweeds, chest X-ray photograph, and my now not-so-mint thesis, and made a hasty getaway – though evidently not so hasty that I failed to catch up my precious copies of *College English* before I left. Aboard the R.M.S. *Grand Cham* as she sailed for England, this time packed with American tourists (I thought I recognized the Lowboy family), I was decidedly silent, chastened and withdrawn. Back in England, I duly joined a British academic world in which, so far at least, Freshman Composition is not taught, where I could sit or stand as I chose, and no students bounded into my office saying: 'You got a problem here, Mr Bradberry; it's me.' And here, more or less, I have remained, trying to study hard and also keep the lawn well-mown, for you never know where literary appreciation comes from.

But just occasionally – as when I happen across some old pile of *College English*, for example, or when your own letter arrived – I do indeed recall those Composition days, now well into the past. Indeed, as I was saying only the other week to my wife (who is *not* from Sheffield, though of course she does have money in her own right), it was all by way of being a very formative period in my life. Even so, it is hard to recover all the appropriate emotions. Just a couple of days ago there came a tap at the door of my room – on this side of the Atlantic we prefer not to call our faculty rooms offices – and a youth, wearing a sickly smile on his face, popped his head in. 'I have just arrived on your campus, fresh from graduate school, for my first full-time teaching assignment', he said. He ducked, but not before a dictionary had raised a nasty weal on his brow. It was a cruel gesture, but I do think I did it for the best.

Even so, if you are still interested, let me know. We are very keen on foreign students these days, and if you can reassure me on the matter of how you are placed financially I will see what can be arranged. However, I do feel that, especially since the success of the film of *A Passage to India*, the field of Forster has been a little overworked these days. May I suggest a topic here, 'Cross-Influences between Anything and Nothing: An Interdisciplinary Study', which a rather nice girl who has just married her tutor has now discarded. I think it might suit you rather well. All things being equal, I shall be perfectly happy to supervise, and if you should ever want a word with me, I should have no difficulty in fitting you in on three or four occasions over the next two years or so.

Yours, etc.,
Malcolm Bradbury

Time Called While
You Were Out

These days, I suppose, I am one of the more high-minded sorts of writer — ever ready to advise a close friend on experimental paragraphing, or lecture any passing journalist on the meaning of art, the confusion of life, the promise of literature, the future of the novel, the nature of the liberal dilemma on the horns of which we now, rather uncomfortably, sit, and other matters of like weight and moment. I write more or less what I like. What I write I believe in. And give or take an editor's intervention, or two, or three, the way I wrote it and meant it is the way you get it. But I have done my share on the downside of writing, sweated on the hard rockface where most writers have been tested at one time or another. The youngsters don't realize it now, but in my early days writing was tough, really tough. We had to rise at four, wash in cold water, stoke the furnace, and then work on hard, heavy manual typewriters that brought the blisters out on your hands, for all hours God sent. Lunch was bread and dripping, and the reviewers used to come and lash us every single day, one thing that has somehow not changed since.

I am reminded of all this by a letter I got the other day from some young writer who was in a considerable lather because someone had approached him and asked him to, well, 'collaborate'. The idea of co-authorship appalled him, he said, though his publisher was all in favour, pointing out how well such things had gone in the past: Beaumont and Fletcher, Gilbert and Sullivan, Masters and Johnson, Morecombe and Wise. Would I guide him through the morass? Naturally I understood his nervousness, and tried to think of a way

of dissipating his worries. Would it be enough to remind him that in
my young day, when writing was 'ard, really 'ard, we had to
collaborate all the time? But then so had some of the French during
the war. No, better to tell him a little tale – the tale of the time
when, once, I was Nathalie Pelham Barker.

Dear Young Writer,

Thank you for your letter, asking whether I would ever consider
collaborating on a work of literature. The truth is not only that I
would, but I have. From the experience I learned a number of lessons,
about how to do it, where to do it, why to do it, and when to stop.
Whether the story will be helpful to you I am not sure, but I can assure
you that apart from an odd graduate course on the *The Last Duchess* or
two, the process taught me a good part of what I think I know about
life and literature. The tale takes us some way back in time, back to my
early literary youth. For like many young people I was determined from
an early age to be a writer. I didn't know what it would be like, I didn't
know what I would write about, and nothing much had happened to
me. But the dedication was there, and somehow it led me into academic
life, where I duly became a research student, desperately trying to
reconcile art and scholarship. It was not surprising that this quest led me
onto the campuses of American universities, where this kind of double
life is more common and more readily accepted. As you know, British
universities do accept and study writers, but with one stern proviso I
was not prepared to accept: they must be dead first. American
universities seem to have the opposite attitude, filling their campuses
with errant poets and wandering novelists, who write their work in one
room and teach it in the next, so short-circuiting many of the problems
of reaching an audience.

So, for much of the Fifties, if you wanted me you were likely to find
me on some American campus or other, where the double business of
my life seemed to fit in best. It was not just that American universities
were very tolerant of writers, but that among the friends I had there –
most of them brilliant fellow-graduate students, fresh from doing
Ph.D.'s at Columbia – literary ambitions ran rife. All of them seemed

to be planning Great American Novels that were even Greater than the Great American Novels they were teaching in class, or if they were not doing that they were planning the Great American Screenplay, which meant lowering your standards slightly, but paid a lot better. There were, as I say, many of us, far more, to tell the truth, than the world of letters could bear. But with one of these writers, a young man from Philadelphia called Barry Spacks, I struck up a particular friendship, forged through working together in editing the campus literary quarterly, a journal called *Folio*, where articles on Christian imagery in *The Red Badge of Courage* jostled for recognition side by side with the literary outpourings of our friends.

Both of us had the highest literary ambitions. I was determined to compete with Saul Bellow on his own terms, while Spacks was resolved to dominate the world of poetry and pick up the mantle so carelessly cast down by Ezra Pound. We shared that in common, but also something else, called penury. The problem is common among the literary fraternity, though we couldn't afford the fees to join even that. Nonetheless, Spacks was a man of great resource, and was determined to finance his talent through engaging in various avant-garde commercial enterprises. It was Spacks, for example, who with characteristic Tom Swift cunning invented the first gramophone record that could be used as the lid of spaghetti cans in supermarkets, so providing pasta and the Pastoral Symphony at one go. Due to lack of venture capital, it got nowhere, and as far as I know the idea, even more suited to the compact disc, has yet to be tried. It was Spacks, I recall, who first thought of the Dial-A-Poem service, where you called Bell Telephone and got a breathless voice on the line reciting *The Waste Land* at you, a fine and worthy idea, though not necessarily what you want when you are actually trying to get a taxi.

Spacks was also a great literary innovator, determined to gather great writers around him and transform the literary scene once and for all. He was constantly planning new literary magazines, which had titles like *Transmogrifications* and *The Better Mousetrap*, and then, picking up the telephone, he would begin hunting out gullible patrons to finance them – though these, alas, proved curiously difficult to find in the cornfields of Indiana, where we happened to be at the time. Nonetheless, we were not dismayed. Our literary friendship prospered, our ventures multiplied, we wrote articles of high critical moment together, and there was a feeling of promise in the air – a bit like that in Paris just before the coming of Cubism. And it was with a feeling of tragedy and creative loss that, at the end of the year, we separated, Spacks to make his way to some new American campus, and I to return to Britain, my grant exhausted, to spend the next year overhauling my thesis and making a very indigent living teaching the odd evening class on Montherlant to anyone who was interested, and few, it proved, were.

It was one day the following summer when my telephone, or rather my landlady's, rang. I picked up the machine and a voice vibrant with American enthusiasm greeted me at the other end. It was, of course, Spacks. For a year he had put his literary invention to the best of uses, writing applications for travelling fellowships to be held at British universities. Now he had won one, and was on his way to Cambridge, no less, to write, of course, a thesis. He bade me come to London at once, and show him the literary scene, and we spent a happy few days looking for it, not realizing then that the British literary scene usually lives in the South of France or Tuscany. Spacks had not lost his zest, and made it his custom to accost strangers in pubs and ask them to finance a new literary magazine. I think we raised three-and-fourpence that way, a large sum in those days, though the magazine itself never transpired, largely because other matters attracted our attention.

It happened, I recall, on the fustian seating of the British Railways train to Cambridge – for term now beckoned, and it was time for Spacks to be on his way. He asked me to go along with him, to carry his box files, packed with manuscripts, his two portable typewriters, and a few suitcases full of British sports jackets, for which he had a particular taste. Determined to come to terms, once and for all, with the British literary scene, Spacks had gone into the station bookstall at Liverpool Street and, with customary verve, had collected up all the British newspapers, magazines and periodicals he could lay his hands on. I was myself a stranger to most of them, my idea of a good railway read being the newest issue of F. R. Leavis's magazine *Scrutiny*, where I would turn the pages avidly hoping that yet another new layer of irony had been unravelled in the fiction of Jane Austen.

Spacks's harvest proved to be of a rather different order. They were ill-printed journals with what in those days were called 'bathing beauties' on the cover; the insides were filled with strange, brief nuggets of news of the 'did you know?' variety ('Did you know whales make love by burrowing holes in icebergs?'), small cartoons showing businessmen biting their secretaries, and pages of tips on simple ways of avoiding hair-loss. Others were women's journals, filled with knitting patterns for stringing together Fair Isle sweaters, memoirs culled from old maidservants of the Royal Family, interviews with *passé* Hollywood film-stars, and extensive advice on spots from various agony aunts. It took me some time to understand why all this had detained Spacks's attention. However, he pointed out to me that, tucked away between the tales of sporting achievement, the advice on make-up, the columns on keeping house and, of course, the endless advertisements that held all this farrago together, there were works of fiction.

For this was the time when every magazine carried short stories – detective stories, adventure stories, romance stories, doctor and nurse stories, and so on and on. Somewhere between Audley End and Bishop's Stortford, Spacks began reading some of these out to me, and so we took a momentous literary decision that changed our lives, at least for the next couple of years or so. For, as Spacks pointed out, all these tales were simple in the extreme. Indeed they were constructed by untrained authors to formulae so simple they made the works of Enid Blyton appear great literature. There were no more than three or four basic plots (this was in the days before literary critic Propp, who was to reduce all literary plots to seven), three or four simple character types, and a couple of endings. A small wallchart could lay out the configuration, and Spacks drew one on the spot. All that was necessary for a young author to do was to take the conventions, which were as ready prepared as a Betty Crocker cake mix, throw them in the pot, heat and stir them a little, and serve the results to the breathless publishers; and he could be rich beyond the dreams of avarice.

So our fate was sealed. By the time we descended from the train, Spacks had a plan of campaign all ready, and no sooner had he unpacked his footnotes in the flat which Cambridge University, ever obliging, had secured for him we found ourselves at work. Cambridge is a city famous for its congenial hostelries, and each night found us settled in one or another of them, supping ale and working on the master plan. All we had to do was to devise ten simple story ideas, following the chart we had devised on the train. These we jotted down on six-by-four file cards, numbered each card from one to ten, and returned to the flat. In the morning we rose early, and set to work. We placed two desks opposite each other, a small portable typewriter on each. Then one of us took file card number one, and the other file card number two. We sat down, facing each other and began to type.

In the course of the day, perhaps of the morning, we determined to finish ten stories. To speed matters, we evolved an effective working system I can recommend to this day. When one of us blocked, he shouted 'Stuck!' At this signal we each ran round the desk, sat down at the opposite typewriter, and resumed the other story at the point where the previous author had left off. Whether this was how Beaumont worked with Fletcher, Gilbert with Sullivan, Tristan with Isolde, I am not sure. Certainly it worked for us, and would be the envy of any Japanese production line today. In fact news of our literary efficiency quickly spread, and neighbours used to come by to watch us at our writing, gasping with amazement as the two of us typed furiously for ten minutes or so, cried 'Stuck!', switched seats and began again without wasting a single second.

Spacks's great gift for literary innovation soon had the process refined even further. He persuaded a local stationer to provide us with perforated rolls of continuous paper which reeled steadily into our typewriters without our having to put in new sheets. Thus at once he invented both the principle of bathroom tissue and the basis of modern computing; if, today, there is a hi-tech marvel known as the 'Cambridge phenomenon' which has made that fenland city into the British Silicon Valley, you now know just who to thank for that. More awesome still was the distribution system he devised to deal with our product. For, at the end of the first week, we halted to reflect on our progress, and discovered that there on a table in a corner sat fifty completed stories, ready for submission. Suddenly we were struck with the dismaying revelation that, if we maintained production at this pace, and there seemed little reason why we should not, we would have, by the end of the academic year, something like 2,500 stories, a formidable prospect even for a Charles Dickens. It was true that the supply of magazines appeared plentiful, if not endless, but the thought that they would fill their pages with all the products of our joint byline seemed improbable.

Then there was another worry, as it occurred to both of us that, if our thesis-advisers chanced into the popular corners of the media and found them filled with stories of the type of our very early 'The Stain of Guilt' ('Sergeant Philpott was a sanguine man, but today he was worried. The case seemed an open-and-shut one. Except for one worrying thing. The stain, the small red stain, on Joe Harrison's horny hand'), they might wonder about our academic competence. Indeed it might damage altogether the credibility of the work on 'Christian Imagery in the Koran' with which Spacks hoped to become the toast of the Cambridge colleges. Nonetheless academic life itself suggested the solution. Many a great don has written stories under a *nom de plume*, and there was no reason why two young research students should be any different. So, retiring to the newest hostelry we had discovered, we devoted the evening to devising, not plots, but a gallery of pseudonyms, various enough to prevent editors from feeling that they were overwhelmed from one single gushing creative source, well-flavoured enough to be associated with very different types of work – for the fact is that we were devotees of all the genres, from the most rugged of detective stories to the most sensitive kinds of romance.

So, that night in a pub by the river, there was born our stable of authors, and a varied and fascinating group of talents they were. There was, for instance, Norman Blood, whom we came to imagine, as time went by, as a rather sweat-stained fellow, in late middle age, and definitely running to seed, though his rather sleazy detective stories about the mean streets of London and Los Angeles suggested a decidedly feisty past. He was evidently quite unlike the open-air, sports-loving Millingham Harshly, whose name came, in fact, from the conclusion of one of Blood's own earliest and finest creations, 'The Gorilla That Cried', which ended with the notable last line: ' "He was merciless. Well, the law, too, can be merciless in its own way," said Inspector Millingham, harshly.' Millingham Harshly, evidently widely travelled, stocky, and a little grizzled about the ears, wrote powerful tales of distant, exotic, Bessarabian adventure that thrilled even us as we thought his stuff up over crisps in the Baron of Beef ('There are parts of the desert that few men have know. Towards one of them, as the terrible desert wind called the *muezzin* dashed sand into their faces, there steadfastly marched a small, brave band of foot-weary legionnaires ...'). But even Harshly lacked the suave, knowing charm of Peter Eton, the famed clubland dilettante, with his thin, hairline moustache, his red-silk-lined cloak, and his talent for tales of upmarket romance in an ambiance of adventure, gambling and espionage ('He was walking through the cocktail bar at the Morocco Club, a silk scarf knotted carelessly into the neck of his expensive Pierre Cardin shirt, when Corinne looked up from the roulette table and caught his eye for the first time').

It was not hard to imagine Peter as the darling of the women who also shared our literary stabling. Certainly he would appeal to the sweet, romantic heart of Faith Simple, matronly and sympathetic, with grey-ing hair, a large bosom, and tea-cosies over her teapots, who wrote tales of romantic life among typists ('It took me a year to get over John'). Possibly he got on somewhat less well with Barbara Bingley, whose sad and seamy life came authentically out of the narratives she told of rise from northern poverty to blue-rinsed success ('There was nothing to eat that Christmas when I discovered I was adopted and an orphan'), and who probably rather preferred Millingham Harshly. It was hard to imagine any of them getting on well with Norman Blood, and there were moments when we ourselves found we were liking some of our authors more than others. Happily there was one of them that no one could fail to take to. Indeed it seemed unlikely that our little creative family would have survived at all had it not been for Nathalie Barker – or Nathalie Pelham Barker, as she would later become when her, and our, circumstances changed.

What can we say about Nathalie? A petite brunette with brown eyes and an excellent taste in clothes, she was author of such touching tales of female romance as 'A Kiss in Time!', 'Just for You!', and 'Don't Let Him Get Away!' – tales filled with girls running across heaths with hair blowing in the wind, handsome architects of thirty-five left widower with a small child of five and a droptop Mercedes, and an unusually vast number of loose exclamation marks. Yet she was the one who was the hub of our rather large household – a household that began to worry our postman, as his sack grew heavier by the week. 'I don't understand how you fit all these people into this little flat,' he would say suspiciously as he handed over a great pile of self-addressed envelopes that bore the names of Norm and Jack and Mill, Peter and Faith, Barbie and Nattie, as we came to call them. But there was no doubt it was Nathalie who held us together – Nathalie with her winsome ways, Nathalie who never lost faith, even in the dark days when the return manuscripts rolled back in and the outlay on paper and typewriter ribbons was greatly in excess of the profits accruing to the enterprise.

For it was not always easy, being a writing factory. Spacks had devised a system of submission as efficiently organized as the one we had for creating the goods in the first place, though in the early days it was decidedly less productive. Up on the wall, above the little mailboxes labelled Norm and Nattie, Peter and Barbie, was a large flow-chart which listed all the many magazines that might be a market for their various wares. Each day each author sent out a story to one of the magazines, and we all of us sat back to wait. To this day I sometimes wonder whether the editors of Britain, who serve us so selflessly with reading matter, ever understood the reason for the spectacular increase in their workload that year. For, no sooner did a story come back, and all too often it did, than it was in the mail again, on its way to another magazine, while a fresh story was sent to the previous one. Our system indeed ensured that no desk in, to recall one crucial address, Bream Buildings was ever without something from one of our family, and possibly all of them. In fact it was a busy year for the British postal system indeed, and I'm told that in retirement resorts round the country old sorters still talk about it.

In the early days it must be admitted that we did not do well, our stories returning to us with the same regularity that we maintained in submitting them. The sheer mechanics slowly began to overwhelm us, as we spent much of the day stuffing stories into envelopes and writing the self-addressed envelopes required by the magazines for their all-too-frequent return. Our production began to drop alarmingly, especially as we grew overcome with a disease familiar to all writers, known as the 'mail-fraps'. The mail-fraps is that disabling state of mind that comes to authors when they find they cannot begin a day's work until the mail has arrived; the symptoms include making the breakfast coffee last all morning, smoking heavily, and standing in lacklustre posture in the window, awaiting the sight of the postman coming round the corner. As if he sensed this, our own postman reacted accordingly, reshaping his round so that he always came to us last, just to ensure that our hysteria had peaked. We would snatch the letters from him with a cry, rip the packages open, drop the rejected stories to the floor, and scrabble through the litter, hunting for some sign that there had been just one acceptance.

It came now and again, but, I fear, all too rarely – far too rarely for us to feel that Norm and Mill and Peter, Faith and Barbie and Nattie, were becoming the household names that we desired for them and they, plainly, desired for themselves. We felt not just for us but for them; they felt not just for them but for us. Now and again there was joy in the household, as Jack had a lucky week, and then it was Faith's turn. Millingham earned eighty pounds in a week once, with three stories; Barbie once earned almost as much with just one weepie cry from the old Northern orphanage. Peter broke the London papers, and was asked for more, though when he sent it the editor had changed and he had to start all over again. Most of them got some acceptances, though never enough. Most of them did, but not Nathalie. Poor Nathalie! Perhaps her style was too exotic for British readers, perhaps her exclamation marks did not strike the popular chord. Whatever it was, she seemed to get nowhere at all, with never a credit to her name.

I think probably had it not been for Nathalie we might well have given up our writing stable altogether. After all, Spacks and I both had other ambitions. There were our theses to consider, and the great novels that each one of us was writing. Then, one night in the yard of the Eagle, Spacks came up with a new project – a musical of *King Lear*, to be called *Crack Your Cheeks!* – that excited us both enormously. But there were other people to consider; we were not just writing for ourselves. We worried and fretted about the writers we had nurtured. Perhaps Norman was drinking too much, and Faith getting tired and

depressed. How was Barbara, with her sad orphanage history, taking
yet another experience of rejection? And wasn't it getting time for
Peter, now well past his great days of hunting the whale and
harpooning the rhino, to think of settling down a bit – possibly,
indeed, with Nathalie, who was admittedly a good deal younger, but a
delightful homemaker and friend.

Thus, as often happens with writers, the greater the rebuffs, the more
frenziedly we wrote. And, as the atmosphere grew more frantic, the
more frantic, too, became the kinds of tale we devised. Our plots began
to display greater and greater extravagance, in a mute appeal for
recognition. Then came an unhappy moment when we had Peter Eton
resolve some complex narrative crux by having one of his exotic French
heroines raped by a Russian spy suspended on wires from an Ilyushin
aeroplane. It bore all the marks of desperation, and we realized that it
was time to take stock. As usual it was Spacks, who had spent a gloomy
day studying a pile of writers' magazines sent from America by his
cousin in Chicago, who spotted the nub of our problem. Here we were,
two authors who had had our share of successes, with a score or so of
our tales in print. Yet the fees of twenty-five pounds a throw still did
no more than pay off the bar bill and the supplies of Tippex required for
their invention and creation. Being a commercial writer in Britain, he
explained, was simply not economic.

On the other hand, according to the magazines he held out to me,
commercial writing in the United States was a very different affair.
There were magazines by the score that would pay thousands of dollars
for just one short story. American contributors were reporting tales of
riches galore, and endless holidays in Bimini from their creative earnings. We were, after all, a transatlantic collaboration, if not a multi-
national corporation, and nothing but inertia bound our product to the
British market. No, the answer was clear, and we must transmit it
forthwith to our writers. All that was necessary was for the settings,
rather than the plot-lines of our stories, to change, for the length to
extend a little, and the style become a little more vernacular. Of course
our postal bills would increase, but happily a new instalment of Spacks's
research grant had arrived, and that might well give the necessary capital
injection. So we re-programmed our authors, and our tales now

began to wing across the Atlantic, to the great American El Dorado.

And it was now that fortune began to smile more sunnily on us. It was Peter Eton who scored the first successes. A certain aggressive machismo had always been apparent in his work, but now he put it to good use; various American journals with titles like *Knave* or *Playmate* began to take to him, and several of his tales appeared amid photographs of strange bodily contortions. Norman Blood shifted his locale to the American deserts, and began to attract a little editorial interest here and there, and even Faith Simple sold a recipe or two. But the sun that now shone happily shone brightest on Nathalie Barker – or Nathalie Pelham Barker as, for the purposes of the American market, she had now become. It was as if she had found a world she had always been made for. In the magazines for romantic housewives that flourished in those days – *Redbook* and *Good Housekeeping*, for example – but which have changed or gone today, she found those who were ready to relish her talents and her winsome way with prose.

Perhaps our greatest moment occurred one evening when we returned from a story session at the Mill which had gone on rather later than usual, possibly because we had been celebrating some good American sale on behalf of Nathalie, who could not of course be there herself. The landlady met us at the door, in quite a lather of excitement. 'Time called when you were out,' she said. 'What did?' asked Spacks. 'Time did,' said the landlady. 'It wanted to do a feature story about being a writer.' 'Time,' cried Spacks, 'You mean *Time* magazine?' 'That's what I said,' said the landlady, 'Time called, but you were out.' 'Great', said Spacks, 'Which one of us did they want to write about? Him? Me?' 'It wasn't either of you,' said the landlady. 'It was a writer called Nathalie Pel someone they thought lived at this address. But I told Time nobody round here had ever heard of her.' 'You told *Time* that?' asked Spacks. 'That's what I told Time,' said the landlady.

Time never called again. Or perhaps it did, but in a rather different way. For, a few weeks later, the academic year ran out, our theses were due in, and the tickets arrived for Spacks to trans-ship himself back to his familiar haunts in the United States. High on benzedrine he finished off his thesis by night and day, and we retired to the Baron of Beef for our last drink. Staring into the beer, we stared into vacancy. The

71

partnership was over, and it was time for the stable of writers to be dissolved. But could Faith and Barbie survive, out there in the lonely world on their own? Would Norman drink himself to death, Peter retire to some old authors' home or other? And had Nathalie really written her last – dear, successful, Peck and Peck-dressed Nathalie, with her cashmere sweaters and her sorority pin and her brave, brave ways? As Spacks said, there was only one answer. And when, that summer, he took ship for Philadelphia, on some shoebox-sized freighter, I was with him, typewriter in hand, fileboxes of stories under my arm. And a good summer we had of it, a real Nathalie summer, as Spacks and I sat by some swimming pool in trunks and helped Nathalie gush out more and more and more of her lovely stories. Late in the afternoon we went down to the drugstore and wandered among the magazines, seeing our – no, her – byline flashing from the covers.

For Nathalie was a success. Time never called again, but there was fan mail, such fan mail as you never saw. Then came the day when a letter arrived which I have, to my shame, since destroyed, but it went something rather like this:

Hi, Nathalie!!! Remember me? Sure as hell you do!! This is Chet, and darn it I do believe you're Pel, right? – Nathalie Pelham who was sweetheart of Sigma Chi that sunlit year when we were in the same great old class of '48 together at dear old Wholesome State!!!! Yes, I'd know those exclamation points anywhere!! Remember how we practised them all that summer when we decided fate and our grade average had really chosen us for each other!!! Oh boy, weren't those great times, kid? I still ask myself why we never stuck together!! But I always had these big dreams about really making it in the Big Apple!! Okay, there've been good times, and bad!! I tried the marriage stakes, and I guess from the Barker bit you must have tried them too!! Okay, I made my big dream come true, and today I'm one of the biggest architects in town!!! If you look at the building next to the Pam Am you might see a little name on the cornerstone that will really bring back memories!!! But, Pel, I learned one other thing in life – never turn your back on romance!!!

My wife left me last year, leaving me with a dreamy daughter of five and a host of bad dreams!! Right, I've got fame, and the kind of salary check that keeps me in nearly new Mercs, but there's something missing. 'Pel', could it be you?? Listen, I don't like to write like this, but I've been reading your stories, and I think there's something in there that sounds like a message to me!!! Why don't we give it a whirl, sweetheart!!! I mean, let's just meet, how about under the clock at Grand Central!! I'll be wearing a yellow rose (remember how you loved them???) and carrying a copy of *Redbook* ...

I'm wiser now, and I know we should never have answered that letter. And certainly we should not have gone to Grand Central that fatal day to watch all the lovers meet under the clock. For Chet looked a very pleasant fellow as he stood there, for two hours or more, under the clock in his horn-rimmed spectacles, holding up his copy of *Redbook* and flipping his yellow rose from time to time. He was just the kind of guy Nathalie would have loved, and it was with pain in our hearts that, leaving him there, we stole softly away. It was, as Nathalie would say, strange after that. For just as fiction has a way of destroying reality, so reality has a way of destroying fiction. The next day we could not even lift the covers from our typewriters, and, like ghosts, not just Nathalie but all of our writers somehow just began to slip away into the shadows. Perhaps it was as Nathalie always said: you can't play around with romance and get away with it.

Of course it could well have been all for the best. Soon we were back in the deep waters of serious creation again. Spacks reconceived his novel about the Korean war, and I went back to my *magnum opus* on the Fifties in the British provinces. In due time I became a wellish-known British novelist, and Spacks became a very distinguished American poet. And indeed I more or less forgot about the whole youthful episode until, just a few days ago, a large envelope dropped through my letter box. It came from some British magazine and it was returning a short story; I looked and saw it was one of Nathalie's. On the usual brutal rejection slip the editor had scribbled a few words of regret, saying the story somehow seemed a little old-fashioned for them. They apologized for being a little slow in coming to a decision, but apparently the story had been lying under the cat in the office. I did parcel it up and send it on to Nathalie, at the last address I had for her, a very nice-sounding property somewhere in Bel Air, California. It probably never even reached her. But if it did, I doubt it made any difference, one way or another. That was how it was with Nathalie. Like any good writer, she was the kind of girl who could always take a rejection. As for the lesson of the story, that is probably very simple. There is a lot to be said for collaboration; I still occasionally do it. But don't, on any account, assume it will make life any easier.

Yours, etc.

Letter to the
Mid-Century Book Club

Interesting the general populace in the thrills and spills of serious
literature is, I well realize, no easy matter. But it is hard not to be
struck by some of the more flamboyant expedients that are used. Our
literary prizes, for example, are nowadays regularly judged by the
likes of Richard Branson, Ken Livingstone, Ian Botham and
Samantha Fox – bookish souls at heart, no doubt, but somewhat unexpected wanderers in the forest of literary innovation, post-modern-
ist experimentalism, and high poetic frenzy. I have no doubt at all of
the sagacity of their judgement, and the justice done to the winners
they pick. But my mind cannot help taking itself back, once in a
while, to an older way of doing things, particularly one that crossed
my path back in the days when I was constantly teaching in the
United States, where many of the modern arts of book promotion
actually started. In those days I had a very serious literary mind, a
bookish, pipe-smokingish sort of look of a kind that, along with tweed
jackets and button-down shirts, was much favoured by the younger,
untenured academics of the time, and a taste for enrolling myself in
Book Clubs. Indeed in the more distant parts of the Middle West
where I did my academic business, Book Clubs were pretty much the
only means on offer for getting serious books, and seriousness was
what I wanted. I was ideal fodder for their bargain offers: a free cased
set of the *Compact Oxford English Dictionary*, which came complete
with a telescope for easy reading; a great fat book by one of the
several Arthur Schlesingers called something like *The History of
Everything*; and, of course, the inescapable *Alexandrian Quartet*.

So there is little wonder that I glowed bright with excitement when, one day, the American intellectual weeklies and monthlies to which I was addicted filled with news that a new Book Club was starting, the Mid-Century Book Society, and its selections would be made by critics of extraordinary eminence. And no better a set of personal heroes could they have been than the names they announced. One was the poet who probably mattered most to me at the time; he was called W. H. Auden. Another was perhaps the major academic critic of the day, the man whose book, *The Liberal Imagination*, had virtually lured me across the water to America; he was called Lionel Trilling. The third was a major scholar of Romanticism and French literature, a cosmopolitan and defender of the clarity of thought; his name was Jacques Barzun. In a classic advertising photograph they all sat together round a table, fresh and well-suited, evidently caught in some act of critical vision. Of course, being over twenty-one and a genuine lover of art, I sent off at once for the brochure, and put my name down for recruitment. When it arrived, however, I could not avoid imagining the following literary letter, which like most of them I never quite managed to send:

Dear Messrs Auden, Barzun and Trilling,

I have just lately received a very beautiful mailshot from the Mid-Century Book Society – *your* book society, the one where you all sit around the table in those great Brooks Brothers suits and discuss, I guess, all your highest critical thoughts and make up your minds about which books you'd most like us all to get down and read. Well, I like books, and I like the kind of books you like and would like us to like, and I like the kinds of things you say about them, and the brochure says you're going to say lots of things about them. I mean, I really like what you, Mr Auden, think about the Icelandic sagas, though checking out the first select titles I do not see too many of them on offer at $4.95. I like what you, Mr Trilling, say about the sadly neglected William Dean Howells, and I'm sure when the list really gets going he won't stay sadly neglected very much longer. I like what you, Mr, or should I say Monsieur, Barzun, have to say about Montesquieu and all those really subtle French thinkers, whose minds you have unlocked for me, and I cannot wait for you to introduce to me the names of even more obscure French thinkers who otherwise I never seem to hear widely promoted, certainly not out in *this* part of Queens. But honestly what I really liked about the terrific brochure you guys came up with is what I guess you, Monsieur Barzun, would call the *ambiance*. I mean, I really just love it when you say 'The members we seek are persons of independent mind who will welcome an opportunity to disagree with Mr Auden, dispute Mr Barzun's choices, and quarrel with an essay of Mr Trilling, by declining the book it speaks of.' I just can't tell you how much that really turned me on.

My college gym teacher always told me I had a really independent mind, when all the other kids were hanging on the bars the way they were told and there was I, halfway up the rope – so I really think I'm going to enjoy disagreeing with people like you, people really worth being disagreeable *to*, people who are famous and must have got that way for mostly being right. I guess most of us get a few things wrong from time to time, and ought to be glad to grab some spot-on advice, but I think you are being a bunch of real sports to get right up there and admit it. Out here in Queens, we sometimes kind of get the idea that very famous people are so very famous, such celebrated, well, celebrities, that they don't have too much time to listen to *anybody* any more – certainly not to people like me, or is it I. But I can tell the *ambiance* you are giving off is going to be really different, kind of friendly and approachable yet dignified – like when you say 'You are invited to help us celebrate an occasion of some moment'. I really went wild when I read that, because I think that, in this modern world of today when culture is getting crappier and crappier by the *hour*, and everyone is being zonked in the head with all that garbage those people who make the television programs think is *all we deserve*, well, people like our sort of people, the kind who like to talk about modern books and all, really ought to get together and talk literature the way literature has got to be talked if it isn't going to be really wiped out, really *erased*, entirely.

So the other night when it was real nice and spring-like I put on a really blouse-type summer dress and set out. I went to Mr Auden's place

first, because he comes number one on your list. At least the guys round
the fire-hydrant said it was Mr Auden's place. It was pretty dark and
there didn't seem to be anyone at home, or at least no one answered.
But there was a light on and someone, a girl or a guy, I couldn't tell,
but kind of fair-haired, kept passing back and forth at the window. One
time he opened it and threw out a whole half-pizza, if you see what I
mean, which proved when I checked it out, really caring about literary
associations as I do, to be covered with a thick bacterial coating, and to
my judgement had been past it for like several weeks. I wondered if Mr
Auden was looking after himself okay, and waited in the street for a
couple hours. Some very strange folks came by and tried the bell, but
they didn't make it either. Then a great bunch of guys who looked like
actors and laughed and talked a lot, very loud, came and they did. But
while I was standing there I got talking first with a cop and then half
a precinct and we had a very good disagreement about the novels of
Lawrence Durrell, they preferring the *Alexandrian Quartet* and me the
books about zoos and animals. By this time there was quite a loud party
upstairs and a good deal of laughter and weird singing, and people came
out into the street and were, well, I mean, kind of throwing up in the
gutter. So I finally figured that this was not really a good time to get
really into the Icelandic sagas and I took the bus home.

But then the more I thought about it, the more I thought that I
didn't really want to get into the Icelandic hassle with Mr Auden. I
wanted to tell Mr Trilling how much I disagreed with him about Mr
Nabokov's *Lolita*, because in my view that book is really *unfair* about
American schools. I mean, when you read some bits of it you really
wonder if that guy ever really went to one. So I took a bubble bath and
then I tried to call up Mr Trilling on the telephone. The number was
real hard to find and I had to use the operator. Then it rang and there
was a whole lot of noise at the other end that sounded like there was a
kind of upmarket bar mitzvah going on. Someone who called himself
Mr Mailer came on and said Mr Trilling was busy with guests and
actually talking to Thomas Mann, and he'd be kind of occupied for the
rest of the evening but maybe he'd call me back. I knew he was kidding
me and it was real disappointing, but I got talking to the operator, who
was kind of nicely spoken, about John Betjeman. It turned out she liked

him a helluva lot more than I did, but then I never did care too much for tennis, and it was a really good disagreement. But not like the one I'd really been looking forward to having with *you*, Mr Trilling.

Anyway, I sure didn't give up. I sat down and got out my Bloomingdale's stationery and I wrote a letter to Mr Barzun. It was a long letter – I guess around sixteen pages, in fact, because I write this big longhand – and really *disagreeing* with his book *A House Is Not a Home*. I also told him a bit about myself, about how I'm trying to lose weight and how I love horses and how I'm really into Ayn Rand. But I've waited now for two whole days and Mr Barzun still hasn't written back to me yet, although I told him I'd be right round there any time he got free. Okay, well now I imagine you all sitting round that nice table in those nice suits, reading this letter, passing it from hand to hand, I guess. So I hope you don't mind me saying this, but I'm a very upfront kind of person, and what I wanted to say was I'm already kind of disappointed in the Mid-Century Book Society. It looked like real fun when it started, but you know there's a History Book Society too, with selections made by a Mr Plutarch, that sounds just as great and you don't have to keep so many books. So it looks like you could lose me, unless you'd really like to stay home some night soon and let a girl with a really independent mind take you up on your offer.

> Yours bibliomanically,
> Nathalie Pelham Barker

Passencore Rearrived
from North Armorica

Reading the other day about a new book of memoirs, *The Bonus of Laughter*, by Alan Pryce-Jones, the former editor of the *Times Literary Supplement*, and a noted critic, wit and *bon viveur*, I suddenly found my own memory activated, by reminiscences of a literary letter I have for some time intended to write. It takes us all back some time ago, to the later 1950s or maybe the 1960s, at a phase of things when I conducted, much as Mr Pryce-Jones himself did, much of my existence in the United States, in my case mostly at a university in the Middle-Western cornfields. Here, in my few leisure hours, I took part freely in the various regional delights, like looking over the sale of hoes at the local J. C. Penney, or going to the weekly hog fair. But the great day of the week was when all we graduate students and untenured academics used to go down of a Monday to the local drugstore, with its fine display of Mail Pouch chewing tobacco, and await the arrival in town of the Sunday *New York Times Book Review*, for us in those parts an absolutely crucial reassurance that somewhere out in the great cities human thought and critical innovation continued to turn apace. One day, unfolding the pages of this magical supplement, I lit on a fascinating article that spoke closely to my condition. 'It is not so very long ago since I took a freighter trip to Europe in order to make myself read *Ulysses* from cover to cover', I found Mr Pryce-Jones telling his countless impressed American readers. 'I knew that it demanded 10 days of plain living and a deck chair, a total absence of distraction and an over-riding sense of purpose: otherwise I should, as often before, drop the book after 50 pages'.

We all have our problems in getting to grips with really serious literature, so naturally I read on, keen to discover how a major critic went about his business, the task being one to which I had neophytic aspirations. Between New York and Liverpool, Mr Pryce-Jones went on to explain, 'I did what I had set out to – and did it, moreover, with very great delight. Given the right time, space, and opportunity, given an incentive – later I was to teach a university course on, among other writers, Joyce – the difficulties of *Ulysses* fall away. What remains is a masterpiece'. This portrait of the life of the better class of critic provoked in my mind the following imaginary letter:

Dear Mr Pryce-Jones,

Believe you me, I do *know* how bored you famous cosmopolitan critics must get, receiving fan mail from us adoring readers, so I'll try to keep this kind of brief. But this time I just simply *had* to write and tell you how much I *really* appreciated your article in the *New York Times Book Review*, the only pabulum from our so-called free and enlightened press I can stomach these dark days, about all those difficult organizational things you had to do to read *Ulysses* in exactly the right circumstances. I can't tell you how I just *identified* with those feelings, really it was like it was *me*. We both know there are so many dullards around these days – my own spouse is one of them, I can tell you – who just don't have the marbles up there to *realize* what the responsibility of a reader *is* in this age of fast, frantic living and great, fat, difficult books, or even *begin* to understand how hard it is to find the ideal circumstances to read them in. What you said really just encouraged me *so much*, especially because my husband, to be frank, is one of those old-fashioned *gross skimmers* who could read any old thing in a subway train, but does he *really* read it? I can't tell you how many years I've been trying to get it into his what he calls *mind* just what a lot of time, and the same goes for money too, it takes to be anything like a *decent* and *educated* student of the modern novel. But I just stuck your article right there in front of his schnozzle and, even while he was sitting there writing out the check for my big read this summer – I'm off for a month to Honolulu just to *make* myself read Lloyd Douglas's *The Robe* from cover to cover, every line and every word – his face pretty much softened from the way it usually is, and guess what he said? 'You know, Gloria, you and Mr Pryce-Jones must be *twin souls*.'

And I guess – if you don't mind me, a simple suburban housewife, but one for whom the benison of letters is paramount, or is it paradigmatic, associating me in this way with a very famous critic and editor like you – I guess he's right at that. You won't believe this!!, but every *single* thing you said about you was true for me too! Yes, really! It must have been ten years ago – no, I lie, it was eleven, I just went and checked out the stamp in my old passport – when I decided just the way you did I'd have to do something about beating my way right through *Ulysses* from one cover *to the other*! I'm a slower reader than you, I guess, not being a professional and teaching all those university courses and all. So I knew for *me* it demanded three weeks at least of solitude in a five-star hotel with a good pool and its own beach, and that I could never make it unless I had a new wardrobe, a good suntan and an overriding sense of porpoise. Anything less and I knew I'd just drop that great book without even cracking open the bookstore wrappings! On that isle in the Aegean, then – I like to pick my locales to fit *right in with the book* (not that a freighter wasn't a brilliant choice, though I guess that for that I'd have picked *Finnegans Wake*, because in it he says, and I quote, 'Sir Tristram, violer d'amores, fr'over the short sea, had passencore rearrived from North Armorica', just the voyage you took (you see I know the book quite well, after that really great two-year stint on it in Trieste)) – on that isle in the Aegean, then (sometimes when you read great writers it makes your sentences kind of long), I did what I set out to do.

Like you, I did it *with great delight*. I can tell you, it was terrific! The hotel was great, the *ouzo* really something else, and we never saw a cloud the whole time I was there! As for the book, that was nice too, although I found it just mildly, well, confusing. The thing is – I'm not so dumb now – that I'd understood at the time from the lady who advises me on reading down at the Anne Hathaway Bookstore that it was going to be about Greekish history, and about Odysseus returning to the Isle of Penelope. Then it turned out to be about this rather unclean Irish, well, Semitic person, and the whole story was over in twenty-four hours, though not the way I read it (anyway you took ten days!). But once I'd got the right time and space, and also got the story sorted out, or most of it (who was that Stephen?), well, like you, all of the difficulties more or less fell away and what remained was, just as you say, an outstanding masterwork. It was a really thrilling experience, and *being in Lesbos for Bloomsday*! In fact it drained me so much emotionally I had to take a two week holiday right after. What's more, the whole thing gave me a really good idea for the summer two years later, when I hired a palatial hotel-room in Dublin, filled the closet with ten year old Paddy so I wouldn't have to keep running out a lot, and really got down to reading *Zorba the Greek*.

Now, I was wondering – have you made it with *The Magic Mountain* yet? That really is the kind of book you don't have a hope in hell with in front of the fireplace at home! I decided that, with it being philosophical in its tendency, I ought to try and find a really contemplative atmosphere to, well, do what I had set out to, and having already been in Alpine mountains (that was right after the album of *The Sound of Music* was issued), I chose, guess what, a monastery holiday in Tibet for the prodigious read I knew I'd have ahead of me. It was really nice, and the Sherpas are really quite as sweet as everyone says. Unluckily that was the year the Chinese hordes invaded (like you, I take a while to get around to one of these big books; I want to make sure it's really lasting and still being talked about before I get involved in a big expense with it) and I hadn't even reached page 50 before we were fleeing raggle-taggle into India. I left my copy on some yak or other, and I have to admit I couldn't ever work up the enthusiasm to start all over again – so I still have this big *gap* where Mann ought to be.

On the other hand, I did have this really great time with Henry James's *The Golden Bowel*. Everything the advertisements say about the Bahamas is *true*! I enclose some very nice snapshots of me – I'm the one with the neat, well-kept figure in the solar topee with the daiquiri – somewhere between pages 73 and 76. It was taken by a really *charming* Frenchman who was out there with *The Brothers Karamazov*. You probably know him, Yves someone, he works for the literary pages of *Le Figaro*!! It was a great summer, a pretty great book, though James is not too great on the laughs, and between paragraphs I have to tell you

I met some really fun people that year. I'll send you the brochures if you want them. In fact maybe we could exchange snaps, if you're a camera bug too, like me. With all the reading that as a literary editor *and* a university teacher *you* have to do, you must have been to some really *great* places too and I guess we could swop some terrific slides.

Well, I hope all this doesn't sound too forward of me, and I hope you don't mind my writing you this very long letter. I excuse myself by saying I know you'll find somewhere *really* nice to go and read it! Besides, as I was saying, as soon as I started on your piece in that wonderful *New York Times Book Review* I felt *right away* we were already friends, and I had that great feeling that at last I'd met another human being who just like me was *really* willing to make the kind of sacrifices a literate person really just has to make if we are going to properly study the *truly* Great Books of our time. I also liked what you said about how if you're going to read them right you need an incentive. I give these little reports on my own mental adventures in best books to a little ladies' reading group (the group is little, some of the girls are enormous) which meets down here at the Chautaugua Inn, and even though I know it's not *exactly* like teaching a course on 'Tourism and the Modern Novel' in some great university where the students have already read critical theory and stuff like that, I think it's really important to have an objective in front of you. I find it's especially important when a book just starts to *flag* a little in some place when I'm far away from my usual verities; I guess this doesn't happen to you, being an editor and having to read everything with an alert mind, but I have to confess it just does now and then with me. But I really connected with what you said in your article, about how there you are, in some first-class hotel or on this terrific cruise, with congenial people around and maybe a good steel band, and you sit down with one of these really great works after dinner and maybe a Marguerita or two and the words sort of fall away and suddenly what remains is, well, as you put it, a masterpiece.

Oh, before I finish, Mr Pryce-Jones, there's really one thing I mustn't forget, but it's what really made me sit down and pen this long epistle to you in the first place. It's about a problem you must face a lot, and I'm asking for some really good advice from a master.

You know how you have to look *way* ahead with these things, with so many people really into travel these days, and you even have to form a line in the travel agency before you even reach an airport or the customs, and all the cruise liners being packed with all these diamond-encrusted oldies with their walking frames who are travelling just for fun. Now the fact is, in a couple of years I'll be ready for something I've been saving for *years*, and that is Marcelle Proust's *Remembrances of Things Past* – the whole of the twelve volumes, or is it eighteen? Everybody tells me it's going to require something very big, like a year long cruise, with, as you so nicely put it, lots of plain living and a good deckchair. I just thought maybe you would have some very good suggestions. I guess by now you must know all the right steamship lines, the ones that really put themselves out for folks like us, with *our* special needs. Of course, just to name a few quirks and foibles that always go on my list when I go and book down at Diamond-Studied Travel, I like a ship that's fully fireproof and with one of those whirly-type hot-water pools, not to say stewards who really know their French wines and how to treat a lady, and haven't just been swept up by accident from the dockside at Bilbao. Otherwise I know I'd drop the book after about 50 pages. Naturally I mean to spend most of the time there on deck, living plainly and looking for a total absence of distraction, bashing away at Proust's world-renowned masterpiece.

I'm asking you because you seem to be the only literary critic of real reputation who has gone into these things at all properly. I mean, we know the usual travel-pieces in the Sundays are all about topless beaches and all-over tans and surfboarding (try reading on that!) and are never attentive to the problems and needs of people like us! So, please, Mr Pryce-Jones, if you can find the time, drop me a postcard from somewhere nice – I imagine you off somewhere right now, reading *Gravity's Rainbow* – and just let me have all the ripe full-bodied fruit of your masterly experience. (I just bet you smoke a pipe! – there, did I guess it!) You can be sure I'll be *really grateful*. So thanks in anticipation, and if you should happen to be at Waikiki this summer on the beach, I really want you to try and look me up. I don't yet know which hotel I'm going to be staying at, because my travel agent has scoured all Honolulu and hasn't yet come through with anything good enough for my –

our! – special needs. But I'll be there, and easy to spot. I'm the one with her head always in a book.

Admiringly,
Gloria Willicomb III

Remembering the Fifties

One of the problems of middle age, I find, is that one is constantly tempted into reminiscence, there being little else to do with oneself. For the fact is that I have evidently reached that time in my life when the present, by some peculiar process that I do not understand, has become the past, and the is has somehow through no fault of my own become the was. Other things happen; the hair withdraws into a smaller and smaller principality, as if gathering itself up for one last campaign, and the teeth and food no longer quite seem to go together. Girls at parties remain perfectly affable, but seem to move on rather more quickly to the other chaps in the further corner of the room. And of this state of affairs there is another symptom. You begin, I find, to grow a trifle reminiscent and retrospective, as if the past were a little more interesting than the present. Indeed you probably start feeling the obligation to begin work on your autobiography.

Just who it is issues this pre-emptory summons is not entirely clear. Nor is it entirely evident why it should come to myself – a rather sedentary sort of fellow, as you see, always writing letters to someone or other – rather than to someone of a more gamey and active disposition, like Norman Mailer. It is also odd how the summons seems to come when the novel you are writing seems to be proving troublesome, or the scholarly work one is doing – the life, say, of Mrs Aphra Behn – begins to lose some of its sparkle and charm. But at times like this the fiction of one's own existence does come to seem rather more interesting than that of one's invented characters, and the life one has sort of lived grows more engrossing than that of Mrs Behn, if only because she is and indeed has been a long time dead, unlike oneself, or so one hopes.

The temptation, I must admit, is dangerous. Somehow, once the idea of writing an autobiography arises, one grows a little more sententious in all one says and does. One starts sitting up very straight in the car, talks differently to one's children, in a tone of nostalgia and reminiscence, and looks at one's old friends in a quite new way, wondering whether they are more page 17 or page 120. At the same time one begins to lose panache. One breathes harder when chasing the wives of one's friends up the stairs, and the past somehow grows more patchy and luminous, filled with glimpses of summers when the sun always shone, and of perfect British Rail kippers. You probably know the feeling, and do beware of it. It means it is autobiography time.

You will be happy to know that I have resisted the impulse, but it cannot be escaped altogether. For there is, I notice, another aspect to being a writer of middle years. People come from the radio companies with tape-recorders, asking for recollections of times when you were alive and they had not even reached the point of conception. Students who have been compelled by some sadistic academic institution to write a thesis on 'Anger and the Nineteenth-Century European Novel' appear barking on one's doorstep, and will not go away until they have been thrown a reminiscent bone or two. Journalists ring, and ask what was the name of the Egyptian chap who snitched the Suez Canal off us in, what was it, 1936? Scholars and biographers write asking for literary recollections, wanting to know, for instance, whether it was indeed Iris Murdoch who was seen cycling at speed through Shropshire in the spring of 1951. All in all, one is kept very busy, and the letters certainly fill up the letter tray. That is why it is as well to have a reminiscence or two to hand, and I do have a letter in reserve of just that kind. Here, then, it is:

Dear Thesis-Writer,

Thank you so much for your letter, asking for my reminiscences.

Actually it comes at quite the perfect time, because tonight I'm asking just a few old and trusted friends to come round and remember the Fifties. So do get on your bicycle in Cardiff, or wherever it is you live, and try to get over here as quickly as possible. It's nothing fancy, of course, just ginger wine and a few small snacks, and I expect, if it's really like the Fifties, we'll be finished shortly before ten. But I think I can promise you a really fascinating evening, and I'm sure by the time it's over all your very interesting questions will have been answered.

For instance, Crispin's coming, and he's going to recall National Service; he was in Cyprus, you know, or at least he thinks it was Cyprus where they sent him. John will recollect the Festival of Britain, Leslie will do Suez, and Gloria has some fascinating memories of Bill Haley and the Comets – whoever or whatever he, they, or it turn out to be. Oh, and Winston – of course he was born in the war, as I expect you will have guessed – is going to reminisce about suspender belts. Henry will give his imitation of the Goons, which he's been doing for forty years and of which none of us ever grow tired, and Dorothy will undoubtedly offer us her very passable F. R. Leavis, because she was a student of his at Cambridge, of course, and I know it will have us all in stitches. Jim has promised to reminisce about the time he couldn't get tickets to see *Look Back in Anger*, Peter has been round the bric-à-brac shops and is bringing a genuine bottle of Camp coffee, and Millicent believes she's got some real Ovaltine.

So it should all be just like old times, the most tremendous fun – and not the only celebration of its kind down this end of our smart and very nicely gentrified terrace, I'll bet an old-fashioned, full-sized British penny. The fact is that, despite the satellite dishes outside the houses, we're still quite a warm and well-established community down here in Austerity Gardens. And there is no doubt, what with sex getting more lethal, values getting stricter, hair getting shorter and morals coming back apace, the Fifties are well due for a revival. In fact the chat shows, magazine colour supplements and the fashion correspondents are well on with the vogue already – just like yourself – and naturally none of us wants to be left out of something like that. As for myself, I have a few literary reminiscences from the good old Angry Decade I thought I'd delight people with. So if you're not staying in to watch the commercials for AIDS, why not try and get round? I do assure you, you'll be in for the most amusing evening.

Yes, the Fifties, our Fifties! What times they were, weren't they? Or, on the other hand, were they? For the only trouble is that the more I think about it, the less I can actually remember anything going on, though whether that is a function of the declining brain cells or the nature of the period I find it hard to say. There was the end of butter rationing, I recall, and someone invented the washing machine, though I think not for the first time. There was a lot of activity in the field of state dentistry, some of the marks of which I bear to this day. I remember the excitement of going to the Festival of Britain and looking for the Dome of Discovery, though thanks to the crowds I never actually discovered it. With the war over and the welfare state come, we all started brylcreeming our hair, I recall, in preparation for the New Elizabethan Age, which duly came with the Coronation in 1953, though it proved not to be quite as exciting as the first one, with far fewer public executions, for instance. In fact it turned out rather the sort of time when everyone felt the need to go to bed rather early, right after *Take It From Here* had ended. There were, I remember, bikes with dipped handlebars and derailleur gears, crêpe-soled shoes and Denis Compton. And then of course there was Suez – the great historical moment when the British Empire ended, and was duly replaced with the British Council.

It was a new age, filled with dangerous new ideas. There was the Bomb, and the Holocaust, and the Cold War, and the Crisis of Being. There was Beckett, there was Existentialism, there was Plight, there was Anguish. Everyone wanted, I remember, to be a writer, the number of vacancies in jazz bands having proved very severely limited. Anger came, and enraged loudmouths began shouting on the stage about the corruptions of nostalgia and virginity, as indeed I see they do today. On the other hand, where nowadays everyone wants to be an insider trader, in those days they all wanted to be outsiders. Indeed it was the done thing to try to contract out of everything on offer, even one's blood-group. It was a time of great literary scandals, when the critics frequently fell to fisticuffs in the bar of the Royal Court, though whether this was about the purpose of art or whose turn it was to pay

I cannot remember. Someone horsewhipped Colin Wilson for a careless remark about Nietzsche, and Dylan Thomas constantly toured America, bringing some delight to the coeds and even more, it was murmured, to the faculty wives. The espresso bar was invented, and suddenly it was possible to sit up until as late as ten-thirty discussing Existentialism over a cup of coffee with a lot of fluff on top. There was a vogue for Commitment, and writers were constantly seen on marches or sitting down in the streets with placards, until it came time for them to vote for the Tory candidate at the next election.

So I suppose there was a lot there after all, when you think about it. And no doubt you are right, and it is indeed time that some of us started getting down onto paper just what it really meant to be a budding writer and intellectual in that austere and sparkling postwar world. Indeed one or other of us – and, given your acned youth, it looks as if it had better be me – ought, before we get past it, and total amnesia sets in, to pin down in a glittering phrase or two the distinctive and special qualities of that austere time. Yes, someone should capture all the characteristic ennui and monotony, all those parties that almost but never quite did take place, probably because of the power-cuts, all the cafés and pubs where one always expected to meet (though one never actually did) such leading sporters of the age as Angus Wilson, Colin Wilson, Sandy Wilson and Edmund Wilson, to name but a few. It would indeed make a devastating tale, and if someone could drop a madeleine or two in my tea and come up with a really interesting publisher's contract I would not be at all averse to it.

On the other hand, when I really think hard about it, what I mostly remember people doing in the Fifties was remembering the Thirties. For it was an age of great reminiscence on its own account, when the only reading matter available were the war-scarred memoirs of the veterans of the Thirties, the dear old low, dishonest decade. Indeed, our prime reading matter in those days, as we sat in our National Health spectacles on our conscript bunks in the army camp at Catterick, or else on a very similar bunk in a provincial redbrick university – the only two places where the members of our generation could be found, as you will know if you have read the literature – were the endless memoirs that poured from the presses every week, probing the commitments and apostasies, the loyalties, the treacheries and the buggeries, of the giant race before the flood.

For those were great times, quite unlike our own. They were times when the great burden of history had fallen like some collapsing factory chimney over a slagheap onto the young people of the proletarian decade. For the Thirties was, of course, an age of the workers, or rather an age when ex-public schoolboys wrote about what they felt about the workers. It was an age of travel and low sexual adventure, when every young author felt the need to go to the beaches of the Friesian Islands to study Nazism and find out why Nazism compelled all of German youth to take their clothes off. It was a time when every writer was a camera with the shutter open, a time when everyone felt the need to walk through the Abyssinian Kush, report some small foreign war, and spy for one's country, or preferably someone else's. It was a time of nightmarish atmospheres and general foreboding, with the aircraft flying low overhead and the nightmail express steaming for the north.

No wonder then that, reading all this, we felt ourselves to be faint and pallid souls, far too enfeebled – possibly by the watery cabbage in the wartime British restaurants, by the coddling of the Welfare State, or by the X-ray machines in all the shoe shops, which made your feet drop off – to be capable of aspiring to anything of this sort. There were no more wars to go to, and if there were there were travel restrictions that prevented you from going to them. The public schools were out, and the grammar schools, which produced only ink-stained swots, were in. It was no use being a camera with the shutter open, because you couldn't get the film. Theirs was a generation that really knew *how* to be a generation, while we by comparison were total amateurs. Unlike ourselves, who mostly stayed indoors, *they* had not just sat at home and waited for history to happen. In fact – probably for perfectly good reasons, but we will not go into that – they clearly found themselves totally incapable of sitting still anywhere for very long. No sooner had they scouted out the decadent *boîtes* of Berlin than it was time to go, probably by way of Cape Wrath, and fight in Spain, a tradition now virtually vanished – except, of course, among the ranks of soccer hooligans.

Thus it is not surprising that we looked back – and not in anger but in wonder – at that age of pylons and power stations, treacheries and transvestites, journeys to the border and across the frontier, and especially at its great writers, whose biographies virtually extinguished any thoughts we might have of writing our own. Indeed, as it happens, I was looking at some the other day; I did think of writing a book about the writers who refused to join the Left in the 1930s, but I could not find any. I picked up the old classic volumes – Christopher Isherwood's *Lions and Shadows*, Stephen Spender's rather more sensitive and introverted *World Within World*, John Lehmann's *The Whispering Gallery*, John Pudney's rather more robust *Home and Away*, and several more of the kind – and once again I found myself embroiled in the old magic. For here I was again, in the era of politics and psycho-analysis, of Isherwood's neural itch, Spender's endless doubts, and above all of the ubiquitous Auden, who dominated everything and everyone, and even got the age named after him. Here he was again, complaining that he smoked so much because he had been imperfectly weaned, throwing Isherwood into a state of psychosomatic influenza at every meeting, and generally behaving as a literary hero should. In fact the truth is that the age could not have worked as it did without him, and to tell the truth it is probably the lack of a really good Auden that has made the task of Fifties memoirists so impossible. Certainly, without him the Thirties would have been scarcely worth a backward glance.

How did Auden do it? Here he is at work. 'He rolled up Swinburne like a carpet from under my feet, threw the books out of the window, delivered urgent monologues about D. H. Lawrence, Havelock Ellis, Wilfred Gibson, psychology, sexual hygiene, homosexuality, and social-ism,' explains John Pudney, who shared a difficult pubescence with him at Gresham's School at Holt. 'For a person of my age and environment, this was an explosive experience,' he adds, to my mind a little frantically, and this is not hard to believe. For Pudney goes on to recount his adventures: furtively sneaking out into the night to recover volumes of Swinburne that Auden had defenestrated, hiding his own poetry under the Scotch grouse in the tuckbox because Auden had a way of dumping poems he disliked into the school pond, and so on. Indeed it seems that the terrorized Pudney was never safe. 'He would climb up a pipe into my study in the early hours of the morning before anyone was awake, to leave a message and to make a few corrections to the prep which was left out on my desk,' he notes, displaying the classic problem of the memoirist. For while, on the one hand, simple common sense would commend shifting to another school entirely, on the other you will never be able to write much of an autobiography simply about pressing flowers.

Similar problems bedevilled Auden's contemporaries at Oxford, when that institution took upon itself the evidently considerable risk of admitting him. It was Auden's modish way to sit in his darkened set – as rooms in Oxford were apparently called – conducting classes in advanced literary criticism with a group of acolytes, whose folly never ceased to infuriate him. 'If there's anyone needs kicking in the pants, it's that little ass,' he would comment, as the throng he had gathered there to consider who was the best poet of the day mulishly failed to see that the answer was self-evident – indeed it was staring them in the face. 'Written ravishing lines, but has the mind of a ninny', he would shout with growing impatience, as the company persisted in feeding him with names other than his own. Happily, though, critical sense won out, and the matter was settled. Auden, it was decided, was to be the best poet of the generation, Isherwood, sneezing away over there in the far corner, was to be the best novelist, and Spender, always willing, was to be the memoirist and recording angel, his notebook open at all times, especially when Auden was about. Isherwood was assigned similar duties, one amanuensis not being enough. He recalls Auden walking down the Broad in Oxford in an absurd felt hat, while the girls sniggered at him, and recorded Auden's witty *bon mot* on the matter. 'Laughter is the first sign of sexual attraction', he observed. It was one of those profound truths that was self-evident in the Thirties, though perhaps it is not quite so clear in the more obscure and confused world of today.

For, though the Fifties may have been like something or other, the one thing I can say in all certainty is that they were not like that. As people said in a famous phrase of the time, fings ain't what they used to be, and it was perfectly true that they wain't. Undoubtedly, by comparison with what went before, ours was a notably palefaced if not totally anaemic age. For ours, after all, were the austere days that came *after*, in the season that Cyril Connolly – no mean hand with a Thirties reminiscence himself – called 'closing time in the gardens of the West'. Modernism had expired, and the avant-garde was over and done with, apart from Colin Wilson, who maintained the Latin Quarter spirit by living in a sleeping bag on Hampstead Heath. The 1940s spirit of Romanticism and Apocalypticism, which had spread like non-specific urethritis through Fitzrovia, had died out too, except for an odd pocket in South Wales. Politics had quite discredited itself, and Marxism was the God that had failed, except of course at MI5. A buttoned, despairing stoicism was the only mood worth cultivating, given the circumstances. Now it was time to try morals again, since they had been out of circulation for some time. And a mature high seriousness was the thing to have, especially if you happened to be studying English with Dr Leavis at Cambridge, which in the Fifties, of course, everyone did.

Thus, by comparison with the Thirties, little seemed to go on, and there was nobody much about anywhere at all, since, after all, they were all either doing their National Service or learning how to become Scholarship Boys, who were like the Bevin Boys of wartime, except that they slaved above the ground rather than below it. Nobody did much to anybody at all, for virginity was back, after a fashion. The girls all wore thick vests and supercilious expressions, as well they might, and sex was virtually abolished in the postwar shortages, what little of it there was available being exported to the troops in Germany. Treason was no longer in fashion, now that Auden and Isherwood were in America, Burgess and Maclean in jeopardy, and Spender in confusion. Public schools were quite out, and those who went to them carefully adopted regional accents and the common touch; you either went to grammar school, or pretended you did, just as everyone pretended to come from the North. Abroad being out of bounds because of the travel restrictions, everyone had to make shift, as best they might, with Cardiff and Wakefield, Leicester and Nottingham, and the suburbias of these provincial cities became the main settings for the fiction and drama of the period. All of this was part of a revolt against Bloomsbury, the postal district behind the British Museum where the upper-middle-class writers of a previous generation lived in an atmosphere of modernism and fornication the new generation was determined to destroy at a stroke.

This was why – having previously made artful arrangements with the *Zeitgeist* – I took care to grow up in Nottingham, my home for the earlier segment of the crucial decade, up to the first commercial break. Thus, while all the publishers were busily shipping off their protégés to various provincial locations to enjoy a fit of anger in Barnsley, or a spot of sheetburning in Widnes, I was there already, a youthful figure in the great Nottingham Renaissance. For suddenly the city had become a kind of Midlands Vienna – though a little short, perhaps, on *Sachertorte* and *Gemütlichkeit*. There was no lack of an avant-garde. The city filled with Jewish girls called Grizelda, who wore black stockings and played the harp, and a whole body of strange, rootless and very literary young men who slept on the pipes in the public library. They were known as the Beet Generation – the only paid work they ever did was work at harvest time on the sugar beet harvest – until the phrase was borrowed, totally without acknowledgement, by the likes of Kerouac and Ginsberg, and we had to call them something else, probably shiftless. At other parts of the year they cadged drinks in the Nottingham milk bars and, sitting on park benches, wrote their novels, all of which began: 'The agony continues, unabated'.

Shortly after this, however, Bohemia moved upmarket and became widely fashionable, thanks to two events which coincided – the invention of the espresso bar, and the arrival of Sartrean Existentialism, two continental innovations that were often confused, so that there were many discussions as to whether the word for Nothingness was *néant* or *capuccino*. The espresso bars brought the continental spirit into Nottingham life, along with waitresses such as the city had never seen before – flute-voiced débutantes, slinkily attired, who talked all the time about Daddy's yacht as they spooned out their frothy ambrosia. It was in such steamy *boîtes*, amid the imported tropical greenery, as the thrilling beat of Spanish guitars pulsed aphrodisiacally on the Tannoy, and the *gaggias* hissed soulfully in the background, that I sat each night, feckless, rakish, tossing a mop of wine-dark hair, and wearing the obligatory duffel coat, holding forth to many girls in berets about the things that really mattered: Schopenhauer, the Modern Jazz Quartet, my novel-in-progress, my unfinished chemistry homework.

Let no one say that Nottingham, or for that matter the Fifties, which were much the same thing, lacked experimentalism. Its boulevards were filled with *flâneurs* and its *demi-monde* was almost as good as the real *complet-monde*. Everyone wrote novels, poems, and especially plays. For one day, capitalizing on their successful reviews of John Osborne, the *Observer* newspaper announced a playwriting competition, open to anyone of any class, colour, creed, or gender, providing only that they were angry enough to satisfy the high irritation level set by Ken Tynan, their drama critic. Old ladies cowered behind the lace curtains of suburbia as, for weeks, anger ran rife through Nottingham. Friends of mine normally too timid to order a meal in a restaurant suddenly became raging rebels, and you could see authors sitting in every window in their jockey shorts all over town, beating their masterpieces out of their typewriters.

Were we angry? We were not entirely pleased, I can tell you, and we were not afraid to show it, though in my own case it was less anger than *Angst*. For, as I say, this was the time of Existentialism. We all accepted Sartre's view of Being and Nothingness, and guessed that he must have been in Nottingham at some point himself. Absurdity, too, surged through the city, and could very well still be there, in some undiscovered corner or other. Novel thinkers and radical intellectuals crowded each other in order to get on the buses. I knew them all – a man, name forgotten (it might have been Ping), who wanted me to sail down the Grantham canal and then round the world on his wherry, and a girl named Ernestine, a long-legged, toothsome morsel who wore black stockings, smoked green cigarettes, and rode everywhere in taxis, tossing gloves out of the windows. We had a heady courtship, and planned to flee together to Madeira, where I would finish my novel and she would open a flamenco parlour. Alas, when I counted my entire pocket-money it proved inadequate. She took up with various smart-looking men in hacking jackets who said 'Pip, pip, old chap' and were definitely not of my type. And I set to and passed my Higher School Certificate with a distinction in geography. It was getting time to move on.

But still there was no Auden in my life; that was to come a little later. For, thanks to my scholarly achievement, I set off to university. Naturally, the times being what they were, it was a provincial university, a former local lunatic asylum that had preserved its tradition by becoming a seat of learning. For an aspirant writer like myself, it was not, to be frank, a place of great literary activity. But there was a literary magazine, edited by a fellow called Orsler, who indeed became my Auden, or the closest approximation to him that was available in the circumstances. I well recall my first encounter with this extraordinary figure, who was already deeply embroiled in the world of letters, having once seen T. S. Eliot leaving Faber and Faber. For months I bombarded him with poems and short articles on Plato, which he regularly returned to me with small notes covered in scatological abuse. Then one day he asked me to come and see him. I still recall the details of that momentous encounter.

Unlike Auden when Spender first met him, Orsler was not sitting with his eyes shaded in a darkened room. In fact he was standing buck naked in front of the fire in his digs, eating a piece of cheese and dictating a proposal of marriage, I believe subsequently rejected, to a friend and amanuensis. 'Young man, you're a bloody genius', he cried, rather as Auden did with Spender. 'Almost as great as me!' Spender records how on a similar occasion Auden then began to read some passages from his, Spender's, work in his own voice; they sounded so good that he failed to recognize them. Much the same thing happened to me – though in this case because Orsler, as was his frequent habit, had totally confused my work with someone else's. It was indeed one of the great achievements of his editorial reign that almost everything in his magazine appeared under the name of some other contributor. Some considered it to be evidence of his mental confusion; in my own view it was part of his challenge to the cult of personality that, he said, bedevilled Western literature, and prevented people from seeing how important he was himself.

Nonetheless, from that moment on, Orsler became my patron, and I his protégé, and a dangerous situation it all turned out to be. 'You must write poetry, we do not want to lose you for poetry', Auden told Spender, and then explained how he should be a poet. This meant dropping 'the Shelley stunt', he said; the modern poet was Mr Every-man, and Spender should therefore cut his hair short, don spats, and go to regular work in the city by suburban train. This resembled the tack

Orsler took with me. He made me burn some newly bought trousers because, he said, they made me look like a pier-show minstrel, and gave me a somewhat unpleasant suit of his own which he had discarded, for what I take it were excellent reasons. He had no truck with my avant-garde Nottingham mannerisms, and taught me to live in great simplicity – encouraging me to cook for him and wash his dishes, entertain his friends in my rooms, and remain in the background whenever he wished to pontificate on any matter, as he always did. It was thanks to this useful training that, from that time on, I have always been the kind of modest person no one would ever notice even against a light background, and I have managed to remain more or less invisible – especially when awaiting service in restaurants – ever since.

Yet, as again with Spender and Auden, Orsler's approach to himself was a little different. His own literary hero was Lawrence – naturally I mean the D. H. one, not the T. E. – and he had come to model his life on him. 'Lawrence – D. H. rather than T. E. – was right', he would shout in public places. 'Sex rules the world'. During the Fifties it was an irritating message, and the number of public places he was permitted to shout it in diminished week by week. Nonetheless he remained steadfastly Lawrentian, believing like his own master that instinct was everything. Once he asked me the time of some train it was important for him to catch. 'It leaves at 3.15', I advised him. 'No, it doesn't', he replied, putting his hand on his heart, or perhaps some other part of himself, 'I don't feel it *here*'. He missed the train, and it was shortly after that that he became a devotee of Proust – lying for weeks on the bed in his cork-tipped-lined room, beginning a novel that he intended should last a lifetime. He was still there when at last I left university for the even bigger world; indeed he could well be there now. I still remember our final exchange. 'When are you going to put me in a novel?' he asked, as I held my hand out in farewell. I must have demurred a little, for he said sharply, 'Now, look here, I discovered you, didn't I?' I had to admit that, in his peculiar fashion, he had. 'A memoir, perhaps', I said, and a small smile came over his face as I left him.

It was a momentous farewell, because after that things changed very quickly. *Lucky Jim* came out, and not too long afterwards *Look Back In*

Anger. It was clear we were getting to be a generation at last, mostly by shouting a lot at each other. It was around this same time that Colonel Nasser snitched the Suez Canal, and the youthful crowds rallied in Trafalgar Square, howling for change and looking at each other's duffel coats. The mood of triumph proved a little short-lived, however. In fact shortly after this everyone began to turn Anglo-Catholic, and the Vespa motor-scooter was invented. People who had been proud of being rank outsiders now started becoming respectable. Back in Nottingham, even the members of the Beet Generation, who used once to gather outside the Registry Office and throw stones at the windows, to show their utter contempt for marriage and bourgeois respectability, suddenly, and probably wisely, threw away their novels, essayed various forms of matrimony, started small businesses, and were soon employing accountants.

Nonetheless, always true to my principles, I remained a thesis-writing vagabond for the rest of the decade, living out of suitcases and travelling the world. Orsler, of course, was conscripted for National Service, and ended up preaching Lawrentian values to squaddies in the heady surroundings of exotic Singapore. I went on with the novel I was writing, and even tried to put Orsler in it. Alas, he proved an unwieldy fit, and I resolved to save him until I set down my memoirs. As this shows, I have not forgotten what I said. So, if you should get the impression that we men of the Fifties were a dull crew, a bunch of gangling provincial intellectuals tiptoeing into culture in stockinged feet, you now see how wrong you were. They were good old radical days, the Fifties, definitely worth all the remembering. In fact one of these days we ought to do it again sometime. I just hope this helps.

Yours, etc.

The Spouse in the House

Now and again I get a letter in my mail which is a perfect pleasure to answer, and one of these arrived just the other day. There is no need to explain its subject. That should be perfectly clear from the reply I have been drafting, and will probably send − if, that is, my wife approves it:

Dear Miss (?) X,

Many thanks for your letter, which I read with very great interest − not something that I say about all the letters I get these days. Many of these come from people who want to become writers − a very humane and worthy desire, of course, but one which now seems to be reaching epidemic proportions, and I fear we shall all soon be crushed under a mountain of paper unless something is done about it. There are times when I wake in the blackness of the night and think that what we need is not more books but less of them. I have even turned towards the view that the reason wicked publishers reject so many manuscripts is that they are right. Of course I do try in all cases to be as helpful as possible, but quite often my heart is not completely in it. In any event there is no shortage of handbooks and creative writing courses to help with the matter. You will see now why I am grateful for your enquiry, which is quite different − and on a topic about which there are, as far as I know, no handbooks or courses at all. For you do not ask me how to become a writer, but how to become a Writer's *Wife* − a much more interesting question.

Your letter does not tell me which sex you subscribe to, though really that does not matter. For, of course, Writers' Wives, like writers themselves, can be of either sex, though admittedly in the folklore it is almost always women who are famous in the role – with the possible exception of George Henry Lewes, the literary wife of Marian Evans, also known as George Eliot, to confuse matters further. Nor do you explain whether this is simply a general, speculative enquiry about your career intentions, or whether you have a specific example of authorship already firmly caught in your sights. Again, though, that does not really matter. The important thing about your letter is its wise, clear-headed assumption that marriage to a writer is like no other known form of matrimony, that writers themselves are a breed of person quite unlike any other, and that the whole project therefore requires intensive fore-thought and research. In that you are absolutely right, and you will go far – though whether you are wise to is another affair entirely.

The fact is that, in the hard commercial and bureaucratic world of today, there are few writers who would survive for very long without the support and activities of a really first-class Writer's Wife. May I offer you my own case as an example. I am, like quite a lot of writers, though not all, quite a sensitive sort of person, and therefore not greatly at home in reality – one reason, doubtless, why I became a writer in the first place. After rising of a morning, I spend most of my days and much of my nights bent across a typewriter, locked in a universe of literary fantasy. Most of what I know of real life comes to me from very old newspapers, or odd remarks dropped incautiously by the people who bring me my food and then collect the soiled plates afterwards. I go out rarely, my wife having warned me that the risk of infectious disease in our neighbourhood is absurdly high. The telephone makes me jump, and as for that complex world of tax accountancy, VAT regis-tration and royalties that bedevils writing and keeps so many nice young men in Porsches and riverside apartments in Dockland, I really want no truck with it at all.

Happily I am partnered in my enterprise by my really first-class Writer's Wife, who looks after reality for me while I am absent from it, which I am most of the time. Superbly combining, as she does, the roles of sexual companion, confidante, literary agent, solicitor, accountant, libel lawyer and doorstep bouncer, and somehow managing to run several other careers of her own as well, she turns me from a person writing into an actual writer. Thus the mountains of manuscript I produce during my long and industrious day are always carefully collected, wrapped into bundles, and sent off to persons unknown, who quite frequently then ensure their publication. Changes of clothes are quite often provided, and I am fed on most days with a reasonable frequency. Ashen-faced accountants occasionally pass through the house, and she has somehow talked them into letting me have pocket-money of ten pounds a week, which enables me to send out quite frequently for tobacco and the occasional box of chocolates. She is in short the ideal Writer's Wife, a paragon of the kind. Not surprisingly, other writers are constantly attempting to poach her from me, or otherwise seeking a share of her services. Very fortunately, she confesses herself of the opinion that to manage one writer in a lifetime is quite enough, if not far too much, for any human being, and I quite see what she means.

All this, I think, confirms my point that literary marriage is a very specialized form of matrimony, and certainly not something to be entered into lightly. I am afraid, though, that the whole area has been bedevilled by many false impressions, largely fostered by the press, various sycophantic biographers and Hollywood movies, in which writers are depicted as charming, witty people who but rarely sit down to a typewriter, and usually keep on chatting even when they do so. That is really not the way of it. It is often assumed that because writers are sometimes, though not always, sensitive, intelligent and creative people they will therefore make attractive and exciting partners. A few moments' thought should shatter that notion. Remember, it takes a person of distinctive psychological traits – obsessive, narcissistic, egotistical, self-excoriating – to become a writer in the first place. If that person is successful, other qualities will be needed as well – probably including jealous combativeness, paranoia, and profound self-love. Nor is life in the presence of literary creativity the load of fun it may sometimes appear. There can be much pleasure gained from watching a potter pot a pot, or a painter paint a painting. But writing writing is an activity that goes on largely within an inaccessible location, the writer's own head. The results are then transferred onto paper and duly published as a book, which can be read by anyone. I think you should ask yourself the question whether you really want to marry a writer, or are looking for the address of a really good bookshop.

But if you are determined, and you strike me as the determined type, I can indeed give advice on the care and management of this peculiar breed of person we call writers. I have studied the species quite intensively, and know a good deal about their maintenance, social customs, mating habits, diet, and so on. Briefly, writers, as you might expect, spend a good deal of their time writing. This is especially true when the roof has to be fixed, when there are children to be fetched from school, and such like. Strictly speaking, for their work they need no more than a pencil and piece of paper, but in the age of the word processor and advanced office equipment their desires have increased alarmingly; this needs watching carefully. They require, I find, light, airy rooms, a fairly warm temperature (that of Corfu does very nicely), and supplies of food and, especially, drink; personally I recommend a constant flow of coffee for creative stimulation without intoxication. An ideal diet is a light midday snack, which can be served over the word processor, so not greatly interrupting production; then perhaps a heavier meal in the evening, when the odd guest may be introduced to the house, preferably a publisher with another contract.

Of course different kinds of writer do have different needs. Novelists need to work longish office hours, or they will soon turn into short-story writers. Poets, on the other hand, unless they are writing Miltonic epics, usually work best in short, sharp bursts, and have decadent needs for inspiration, which usually they find in low public houses; on the whole this tendency should be discouraged. There are, in my view, two distinctive kinds of writer, the failures and the successes. The failures, not surprisingly, are in a permanent state of depression, believing themselves despised, neglected and rejected by publishers, the world, and probably you as well. The successes, on the other hand, are quite different. They live in a permanent state of depression, believing themselves despised, neglected and rejected by much the same parties, but also by the judges of the Nobel Prize, the compilers of the New Year Honours List, and above all by posterity – which of course does neglect them, not even having managed to arrive yet. Two other classes of writer can also be distinguished. There are those who work best early in the morning and grow lethargic later in the day, and those who work the other way round. It is very important to discover what pattern suits yours best, because the really fundamental thing about writers is to keep them writing.

It is when writers stop writing that all your troubles will start, so it is crucial to keep a careful eye on this. Briefly, writers stop writing for two reasons. One is when, like drains, they become 'blocked'. As with drains, it is of the utmost importance to get them unblocked at once, or the whole house will soon no longer be fit to live in. Always keep by the telephone the numbers of their literary plumbers who specialize in this kind of thing; they can be anything from an agent to a psychiatrist. Even more worrying is the other kind of stoppage, which occurs when a writer suddenly decides he or she needs to 'start living', or 'gain experience.' This, I am afraid, can lead to anything – a trip up the Amazon, a British Council lecture tour abroad, an orgy in the brothels of Cairo, the start of a spectacular affair, anything, indeed, that can later be explained to journalists, magistrates, or the tax inspector as 'gathering material'. Fortunately the symptoms are easy to spot, since they almost always occur between books. Good Writers' Wives, needless to say, know exactly how to deal with such lapses. They know it is necessary to take writers for walks from time to time, so that they can 'see life', and even be allowed a reasonable number of parties, to 'keep in touch'. I would particularly recommend ladling the writer suddenly onto a plane for a surprise summer holiday, so that afterwards they can say they have had a 'rest from writing', something all writers claim they need constantly, though why I do not know.

As I am sure all this makes very plain, a literary marriage is not something to be entered into with many illusions. I am afraid, however, that many abound, particularly among young literary groupies, who have the notion that they can become the writer's 'best critic', or 'fellow writer', or, even worse, 'muse'. Let us be clear about this. Most writers do not like critics, and the last thing they wish to do is share a bed with one. Nor do writers like other writers, and certainly not someone who wishes to work in the same field. When two writers do choose, as they sometimes do, to live together, it should always be quite clear who gets which material, and for how long. This simple but golden rule was unfortunately overlooked by Scott and Zelda Fitzgerald, with very unfortunate results. When Scott started *Tender Is the Night*, Zelda apparently started in jealousy her own novel, *Save Me the Waltz*, about something they did indeed share in common, their own lives. He took seven years, and she took six weeks. Unfortunately the competition was not a success; Zelda ended up in a mental home, and Scott in Hollywood, much the same sort of thing. There is no reason why a Writer's Wife should not be another writer, but I would recommend a rather different genre.

As for the question of being the Writer's Muse, this should be avoided at all costs. Many young Writers' Wives cherish the hope of having a poem addressed to them, or being put into a novel. Experienced Writers' Wives – and I checked this at a party I was allowed to go to just the other day – are terrified by the very thought. The truth is, of course, that there is no escaping the dilemma, since readers will always assume that characters of the opposite sex in any piece of writing will either be representations of the Writer's Spouse, or else a much desired alternative. There was a time when writers were able to escape all this by claiming that all their characters were purely imaginary, and they wrote notes to that effect in the front of their books. Alas, since Sigmund Freud came on the scene, notebook at the ready, all alibis are off. In fact the problem of Spouse Representation is possibly the biggest crisis in literary marriage, many of which have foundered because the Writer's Wife became jealous of one of the partner's characters, or even worse, fantasies. Once suspicion starts in these matters, there is no stopping. Depict a drab, monogamous marriage in a novel, and this becomes a depiction of one's own; depict rhapsodic couplings and adventurous fornications, and this becomes evidence of having it off with someone else, or wanting to. This is why writers frequently set novels on other planets, but it does not help. A truly jealous wife can become suspicious of anything, even rabbits.

In these matters I can warmly recommend the elusive strategies pursued by my own Writer's Wife, whose habit it is to insist to all and sundry that she has never read a single word of my novels, would never dream of discussing or criticizing their composition, always delivers them to the publishers with averted eyes in a tightly sealed envelope, and therefore has no notion whatsoever whether she or for that matter anyone else has been depicted therein, though she is quite certain she has not been. Just who it is who moves silently through my study of an evening, shifting papers, correcting typing errors, and leaving notes to indicate when a character's eyes change suddenly from blue to brown without good reason, therefore remains a total mystery to me. So, too, does the content of those long, mysterious and late-night telephone calls that occur between my wife and Mary Lodge – a fellow literary wife who has also never read her husband's novels, and is equally certain she is not in them – after one or other of our books has just come out. However it would appear that some notes are being compared, since there is now talk in that quarter of something called a Union of Concerned Writers' Wives, the aims and policy of which are not yet fully clear – though you will know very well whom to address if you wish to receive a leaflet.

You will see from all this that my field of research has extended, for reasons I do not care to go into here, not just to writers but to Writers' Wives. I can fully confirm that they are indeed a formidable breed on their own account, as anyone who has ever met a phalanx of them, perhaps, say, at the Booker Prize dinner, will know, and probably to their cost. My findings show that there are as many kinds of Writer's Wife as there are of writer – indeed more, probably, since many writers I know have been sufficiently fond of the species to have had more than one of them. However they do fall into a distinctive number of types. There is, for example, the Deferential Wife, who possesses a wonderful respect for her partner's genius, nourishing and respecting it, feeding it with esteem and hot coffee, always busily answering the telephone and preparing the syllabub. They are widely to be found, and they appear perfection; alas, like perfection, they often do not last long. For as their spouse's fame and ego grow, they soon appear not to respect fully the *profundity* of the genius, the *depth* of the talent, the *transcendental meaning* of the work. Good as they are, they are frequently displaced, as often as not by someone with an M.A. in Literary Theory and a more advanced critical vocabulary.

107

Deferential Wives can be contrasted with their opposite, the Utterly Contemptuous Wives, who appear to be destined for some other and quite different activity, like success on the stage or marriage to the aristocracy. 'Oh, God, if only they knew', they say, as their spouse brings out a new book, and they stand there at the signing, watching him surrounded by literary groupies. 'They think he's so clever and artistic. If they only knew he never gets up before midday. If they only knew the book was completely rewritten by the editor. If they could only hear him trying to explain snooker . . .' The odd thing is that the Utterly Contemptuous Wives often manage to last a good deal longer than the Deferential Wives, and often it is not their spouses but they themselves who finally grow totally bored, and marry someone else altogether whom they can despise even more.

Far more impressive, in my eyes, are another class, the Sexy Wives – those literary companions who, male or female, have a sexual splendour so palpable it seems like inspiration incarnate. Often they are so obviously stimulating that it seems that they are art and style itself, and writer and spouse go about together, two beautiful people, in a kind of glowing wonder, splashing each other with champagne, transforming parties, giving each other necklaces and wristwatches, and living in a narcissistic self-fascination so great it often becomes part of the art itself. This is what happened to Scott and Zelda Fitzgerald, two beautiful stylists who became the fashionable figures for their age. Unfortunately style does have a way of being evanescent, and it is often not long before the Sexy Wives are replaced, by even Sexier, and certainly younger, equivalents. Nonetheless there is much to be said for them, and they are greatly to be preferred to their opposite, the Genteel Wives.

The Genteel Wives are, I fear, to literature roughly what dedicated teetotalism is to a really good party. Like the Yuppies of Greenwich, their main aim in life is gentrification, and the chief role they perform in their spouse's work is to bowdlerize it. They were perhaps more common in the nineteenth century than this one, though many examples of the species persist. There was, for instance, Mrs Nathaniel Hawthorne, who used to read Nat's manuscripts and remove from them anything that looked too much like a gratifying fantasy. There was also Mrs Samuel Langhorne Clemens, who married Mark Twain, the naughty boy of the Mississippi, and tried, like Aunt Sally, to 'sivilize' him. The fact of the matter is that all art is filled with erotic secrets, and happily most of these have passed on to posterity more or less intact, the Genteel Wives being too genteel to notice them all. It seems fairly certain that Genteel Wives should not marry writers, and probably not anyone else for that matter.

The truth is that there are many, many kinds of literary marriage. But, literature indeed being filled with erotic secrets, the marriages frequently have a great deal to do with the kind of literature an author produces. This is one reason why writers of the more experimental type often try several, changing their styles along with their spouses, while other writers claim they can write only when they are between wives. In this matter Ernest Hemingway was a fascinating example, marrying four times at different points in his career. A careful study of his understandably posthumous novel *The Garden of Eden* may explain why, since it largely concerns a Writer's Wife who wishes to be a man and turn her spouse into a woman, thereby discouraging his talent. Like Fitzgerald, Hemingway clearly saw a complex relation between matrimony and art. His early and possibly happiest marriage ended quickly in disaster, perhaps because his first wife lost a briefcase of his manuscripts, one of those solecisms better avoided in any creative ménage. Two later marriages pushed him into big-game hunting, deep-sea fishing, and fighting in wars. Finally, at the height of his fame he married his fourth wife, Mary, whom he wooed by shooting up the toilet at the Savoy Hotel. Thereafter followed physical deterioration, increasing depression, and finally suicide. Mary Hemingway, as she confessed herself, was not always entirely happy with her Papa, but she did survive him. Thus she became the final apotheosis of the Writer's Wife, which is the Writer's Widow.

Of course, my dear Miss (?) X, this may not now be the first thing in your mind as you contemplate your marital and literary future, but it is worth a thought or two. After all, the Writer's Widow is one who attains the apparently unattainable prize of literary marriage, which is the Last Word. Now one becomes the final arbiter, the one who sifts and sorts, shapes and changes, burns and selects, scraps the diaries and sorts out the letters, authorizes the publications and the disposition of the manuscripts, and generally determines how one's spouse is to be seen, which is, of course, in the light of your own great part in the author's achievements. The Writer's Widow is the one who knows the secret intentions, the unexpressed desires, and takes every advantage of that fact – until, of course, the triumph is over, for Widowhood itself is transient, and the last word is not quite the last. For now comes the moment that was always intended, and the writer, if posthumously, contracts the most destined marriage of all – with the Literary Biographer, for whom, in the end, all the doings were really done, the writing written, the life so carefully lived.

Well, there, Miss (?) X, that is all I can tell you, and from this point onward you are out there on your own. All I can now do is to wish you all good fortune in the arduous career you are on the brink of choosing, and hope that all your doings become publishable. You seem to me to have the shrewdness and sense to do it right, so it is very possible that we shall meet one of these days, perhaps at some literary brunch or prize day or other. If so, do please get in touch; I should love to hear, in confidence, how it has all worked out. Perhaps, though, you should be just a little cautious about how you approach me. The fact of the matter is, I rather think I shall have my wife with me.

Yours, etc.

The Serial with the
Little Extra Ingredient

Now and again, various literary or writing friends of mine call or write to say that they have just been commissioned to write some popular television series or other. For the price of a racehorse's ransom, they simply have to turn their minds to the production of a major television project, which will make their fortunes, change the entire ideology of the culture, attract audiences in the millions, and somehow, in classic British fashion, become the great upmarket product of the age as well. It is not surprising that this invitation causes them some anxiety. For the truth is that, in the modern world, there is no task more onerous, or more terrifying.

They write to me, I take it, because they believe I have had some experience of this kind of thing, and they are not quite wrong. I have spent time amid the splendours of television writing, as indeed among its miseries. I have done adaptations of this, originals of that. I have worked with directors of great talent and actors of genius – if, that is, you can actually work with people of this sort. I have had television serials that flowered and bloomed, and others that collapsed from lack of the ready just before the first day of principal photography. I have had pleasure, and pain, and above all something you could indeed call 'experience'. It has not made me much wiser. I can spin you a theory, give you a version, of what makes a good television series at the drop of a contract. Nothing in the world is more exciting than the television series that goes more or less right, nothing more frightening than the one that goes wrong. The unhappy fact is that, in the early, hopeful days of these adventures, there is usually no way of knowing which one is getting into. For that reason, I am cautious about offering advice on these matters. Nonetheless my postbag quite often contains queries on the topic; my replies, ever sceptical, tend to take something like the following form:

Dear Mr Potter,

I was so glad to hear that the British television service had commissioned yet another television serial from your pen, word processor, or whatever. Thank heavens they still turn to serious writers to perform the task, when every temptation exists to take British television into the only direction it can go, which is downwards. You ask me to reflect on my own experience of the medium, and to say whether I have confidence in it. To a point, I do, but nonetheless the most honest answer I can give you, or anyone else interested in the matter, is to recount the following rather sombre story, which has to do with my own harsh discovery that writing for television is by no means a simple matter, but is laden with many curious ambiguities.

This tale takes us back a few years, a good few years, when a certain young writer whom I propose to call Alexander Pope – a gaunt, pale-faced, gifted sort of fellow with a book or two behind him, but no real experience of what we call the media – was sitting in his study, writing a review of the newest Iris Murdoch, her eighth or ninth novel to appear that year. Pope – a young author who bore a strange relationship to myself – was a very solemn and serious sort of fellow, whose life had been largely spent within the academic world. He had a hard line in critical theory, a lot of mysterious theses about the role of the media in contemporary society, and a few works of fiction, mostly of a somewhat satirical kind, to his not totally creditable credit. So there he was in his study, in a high state of critical alertness, reflecting on literary matters, and working on a course of lectures on some complex topic – I think it was the Dwarf in Shakespeare – on which he would have to teach in the following term. His mind was in ferment, his thoughts in a state of refined complexity, when suddenly the telephone downstairs began to ring abruptly. Thinking this was about some important academic matter, the choice of the right Aloxe Corton for the university wine cellar, for example, he ran to the receiver. He announced his name, and a new phase in his life began.

'Hi, Popie, baby,' said a very jolly-sounding voice at the other end, against a background of clattering typewriters, secretarial shrieks and a general mood of spilled Tippex, betokening some very large office. 'Who's there?' asked Pope, mystified. 'This is Colly Cibber,' said the voice. 'Remember how we worked together?' It took Pope a moment to gather his thoughts, but the enormous weapon of his memory functioned, and with great effort he culled into thought just who the unexpected caller was. Cibber was a television scriptwriter, researcher and satirist with whom, a couple of years earlier, Pope had had some dealings; this was when, in the spirit of the season, he had become part of a fashionable activity known as the 'satire boom', designed to bring irony and general scurrility within the reach of the masses. As a result Pope had somehow found himself a contributor to a late night television show called something like *Was That the Week or Wasn't It?* In this heady season, he and Cibber had somehow ended up writing a script or two together – an enterprise they managed by meeting in London pubs in the region of Shepherd's Bush, having what they called ideas, and guffawing a lot. Time had passed, the spirit of seriousness had grown, and Pope now associated all this with a misspent student youth. Nonetheless there was something exciting about Cibber's call, indeed the very sound of his voice, that put him into a tizzy.

'How are you, Colly?' he asked cautiously. 'Great, fine, very good, buddy baby,' said Cibber, 'and I've got this really great project on my hands that's going to be right up your little street. So grab yourself a notepad, old son, and write this down.' Pope thought of Iris Murdoch, the Dwarf in Shakespeare, and academic promotion, which they still had in those days, and felt second thoughts passing through his head. But he was an amenable soul, for all his gaunt features, always pleased to help the passing lame dog over the local stile or go along with the enterprises of a friend, or almost anyone else, for that matter. 'Go ahead,' said Pope. 'Okay, bud, gather this,' said Cibber. 'I'm working at Limehouse Television now as script-editor. And we've just commissioned this really fantastic new project, you won't believe it. It's the television serial to end all television serials, no less.' 'You mean a series?' asked Pope. 'I mean a serial, like what you have for your breakfast,' said Cibber. 'I mean something that lasts for ever, goes out twice weekly, peak viewing time, with more ratings than the American navy. It's a brilliant idea, a serial with a really new ingredient, you know, formula 4X, the first soap with all-in freshener.' 'What does that mean?' asked Pope. 'It means, buddy boy, that this is going to be the first all-satirical television series ever,' said Cibber. 'It means it will turn the nation upside down, pull no punches, tell it like it is. It'll go straight for the political jugular, it'll respond to all the latest news, and it'll be written *right there on the day*. It's what we all dreamed of, right?'

And it was true that, in the bright days of *How Was Your Week and Did You Have It?*, or whatever, the idea of establishing permanent satire on a day-to-day basis had been in everyone's mind. So were ideas of televisual immediacy. Indeed at the time I am recalling television bubbled with such thoughts, and famous writers like Stoppard were being commissioned to open up their daily papers and write plays that would be shot in the studio within two nights, even before they had been rehearsed. Collaboration, too, was the in idea, and playwrights were being made to write their plays with total strangers, some apparently dragged straight in off the street. Pope was a serious soul, but like any writer he had a taste for being a mover and shaker in contemporary culture, a devastating satirist, a voice of rage and truth. He had a taste for all these ideas that happened to be raging through this, to him, enlightened season of television thinking, even though something in him murmured that what was in this week would be out next, and even more out the week after. 'It all sounds very interesting,' he said, 'and very nice of you to let me know. Is there something I can do to help?' 'I'll say there is, buddy boy,' cried Cibber, laughing and apparently squeezing someone nearby who was giggling furiously. 'Haven't you got it? We're going for all the best writers and we want you right there on the team!'

Pope stared at the Murdoch-describing words in his typewriter and thought furiously, feelings of academic scepticism contending in him with another motive which might have been creativity or just possibly cupidity. For, though he was no expert in these matters, he had heard small rumours that those who engaged in this kind of activity tended to eat rather better than most of us, and that payment for this sort of task was rather higher than the contract rate for writing, say, metaphysical poetry. Pope was not a greedy sort of person, but he did have a dream or two. He would have liked to own a pair, or maybe two, of lambs-wool socks, to buy a typewriter with a letter r on it, unlike the one he now used, and to have a coffee grinder for his bottom drawer to increase his prospects of marriageability. But integrity or just possibly nervousness began to win out. 'I'm not a soapy kind of writer,' he said. 'In fact I'm rather into abstract expressionism these days.' 'Great, that's fine!' cried Cibber. 'We don't want typical serial writers. This is a new concept, none of that backstreet naturalism or Yves Saint-Laurent dressed romance. This is new as new and right out of satire. *And* it's been originated by someone whose work you know and respect. And we've given him choice of co-writers and the first name he picked was yours!'

'Who is it?' asked Pope. 'You won't believe this,' said Cibber, 'but it's true. Jonathan Swift, that's who! He's done the format, and written the first six episodes. But with two episodes a week it needs a regular team, and that's why we're turning to you.' 'Jonathan Swift!' cried Alexander Pope. Swift was a writer of high talent, author of stage and television plays which had been compared with Molière – not the Jean Molière who wrote for Granada, but the original eighteenth-century French Jean Molière – for his dissection of wickedness, folly, venery, bourgeois hypocrisy and foible. His gift for scalpelling absurd human nature was unrivalled, his qualities of literary abrasion and scatological abuse were unequalled, and a new stage play of his which had equal quantities of nudity and bitter social accusation had sent the League of Female Decency and Fine Feeling into a state of public rage. Pope revered his work, and for the first time started to feel that the proposed serial could really be exciting, original, everything Cibber said it was, and therefore worthy of his own creative investment. Taken, he asked Cibber to expand on the ideas behind the project, and Cibber responded in roughly the following way.

The serial was to be called *Twizzletown*, and its basic concept would be to explore a provincial town and the venality, corruption, barbarity and sexuality that boiled within the life of its bourgeois citizens. Fascist shopkeepers and bigoted workers, exploitative capitalists and wicked landowners, hypocritical, brothel-owning churchmen, and not a few members of the League of Female Decency and Fine Feeling, would make up its cast of characters. The narrative would be farcical, the tone bitter and twisted. The cast would be wild and savage comedians, there would be no sympathetic characters for the audience to identify with, and all their delight would come from watching the display of their own hypocrisy, meanmindedness and venality, stupidity, bigotry and venery. Swift's first scripts had already sent the Head of Drama Serials at Limehouse Television into paroxyms of euphoric delirium; the cast themselves were so convinced of coming success that they had sold their houses, withdrawn in some cases from their marriages, and moved to the unsuspecting provincial town where the serial would be shot. Network facilities were arranged, foreign rights everywhere under offer, and all in all it was evident that from Pope's point of view it could be a career for a lifetime, even though if the serial flew, an ever larger stable of writers, survivors from Sixties satire, would be hired to develop things as the older hands showed signs of literary wear.

Pope was tempted, deeply tempted. And when Cibber added 'This is the biggest budget Limehouse has ever spent, so you'll never get a better contract,' he slipped and fell. 'Yes, I'll think about it,' he said. 'But if it all works out I'm sure I'd like to try it.' Then he set down the telephone in a whirl, his head filling with strange fantasies. Instead of being an unknown writer, he would be a known one. Instead of teaching dull texts to bright students, or the reverse, he would be himself a text, part of modern literature, in its full flush of satirical rage. Rather than having to ask the girl from the grocer's shop to accompany him when he wished to take in the occasional film, he would be surrounded from here to eternity by stars and starlets. And rather than clad himself from the local jumble sales, he would indeed be able to buy lambswool socks, and probably bench-made shoes to keep them in. Indeed he might be able to buy an expensive device for keeping his feet from ever getting dirty at all – a Porsche sports car, for example. It might mean giving up some departments of academic and intellectual life for a while, or just doing it on the weekends. But wasn't satirizing

the foibles of the nation from a critical standpoint the very peak of the
intellectual life? After all, George Meredith had remarked that the cause
of Comedy and the cause of Truth were the same. There were a good
many sitcoms on television that brought doubt to this engaging thesis.
But *Twizzletown* was something utterly different, and would not be one
of them.

Pope was convinced. He called his agent, discussed his fee, and in due
time signed on the bottom line of some contract or other, not entirely
sure of what would happen next. Quite a lot did. Within a day or so,
the scripts of the first six episodes came, brought by the lady from the
village post-office who hoped she would not have to carry such heavy
parcels again. Pope took them and read them avidly. He had to admit,
in his capacity as a literary critic, that in certain if not most respects the
vision and manner of *Volpone* or *Le Malade imaginaire* were superior.
Nonetheless, they were energetic-enough stuff. Here and there the
satirical vision went over the top into slapstick, and now and again
certain aspects of personal venom seemed to be involved. But satire,
according to classic theory, was always described as a mixed dish, or
salad, and this was a salad with a salty sauce. Pope was more concerned
whether his own powers could ascend to the enterprise, but, sitting at
his typewriter, Iris Murdoch to one side, he found his satirical hand had
not entirely lost its cunning. From somewhere or other he had acquired
a gift for writing fades and wraps, and setting characters up in and out
of a scene without their ever quite saying 'I'm going now.' So he kissed
the grocer's girl goodbye, got on the train, and found himself sitting
happy on the cushions of a car in which a uniformed chauffeur took him
off to the first script conference of the *Twizzletown* project.

In an office at Limehouse Television, Colly Cibber sat behind his desk
in shirt-sleeves, piles of scripts stacked up around him, studio floorplans
pinned to all his walls. There was something a little makeshift about the
set-up, however, and Pope could not avoid the uneasy feeling that the
whole thing could be dismantled at a moment's notice. Cibber was
affable, and introduced Pope to the other members of the writing team:
William Congreve, who wore bicycle clips and specialized in realistic
detail and local patois; John Gay, who smoked cheroots out of a little
tin and was very good on Youth; and Swift himself, who as befitted the

originator sat in the one decent chair next to the whisky bottle. As far as Pope could tell, Swift was already benefiting well from the serial. It was not only the brand-new, fawn twill jacket which fell open lazily to expose the Burberry tag: there was a whole new certainty in his spirit which not surprisingly felt inspirational to the whole team. There was also John Garrick, who would direct, Ben Jonson, who would produce, and Sarah Siddons, who was to play the leading female role.

After Cibber had expounded the writing method – from the first six episodes on, each writer would take a couple of episodes apiece, working from the commonly agreed storyline, in which Swift would have a major part – Swift stood up and explained his vision. 'This serial will be written with complete integrity,' he said, pouring some Scotch. 'And courage. And a mission. Every other serial so far has had cynicism built in. The only cynicism in our serial will be that of society itself. We'll have nothing debased, nothing clichéd. That's why I asked for you three to help me – writers whose honesty I can count on as if it were my own.' Pope glowed with satisfaction, and when, with Swift and Cibber, Congreve and Gay, he slipped out for a sandwich lunch to a local hostelry, he felt the smoked salmon was the best he had ever tasted. There was the odd touch of imperfection: the makeshift nature of Cibber's office, and Swift's increasing complaints over the keg ale that someone in the Limehouse hierarchy had been altering his scripts overnight, so that, for example, Twizzletown's most enterprising sexual hostess seemed to have cut down on carnal pleasures and be largely preoccupied with tea and scones. But as they began to elaborate the storyline together the gloom disappeared, and on the way back from lunch to the afternoon story session he slipped into Austin Reed's and bought himself three pairs of lambswool socks.

Back home, Pope worked for several days on the two episodes assigned to him for early transmission. He added in new characters, fresh satirical complications, and even more profound notes of social bitterness. A week later he returned to Limehouse to watch the live screening of the first episode as it came all the way from the studio 12K. It was true that, thanks to the impromptu nature of this kind of drama, the live presentation and the inexperience of some of the team, who chose to fit in the filmed extracts at curious moments, there was the odd hiccup or two – with, for instance, the camera ending up at one end of the studio and the actors at another. But this was how it was supposed to be with live drama, and wildtrack improvisation, and the general feeling at the party afterwards was that, with its integrity, honesty and its intended and sometimes unintended expletives, the whole thing would go down like a *nouvelle vague* bomb. Everyone kissed and fondled each other, laughed a lot, and waited for the reviews and plaudits of the morning. So joyous were the festivities that the set itself did not survive unscathed, leaving one major location, the front of the town hall, with a major hole in it that would be visible for several episodes to come.

However, in the morning, things looked a little different, and Pope quickly learned that the main thing that spoils television is the reviews. For, it seemed, the critics had found the alienation effect of the serial – Brecht called it *Verfremdungseffekt* – even more alienating than had been intended. Failing to respond at all to integrity, courage and profanity, espousing the cause of dullness, they had debased themselves to the most vulgar literary prejudice. They complained of the lack of lovable characters. They elected suddenly to assert traditional morality and the right of every bigot to enjoy his bigotry without seeing it mocked in art. The odd liberal journalist grudgingly granted the series a certain repellent worthiness, but suggested that no serious standard of vituperation could possibly be maintained in a twice-weekly serial. Gloom multiplied as it emerged that the Limehouse switchboard had been jammed by calls, starting two minutes from the programme's going on air, from viewers who, having sat down in the family nest with their young for a pleasant half-hour viewing commonplace adulteries and abortions, had been faced with portraits of hypocrisies so vile and political corruptions so extreme they might just as well have spent the evening out discussing the lives of their closest friends.

The morning story conference was thus a gloomy occasion. Cibber sat in his shirt-sleeves, the morning newspapers stacked in front of him, reflecting on the unusual pattern of the ratings – which had, he said, gone from some 15 million at the start of the programme to more or less nil at the end. He pointed out that this meant in one sense the programme had done what it meant to do, alienate the viewers, but in another sense not, since none of them were left by the end to be alienated. 'This means we've got problems, duckies,' he said. 'Lord Limehouse himself says we've got to change the storyline. That's from the top, Jonathan.' As Swift seethed in the corner, Cibber read out a list of new management directives. Two of the characters had to be made sympathetic immediately. The head of the town council, with his international mafia connections and his habit of harassing the tenants of all the streets he owned, must be given two beautiful children and told to love them dearly. The town madame, who not only serviced the pleasures of all the major burgesses but shipped small children to Arab harems, should be played with a gamine charm by a different actress. Sarah Siddons, the local honeypot, should be given at least two scenes per episode in which she appeared clothed.

None of this, of course, went down well with the authors. Gay smoked his cheroots with a rising fury, Congreve, taking off his bicycle clips, called his agent and told him to sue, and Swift seized the bottle of whisky from the table, stormed out of the room and was not seen again until the following day. By then, worse had come. For some enterprising local newspaper reporter had managed to collect, from Cibber's informal office, copies of the following six or seven scripts, and thought up the cunning artifice of sending them to various civic dignitaries in the town where Swift kept residence, suggesting that they and their town at large formed the subject of the series. Not only had they in turn rung Limehouse to protest; they had summoned the libel lawyers, alerted the national press, and approached all members of parliament. Already the company legal wizards had required that four characters be totally eliminated. Nor was this all. The League of Female Decency and Fine Feeling had concluded, on the basis of a few bared abdomen, that Swift was up to no good again, and was even settling a score or two with them. They had therefore announced a national switch-off, asking all viewers to turn off their sets and draw small black curtains over their screens each Tuesday and Thursday until the entire *Twizzletown* enterprise was silenced.

Frenzy reigned at Limehouse Television that day, until the Head of Serials put on his best denims, called a press conference, and was reported nationally the next day as having said: 'We think this programme, if completely changed, has got to be a real winner. We're sure that if we make all the concessions we've promised it will be recognized as the example of shining integrity we at Limehouse know that it is.' It was at this point that Swift rose, hurled Cibber's whisky bottle at the Head of Serials, and publicly declared his resignation from the project, calling on the other writers to follow. But in the confusion that followed as the ambulance men came in, Cibber passed round the room, offering the co-authors an emollient extra fee, and the remaining writers then retired, somewhat shamefaced, to yet another story conference, feeling now that a hard row lay ahead of them.

So it was to prove. The series survived for some while, though in a state of continuous revision. While the libel lawyers excised most of the original characters, new ones came in by the cartload, laughing and lovable. They were backstreet charmers, and the publicity department saw to it that they soon had names like 'Lovable Lennie' in all the tabloid press. The mayor became a great giver of street parties, the town madame opened a boutique, and the members of the League of Female Decency and Fine Feeling became a delightful bunch, cleansing the whole town of corruption in no time at all. The ratings rose, and the spirits of the writers went down and down. Gay shot himself, but missed. Congreve became seriously depressed and had to be constantly rescued from ditches. Pope became the recipient of many begging letters from the Inland Revenue, and had to return the lambswool socks. Swift was not heard of again, though his lawyers called regularly; it was however rumoured that a series on a rival channel about corruption in a television company authored by a certain John Dryden was actually by him.

By the end of the summer it was all over. *Twizzletown*, having become indistinguishable from all the other anodyne soaps, was replaced by one – a glossy American buy-in that required no input from the Limehouse drama department, already down to three girls and a very nice-looking boy. It was a tale of corrupt, fornicating *nouveaux riches* in some oil-sodden city, with characters of totally repellent characteristics, but everyone became fond of them, presumably because they wore designers' dresses of silk and satin, were shod by Gucci and vehicled by Cadillac, and there appeared to be no satirical venom whatsoever. Soon the saga of *Twizzletown* was totally forgotten, and I have no doubt that you have never heard of it. It has been expunged from the television annals.

Happily for Alexander Pope, it all came to the crunch before the summer vacation was complete, and he was able once again to resume his teaching career. The girl in the grocer's had not forgotten him, and took 5p off his teabags in a touching gesture of reconciliation. In the first week of term one of his students read him an essay on *Gulliver's Travels*, a work by another, though as it happens totally unrelated, Jonathan Swift. The young man confessed he had not liked the work, and that his contempt for this animal called man, and his 'infernal habit of lying, shuffling, deceiving, and equivocating', was a calumny on human nature. Pope scribbled a long bitter note on the bottom of the essay, gave it a C, and wrote this same young man a very warm reference for a job in the world of television drama – which, as it happens, he holds to this day.

From this narrative, we might learn various lessons. One is that few television ventures start as they finish, the enterprise being so collaborative that every talented person involved in it has a different end in view. Another is that television has the same rough resemblance to a major work of art as the work of Walt Disney has to the ceiling of the Sistine Chapel. But that would be to express a bitterness I do not entirely feel. No, Mr Potter, you yourself once described British television as the best worst television system in the world. You expressed the point with your usual succinct wisdom, and I think you were right. So does Alexander Pope, who still does the occasional play or series, still gets the occasional credit, and still, very wisely, retains his post as Professor of Critical Alertness in some university or other, where it is possible to go on keeping a general eye on matters.

Yours etc.

The Adapter's Tale

Speaking of the media, there is, I can confirm, no better way of ensuring a totally full postbag than to adapt some well-known novel as a series for television. Often these letters complain about the fact that some character or place or other was not in the least how the reader of the novel had imagined him, her, or it. But others are more testing. Why, they ask, should someone who could perfectly well be writing books of his own, or better still teaching several more hours a day, be busily shifting works of literature, like some very heavy baggage, out of one medium and into another? Why is it necessary to move onto the television screen works of art that give excellent pleasure in their original form – books that are written as novels because novels were just what their authors wanted them to be in the first place? Doesn't one subtract from a story more than one adds to it, and isn't rewriting an activity vastly inferior to writing? These are telling questions, I have to admit, and to them I have grown used to offering various answers. But I often feel tempted to probe further and give a very honest one, which would go something like this:

Dear Viewer,

Thank you for your letter demanding to know my reasons for choosing to travesty the work of dear old X, an author we both evidently admire, by adapting it as a six-part series for television. Clearly, rather like young Dr Jonathan Miller, you are inclined to believe that the idea that great books make for good television is an illusion. I do have some views on the matter myself, having adapted the works of others, been adapted myself, and on one occasion having tried to adapt my own work myself. I would grant you it is always a fragile enterprise; nonetheless, there are things to be said in its favour. I could point out to you, for example, that nearly all writing is a form of rewriting, whether with or without acknowledgement, that Shakespeare's plays, most operas and for that matter Joyce's *Ulysses* are all reworking of old myths in a new medium, and that stories do need to be retold to new audiences through our new technologies of expression. I could also point out that I like undertaking the experience as a kind of commentary, one writer making some sort of creative marriage with another, and that this can be very exciting. But there is another reason why someone who is by nature and custom a novelist, as I am, enjoys writing for television in this way. It does get you out of the house.

Let me explain. Novelists, the tribe of which I am a member, live rather strange and unusual lives, not to be compared with the lives of, say, playwrights or poets. Playwrights are, by definition, very sociable and public people, out at all hours, going to the theatre, working with actors, and generally indulging in life to the full. When not drinking in green rooms with famous acting stars, notorious directors and rich backers, or rioting in the bar at the Royal Court, they spend much of their time with the smart and the wealthy – riding the Aegean with them on their gold-plated yachts, playing strip-poker with them in their many Italian *palazzi*, and then going off to New York for their Broadway openings and closings, often on the same night. Poets are a different breed again, living intense, passionate lives filled with complex metaphors, metaphysical desires, and wild frenzies of inspiration. But, modern poems being very short, they are usually through by lunchtime, if not before. After that it is all amusement, and most poets spend a good part of their lives declaiming in pubs and attending literary parties, growing ever drunker and more litigious and putting their hands up the skirts of the wives of their friends.

But novelists, true novelists (and I do mean true, serious, dedicated novelists, not the chiffon-dressed romantic ones who too often represent the breed to the public), are something else again. They are people of distinctive dedication and a special kind of genius, usually sensitive and introverted, if not morose. For it necessarily takes a distinctive kind of person to indulge at length in the invention of totally imaginary events and then spend years, if not an entire lifetime, transferring this onto small squares of paper in the hope that one day someone will read it. Unlike a play, a novel is not performed; it begins and ends as an extraordinary mental adventure. And unlike a poem, it is not written in minutes, and requires an extended working day that goes on up to bedtime and frequently lasts for months or years. This of course is why most novelists, especially in Britain, live in remote country rectories, the more distant parts of Islington, or possibly on isolated foreign islands with peculiar tax advantages. The sun may shine, but they never see it; life may go on, but they never enter it. Naturally they prefer to remain over their typewriters, dreaming of unusual sexual couplings and odd imaginary desires that are performed – and thank goodness for it – nowhere except on the page in front of them. So it is not surprising that, when very occasionally, they emerge into the light of common day – perhaps to accept the Booker Prize, or gratify their publishers by going on a writers' tour – they come out blinking, like feral children who have been reared by the wolves of the forest, and seem scarcely capable of speech.

Writing long narratives is a strange, solitary vice, of the kind that can make you blind, as Homer discovered to his cost. No wonder that many novelists – from Dostoevsky to Sartre, and more recently Adrian Mole – write their books in the form of strange, introverted diaries, speaking of themselves as underground men for whom existence is by definition senseless. And no wonder that the novel as a form is a long way away from those dramatic renditions that appear as adaptations on the silver screen. Now suddenly the private fantasy turns into public image. Admittedly none of this explains why it is that a novelist should suddenly choose to take on the role of television adapter, either of his own work or someone else's; but it should make it very clear why he or she might have the impulse to try. But perhaps the best way to clarify the process is to dramatize it, as it were, by taking a recent experience of my own. I therefore ask you to watch me very carefully. At this instant I am a novelist. You can tell this by the seven pens in my top pocket, the notebook I carry under my arm to jot down a phrase or two if you say anything brilliant to me, and the bat-like, blinking look I give when under a strong light. But in just a second I shall go behind that screen over there. And when I come out you will observe that I am quite different. I shall be affable, amusing, casual and dressed in something informal, and my technique will be different too. In fact you will realize that I have slipped like quicksilver into another medium, another art form, entirely.

1/1. INT. AUTHOR'S STUDY. DAY. (LOCATION)

A busy day. The post has arrived at last, pedalled over by the lady from the post-office twelve miles distant, and it probably ought to be answered. There is a very pleasing request to sit on the pavement for two days outside the Russian Embassy. The figures of my borrowings under Public Lending Right have come; the fees roughly equal the fines I owe to the local library, mobile of course, though not very, and perhaps we can reach an arrangement. There are several invitations to book 'launches', or 'lunches', to promote new works by contemporaries who somehow manage to turn out the stuff a good deal faster than I do. These things these days are held in the most imaginative locations, though the party at the abattoir to celebrate S.C.'s new novel *Flesh* seems to me going a bit far. I shall not go, of course; I never do. London is far too far away, especially by bicycle, and I can never find my way about in it. In any case one would only start drinking again, and delay the new novel, *Composition 93*, even further. There are also several invitations to attend the memorial services being given for several more of my contemporaries, though I suppose I should stop calling them that now. Though by definition far more satisfying than learning they have published a new book, these occasions too can be depressing, making one feel older than one thought, and I shall not go up for them either. I am in no mood to trade anecdotes with the many would-be biographers who always haunt such events, or start rooting out letters for their Collecteds. I am a novelist, and I must not, as my bank manager reminds me, be distracted from writing my novel.

Alas, it is not easy. Two reviews to do today, and then an Italian student is coming to talk about a thesis on my work, which she intends to compare with someone else's. I dread these occasions. These girls usually have an imperfect command of English, and an even more imperfect command of the list of questions they ask, for they have usually been written down for them by an English boy-friend. She will open a big bag, produce a tape-recorder, accept tea, and then ask inordinately long questions which I in turn will politely answer at inordinate length. It will then emerge that the tape-recorder was defective, or wrongly operated, and the research student will cry, so we shall have to go through it yet again. Sometimes I have recorded these interviews five or six times, had to put the poor girl up for the night, and then give her a fiver to upgrade her day-return ticket in the morning, so she can return to her London hostel and the various other Italian girls who have all in their turn been out doing John Fowles, Doris Lessing and Margaret Drabble. It would be better if these girls proved to be the same ones who turn one's head so readily on the Via Veneto, but it is never or rarely the case; perhaps all those go to Margaret Drabble.

And how can I be expected to write when the telephone keeps ringing so persistently? The shoes are repaired and ready for collection. The newsagent will not wait for payment much longer. My agent tells me that a major journal wants me to review a book by my greatest rival. Unfortunately they offer no payment other than revenge, and my agent will even take ten per cent of that. And now there is a curious call, from someone who called herself an independent production company, asking whether I would care to adapt the work of a writer whose work, despite all rivalry, I rather admire, as a six-part series for the television box. To be frank, I am tempted. It sounds extraordinarily easy, since the author of the book in question has evidently done the best part of the work already. It means putting the novel aside for a week or so, but I think I shall accept. No payment has been mentioned but I am sure they will make some. I believe quite a lot of people watch television these days, and there are quite a lot of adapted dramas on it over the period when there are no snooker competitions. I understand this is one of those. I have not said yes and will not until I have consulted my wife, when she comes back from the bank where she spends most of her time juggling her mysterious investments. She has seen television before, and will be able to tell me what it is like.

1/2. INT. BAR, SMALL VILLAGE PUB. NIGHT. (LOCATION)

A crowded pub, smoky atmosphere, local farmhands and farmers, etc., chatting at small snug bar. The camera pans to a lonely figure in the corner, holding a half pint of shandy.

Yes, it's me. I should explain I am not usually to be found here, but tonight for once I feel the unusual urge to take a small tot of something. Late this afternoon I rang the young lady from the television company and said yes. My agent advised it, saying that writing for television could be more profitable than writing novels, especially in my own case. My wife is in favour too. She tells me a good deal of this television stuff has really been quite passable lately; however, apparently it is all done by a lawyer called John Mortimer and everyone says it is time we saw a change of name. Obviously if a lawyer can dash this sort of stuff off in his presumably minimal spare time, so can I. There are some problems, though. Before I actually write the script, they want a treatment, a synopsis, a list of my writing credits, and the number of my Barclaycard. I have never been asked for all that sort of stuff when writing a novel. It also appears that I must go to London and have lunch with people in various locations in Soho, a particularly seedy quarter of the city if the various detective novels I have read on the matter are any sort of guide. I hope this really is a television project and not some cunning plan to sell my body to the Algerians. However, quite an unexpected sum of money has been mentioned by way of stipend. No doubt it is a mistake, but I shall hold them to it.

I think if you wouldn't mind just tracking this way I'll make my way over to the bar and get another drink. Just this once, I do believe I can afford it. Cheers, squire, and have one yourself.

1/3. INT. L'ESCARGOT RESTAURANT, LONDON. DAY. (LOCATION, IF POSS.)

I am sitting in this small chic restaurant, here where the brightest *cognoscenti* of London foregather, though not today, with a very attractive girl. Anthea is a programme development assistant consultant adviser and chief Filofax carrier to Pronto Productions, and from her warm giggles over the Glenmorangie just now I gather that our television project is definitely on. My 92-page treatment was, she says, more than enough to convince everyone who has found time to skim-read it that this is a hot little goer. Apparently the author is very pleased to hear that I, or indeed anyone, wants to adapt it. 'Throw the book out of the window,' he advised, and so, in an excess of enthusiasm, we just did. I think David Puttnam waved at me from the next table but one, so I must be getting quite well known. London is quite exciting and they have now banned cars from Oxford Street. I expect now I shall have to come here quite often, and I have therefore noted some of the other items on the menu so I can try them next time.

1/4. INT. STUDY. DAY. (LOCATION)

It seems awfully funny to be sitting here at my desk and turning another chap's work into something quite different entirely. I say sitting at my desk, but most of the time I am running out to the telephone. A lot of people seem to be working on this project besides me. It's very hard to understand who they are, but they all seem to have read, or sort of, my treatment, and have all sorts of different ideas about it, like changing it to another country, another century, or having different people in it with a different ending. Some of them have actually read the book as well, but others are afraid it will spoil their freshness.

In fact this whole experience is becoming very strange indeed, and I find it quite unlike writing a novel. With a novel, a vast society, a sweep of history, people, customs, habits, feelings, psychological instincts, landscapes, love affairs, and so on are created within the space of your head. You then sit down and write it all onto some paper, and post it off to a publisher. If he is in a good humour, he then transfers it to more paper, with a nice spine, distributes it to one or two bookshops, and one or two people then buy it for their relatives, if you are lucky. These then sit down in a chair, or wherever, pour themselves a tot of whatever, and read the paper, so deftly transferring it back into the spaces of *their* heads. What a clever method of passing messages it all is, and so much more economical than television.

For the people at television do not simply want to read what I have written; they want, as they say, to *do* it. People will impersonate the characters and go to the places about which I have written. It seems very costly certainly compared with a novel, and I do worry about the expense. For example, I just wrote down the words: THEY OVERTURN THE ROLLS-ROYCE. This caused me great distress, because I realized that they would get a real Rolls-Royce and overturn it. Naturally I immediately rang Anthea and offered to write her a Renault 5 instead. But Anthea says they have something called high production values, as well as something else called co-production money, and so everyone now is really looking forward to overturning the Rolls-Royce, because it will make the programme more prestigious and attractive to the Americans. It is a very odd world. I was just rung by a man who says he is an expert on the year 1973, and wants me to get more of what he calls the 'period' into it. If this goes on I shall not get much written today at all, and tomorrow there is another lunch.

1/5. INT. STAR AND GARTER, CROMWELL ROAD. DAY. (LOCATION)

This is not like L'Escargot. Perhaps they are running out of money. But the rewrites I did to the rewrites I did to the rewrites have at last been accepted and we now have a schedule. Everything has been quite carefully planned. First they will get the actors, then have rehearsals, and then they will try and fit all the diaries of all the different actors together in a way that more or less works, and then they will try and make a film record of it all. A lot of people are taking long holidays looking for places that suit the scenes I have written. The London scenes are being done in Corfu because the light is better there, while the Corfu scenes are going to be shot on a purpose-built set in a large shed in Clapham. It seems they will be using sound and everything. This is going to cost a lot more than I bargained for. I hope they have someone sensible on their team who has got an idea of just what this could run up to; probably hundreds of pounds, if I am not mistaken.

1/6. INT. REHEARSAL ROOMS, ACTON. DAY. (LOCATION)

Pierre Macherey, the French Structuralist critic (out of shot), once suggested that what makes works of art is not the creative gift of the author but the entire system of literary production. This now seems to me, if I may say so, rather true. Today – it is some weeks later (adapt weather accordingly) – I really began to realise what an extraordinary *communal* if not crowded activity writing for television is. It is definitely not like writing a novel at all; that takes only one of you. I got to London (again) very early because today they are having a read-through and this was my chance to meet the cast of the show at last. The cast are the actors who will perform the lines I have written, or, if this morning is any guide, something faintly resembling them. They are all remarkably famous and it is only I who have never heard of them; and they all seem to know each other extremely well, if not intimately. Someone mentioned to me the fees that have been paid to them and they are a good deal larger than mine, suggesting to me at times that perhaps the writer is not all that important. What would Tolstoy have made of that? Or, indeed, of the fifty or so other people, most of them with no apparent functions, who stand about, all of them claiming to have distinguished titles and screen credits.

Despite these crowds of people, the production does not, to be frank, seem to have got very far. Perhaps it is true that too many cooks spoil the broth. The whole affair looks very tacky. Instead of houses, all they have managed to get are tapes stuck to the floor to show where rooms might be. Instead of proper furniture, they are using old chairs and in some cases people are sitting down on nothing at all. They are using small boxes for the cameras. Luckily there is someone called the director here, who seems desperate to sort out all this mess. I have small hopes of this ever amounting to anything. On the other hand, several people I don't know at all have kissed me, so I assume that it is not the fault of my script, and that they feel it is reasonably all right.

1/7. EXT. LOCATION. DAY. (LOCATION)

This morning I arrived in the small town where our little series is being shot, to find my way blocked by a somewhat curious spectacle. A row of large vehicular containers was proceeding very slowly towards the town, and from these stuck the heads, horns and nostrils of a good many large and dangerous animals. A giraffe waved its neck at me, a lion or two roared, and a very unpleasant rhino had its snout stuck right up against my windscreen. It was only when the police stopped me and warned me that a tiger from the production was loose in the vicinity that I realized this had something to do with my own literary endeavours. I had, I now recalled, written one small scene in a wildlife park, during which one of the characters is eaten by a lion. Naturally I had suggested that this scene be simulated, and not done for real, but it now appeared they had not taken my advice. Of course I hurried to the director to explain to him that I had not really intended the actor to be digested, and that I assumed the scene would be artfully constructed with clips from old wildlife films with David Attenborough, of which I was told there are many. The director told me that he wanted to do the scene to the highest level of production values, while the actor who was playing the key role stood close by, being sick in a bucket.

This was not the only surprise. The other main event that takes place in this 'location', as it is called, is a riot, where the citizenry of the town largely destroy it in a fit of collective ill-temper. Again, I had written the scene abstemiously, as is my wont, with a great deal of off-screen noise and two people in a doorway looking very queasy. That has not satisfied our brave director, who has decided, again, to 'give it the treatment'. This may explain why the entire town is filled with policemen, though policemen of a curiously idle kind, who spent their time lounging in their cars drinking Heineken. When asked for directions, they proved incompetent, and I then found that they were actors, or what are called 'extras'. In the event, when the shooting started, they proved to be absolute necessities. The rioters, also 'extras', who came in several bus-loads from Birmingham, proved great enthusiasts. The town hall was stormed and I saw with my own eyes part of it burning down. The windows of the shops were smashed, and THEY OVERTURNED THE ROLLS-ROYCE somehow became they overturned the Rolls-Royce. I retreated to my hotel room in great dismay, and lay down. *Imagine my amazement* when I returned to the market place two hours later and discovered that the town hall was undamaged, the broken windows entirely repaired, and the community had returned to its normal state. Or almost normal. Apparently there was a rhinoceros in Woolworth's that had not been there before.

1/8. EXT. SECOND LOCATION, COUNTRY HOUSE. DAY. (LOCATION)

I had not realized until I started writing for television that all television series are required by law to have large country houses in them. This is stipulated by the Country House Owners Association, who apparently have a contract with the television companies to this effect. How fortunate that in my script there was reference to a smallish house of inordinate Gothic ugliness in which a few of the events happen. In the interests of veracity, the television company therefore availed to its service a vast and most charming Georgian manor, the domain of a gentleman landowner who was in green wellies and a state of severe shock. What seems to have bewildered him is the transformation his property has undergone over the course of the day. A hideous green latex covering has been fixed to the façade. Several vile towers have been added to his roofline by crane. Now he lives in a house of inordinate Gothic ugliness, and even his dog will not enter it.

During the afternoon an interesting if slightly disturbing thing happened. John Blunt, the author of the original novel, appeared on the location, apparently keen to take the opportunity of fondling the female cast. He was courteous enough to seek me out and say a kind word or two about the script, a copy of which he had acquired through some surreptitious source. Nonetheless I am not sure how to read his manner. There was the moment the director asked him if he was pleased with the conversion that had been done to the house. He said the drama would have been better if the house had been left as it was. 'It says in the script a house of inordinate Gothic ugliness,' said the director. 'That comes straight from the novel.' 'Wouldn't it have been cheaper to change the line?' asked Blunt, rather bitterly. 'After all, you've changed every one of the others.' Happily, before we got into a fracas about the accuracy or otherwise of my script, they started filming the scene of the actor being eaten by the lion. It was very exciting, and was handled very well, and with any luck the chap should soon be out of hospital. Luckily, someone with foresight had not put him on the shooting schedule for tomorrow. It's strange: a few days ago I would have been far less professional about these things, probably running to the poor chap as he lay on the ground and giving him succour. But of course that would have ruined the shot, and required a retake; he would not have thanked me for it. 'We got it, we got it,' everyone was shouting as the ambulance came, and a great cheer went up. There's nothing like actual experience on location for bringing everyone up to the very highest professional standards.

1/9. INT. SITTING ROOM. NIGHT. (LOCATION)

My wife and I have bought a small television set to watch the result of my recent labours, and tonight the very last episode is being shown. Quite a few months have gone by, the work having been interrupted by an electricians' strike, a general election, the loss of a can of film, and the desire of the makers to add music to the programme, quite supererogatory in my view. The story does not seem quite the one I wrote, still less the one John Blunt wrote. On the other hand, he seems very pleased, since his royalties have increased by sixfold, whereas I still feel that perhaps I should have been more forceful, discouraging them from adding the car chase, for example. Nonetheless one watches with an extraordinary sense of the power of what one has done. Thanks to what one wrote on the little typewriter in the corner, two million pounds, or so I now gather, were spent to produce these six hours of sitting-room gratification. Riot and mayhem have occurred in several towns and villages. In fiction, and very nearly in fact, an actor was consumed by a lion. Now the final credits roll, mentioning the hundred or so people who have worked for a year to produce this result. What follows is the news. Riot has occurred in several towns and villages. At a wildlife park somewhere a child has been consumed by a lion. Evidently the whole story could have been had for free. On the other hand, I would not have been able to claim I wrote it.

My wife and I switch off, and look at each other. Then on us both a terrible realization dawns. It is over. The community of people – directors and assistant directors, producers and production assistants, actors and actresses, focus pullers and best boys – that has been filling my life for a year has vanished, split up, in some cases returning to their wives and in others to someone else's. There will be no more trips all the way to London, no more lunches at L'Escargot. There will be no more real lions and actual giraffes. All that remains – modestly shrouded in its dustsheet in the corner – is my typewriter: the peculiar instrument which somehow typed the instructions for spending two million pounds and commanding the lives, talents and emotions of a hundred talented people. I cross to it, lift the dustcover, and roll in a sheet of paper. For a moment I wonder what to write – and then, in all clarity, I know. I think I'll do a novel.

I hope this answers your question.

Yours etc.

A Visiting Lecturer's Thank You

This letter, like a number of the imaginary letters that whirl from time to time through my head, arises from an important aspect of my work. Besides being a writer, I am also an academic, a scholarly soul with many monographic studies to my credit and an ermine hood or two in the wardrobe. One of the pleasures of academic existence – not many people know this – is constantly to be invited to give lectures in the universities of one's academic peers, on the basis that if you give one at theirs they can come and give one at yours. This ensures the free flow of knowledge, and often of a good deal else as well. And in fact a significant part of my morning postbag comes from departments, scholarly groups and student societies issuing these generous invitations, usually to a university located in a remote and inaccessible part of the country with no visible means of contact to one's own – or else in a totally other country altogether, normally one with few natural charms or else where the charms just happen to be out of season.

Frequently I accept these invitations with delight, only in due time to be confronted with the reality. Travel arrangements normally prove poor, if not non-existent. The weather proves inordinately inclement, since one is, of course, normally asked in term time, which in most countries, even Wales, is fitted into the monsoon season of the year. Rail strikes are arranged to mesh in with the occasion, and the hotel into which one has been booked proves closed for demolition, requiring one to stay either with the oldest or most incompetent member of the department, according to whichever is the more remotely and unpleasantly housed. Even if the destination is Tenerife or Hawaii, and the sun shines brightly on the gin and tonics, the experience of the visiting lecturer normally consists of being confined throughout to seminar rooms virtually identical to those one has left behind in one's home university – which, in any case, has not forgotten you, and rings constantly to say that Mr Johnson in the second year has a problem and is waiting outside your door in the corridor to see you at once. It is not surprising that, on return, a letter of the following kind begins to form itself in the battered and shattered mind:

Dear Professor Apethorpe-Montpression,

I am writing to express my very warmest thanks to you for the generous hospitality I lately enjoyed at your hands, on the occasion of the lecture, or perhaps better the small and improvised paper, that I gave at your institution to the admirable and friendly students of your department. As you may or may not be able to imagine, it is a visit that will long stay with me, and I want to repeat the thanks I gave to you so vociferously at the time for generously inviting me to your literary 'series'. I can assure you it was one of those honours one really cannot refuse! A summons from the esteemed editor of the *Oxford Book of Scottish Salads* – a work that has of course been at my bedside since puberty, and given me many a chuckle of delight – was naturally temptation enough. Indeed it made totally supererogatory the small point you made *en passant* in your kind letter of invitation, that you had just consented to serve as external assessor on the panel for the Readership for which my own university, after all my long years of painstaking and benighted hard labour, was, at last and purportedly, about to consider me. Naturally an approach from someone of your distinction and long-lived work in the field was summons enough! In any case, nothing would have discouraged me from a chance to visit your famous department, word about the original work being conducted there both in the teaching of the subject and the methods of testing and examining its students having become a matter of fascinated gossip right through the entire profession, as you may or may not be surprised to learn.

In the event, it proved all it was said to be, and well worth the remarkably arduous journey. I ought again to apologize for my rather late arrival, though I fear the fault was not my own. I confess myself foolish to suppose that to pass from one side of Britain to the other by public transport was a journey one could hope to compress into one single day. On the other hand, the fact that railway facilities halted some twenty miles short of your charming yet remote location was something the travel authorities could well have given me advice about. How very fortunate that that good-hearted milkman was on hand and so graciously willing to let me lie down in the back of his electrical cart for that long last lacuna or transportational *mis-en-abîme*. Your irritation on my late arrival was entirely understandable, though the fact that your secretary had for some reason supplied you with a photograph of Frank Kermode did not make recognition any easier (though perhaps he had still not arrived from the previous week!). However, once cathexis had been made the visit could not have been managed in a more generous spirit.

Let me say first how much I appreciated your kindness in inviting me to your own house for dinner. It is perhaps one of the privileges of a distant location that with lower house-prices even we ill-paid academics are able to live very well, and I must say I envied you your fine seat at Glamis. Certainly arrival there made a dramatic and colourful prospect for the total stranger. I hope you did not feel impelled to dismiss that poor incompetent who serves you on the door; I expect his day is long, the work cold, the environment inclement, and a spirituous infusion or two, or more, his only relief in what to some might wrongly seem an unusual if not benighted spot. I was sorry not to meet your wife, of whom I had heard much, and was to hear more; but your reasons for keeping her locked in the attic seemed to me very well judged. In any case, the fine-looking young lady who acted so effectively in her stead seemed to me most gracious, energetic and decidedly full of beans, as indeed we all were after the distinctive meal she prepared. I ought to explain, in case you mistook my manner at table, that I entirely respect your principles as a devout chapel abstainer, and that the hip-flask from which I occasionally gargled was one I have long carried and fill only with the very best Perrier, being very dry-throated before a major lecture and always anxious about what I imbibe in this age of radioactive water-supplies and lethally polluted streams.

In any case, the absence of those conventional libations that those of us brought up in Oxford colleges with outstanding cellars have so absurdly come to consider a commonplace if not necessary feature of academic life in no way diminished the conviviality of a decidedly merry evening, if I recall it aright. The academic colleagues whom you gathered to meet me seemed in excellent form for their very advanced years, and you must send me a copy of the Tridentine form of grace you practise, and I will try to have it published, possibly in two volumes. The extended tale told by the notably senior gentleman about meeting, or possibly not meeting but meaning to, that great Victorian poet whose name, work, appearance, sex, or relevance to the conversation he had such amusing difficulty in recalling also passed, I thought, a very agreeable hour, or was it two? I hope the elderly lady in Anglo-Saxon is now fully recovered from her fit, and realizes that the reasons we all lay on top of her towards the end of the evening were entirely thera-peutic. Yet undoubtedly she will have understood that, given her looks, they could have been no other.

It was a great pleasure after these sumptuous proceedings to have the opportunity to inspect the whole of your delightful campus, albeit in the pitch dark. How lucky you are not to have fallen into the hands of these postmodern academic architects, with their flamboyant monu-mentalism and their love of pouring concrete over delightful rural settings at the drop of Le Corbusier's hat! I can assure you that after departing from my own new university campus, designed to elaborate modular principles that require each room to have some obscure number on it like B17/K/ITAL, it was a positive relief to have it recalled that Socrates did his teaching almost entirely in the open air, and presumably if wet in one of those wooden gardeners' sheds that give such a vernacu-lar quality to your own groves of academe. After all, a university can, as the government keeps saying, be anywhere if the mentors are inspir-ing and the library good. On this last, since you did ask me to drop you a note of advice on the matter, all I would say is that I indeed found your book collection quite prodigious, in these hopeless days of cuts and economies, but that even in these hard times it is often possible to persuade the UGC to release a few meagre funds that might allow you to unpack it from the cardboard boxes and store it in a building, also called a library. Here protection from the weather, while not guaranteed, is possible, and there could be provision for storage, sorting, and even as time went on access.

And then we proceeded to the lecture. Far be it from me to comment on my own performance, but I have always been stimulated by the presence of ten or fewer people in a totally airless room, even if their mutual detestation of each other is apparent from the start and that of any stranger equally apparent by the finish. As for the reception of my paper, the acknowledgement and response I received from you all has caused me to rethink hard and change it almost totally. I was very touched that you as chairman should trouble to wake up from the deep sleep that engulfed you, doubtless from the trouble and energy you had put into meeting me, and ask the first question. I am also glad that the fact that I had been speaking on the work of Jorge Luis Borges (he is foreign and an Argentinian, which may explain why his name provoked so little reaction) did not inhibit you from challenging me so exactingly on the poems of John Skelton, thus making the occasion, I thought, genuinely wide-ranging, if not interdisciplinary. I found equally stimu- lating the questions of the three young men in motor-bicycling suits who arrived so late and so noisily, though I fear I had not heard of *The Star and Garter* and hope I did not make myself ridiculous with the surmise that it was an unattributed play of Shakespeare's. As you said, Massinger is surely a far better guess!

It also seemed to me such a good idea to serve the cold cocoa after- wards, for otherwise I would have lacked an opportunity to talk to those very few of your students who felt themselves prepared to walk outside after dark and engage in intellectual activity. Here I was fortunately able to find out something about the nature of the advanced academic programme you and your colleagues have devised. A few of your best ideas we had discussed ourselves in my own university and, perhaps foolishly, rejected – such as having the syllabus stop with the death of Langland, and making Old Norse an entrance requirement. Others struck me as entirely novel, such as replacing the writing of essays with work opportunity experience. The students seemed

140

excellent – I was particularly impressed with the achievements of one young man who had been getting B + + s and above in mowing your lawn – and I am sure they have no difficulty in getting excellent jobs afterwards, especially in the heavy labouring trades.

I shall carry some of these remarkable ideas into our own departmental meeting, which convenes tomorrow, though I fear they will not get very far. I must say I greatly admire the firm 'steer' you so evidently give to your department! You would be quite amused by our own so-called 'democratic' practices! I remember you told me that as far as you were concerned professors should be appointed to the headship of the department for life, if not beyond, should have absolute power, including the now unfashionable *droit de seigneur*, and that you would have no truck at all with the modern idea of heads rotating. I am inclined to agree! Our heads here rotate constantly, up to three or four times a term! Indeed we now call them 'chairs' and frequently sit on them. At the moment we are in the midst of a feminist upheaval and the present 'chair', a lady who has scraped off most of her hair and is always dressed for parachuting, has insisted that the entire syllabus be 'desexed', which is why I am now teaching *The Magic Mountain* by Thomas Personn. No, one cannot help envying you the older academic spirit you maintain, and the way you sustain so sturdily practices that even Oxbridge is beginning to dispense with, like the requirement of absolute celibacy among the faculty. That could, of course, be one reason why they dispersed so rapidly with the more nubile students once it became fully evident, from the way the porter had turned out all the lights and begun to dismantle the chairs, that my lecture was over, leaving me to assist you over that rather difficult cliff and through the bog to your home.

I should also thank you for the comforts of the night. It is a long time since I went to bed with a hot-water bottle, or indeed in straw, and I hope I did not make too much noise in the middle of the night, but I fear my bladder is a trouble and the latrine proved very distant. I was pleased, around four in the morning, to meet your wife at last, and hope I did not offend her by discouraging her kindly advances; but the tiring nature of the lecture I gave, to which your own somnolence was fair witness, and the vigorous intellectual discussion thereafter had quite worn me out. Happily I was in better shape when the young lady from dinner, who clearly manages the house well, arrived with the morning tea and the local parish magazine, and I hope you will remember me to her, if she remains part of your establishment, and say my name is not Fred at all, as I kept trying to tell her. I greatly appreciated the opportunity to mend your boiler before departing, and though the return journey proved even more hazardous than that which brought me to your campus, and the milkman had already left, I shall not, as I say, quickly forget the occasion.

This brings me to the matter of travelling expenses. I fear your ruse of attempting to make the train journey on the basis of a platform ticket was all too readily rumbled by the railway servant who not only made me pay full first-class fare (for some reason I had stumbled into one of the better compartments) but threatened me with a court case. The disquiet that this occasioned in me needed some rapid soothing, and I hope I may therefore claim for the bottle of gin, which cost me £12.50. When I reached London the spaces under the bridge at Charing Cross to which you recommended me proved full, so I was directed by a kindly bobby to the nearby Savoy, and the bill for their services I herewith enclose (you will of course have to add 15 per cent for VAT and another 20 per cent on that for service, for I am firmly opposed to the notion that because academics are so ill-paid they should therefore be parsimonious tippers). Altogether the expenses for my trip came to £210, and I trust you will not find it large, but I have had to add in the fine for my railway deception. It is, I admit, of a size which in my own university we could not meet, because of our 'democratic' accountancy, but which must be different in your own case, since in an off-guard moment you did make it quite clear that all the departmental finances are totally under your control, and never spent. I have now, fortunately, been confirmed in my Readership, in case you are wondering. I am sure we would both agree that my lecture to those three students and the four or five faculty dotards who were marking exam papers during it was, as they say, a very rewarding occasion for all concerned.

> Yours faithfully,
> Andrew Patterson

142

This is the kind of letter I would indeed have liked to have written and sent on more than one occasion. It was never sent, of course. After all, I am famous for politeness and, in any case, one would not like *not* to receive any further invitations. After all, being able to travel and lecture is one of the great rewards and delights of academic life. So, if I wrote at all (and I may not even have remembered to do so, what with Mr Johnson still standing there in the corridor, and so much to do because his troublesome spots had stopped him writing all his essays), I undoubtedly said, well, 'Thank you for you kind hospitality and the chance to talk to your students. I greatly enjoyed my visit and was greatly impressed with the work in your department. My travelling expenses came to exactly £15.12p. I hope you will ask me again. Yours sincerely, Malcolm Bradbury.' And to tell the truth I rather hope they will.

Notes from the
Carl Stumpf World

Among the many letters in my busy postbag, quite a few refer not to the literary but to the academic side of my life. In particular there is a kind of letter which comes, in quite considerable quantities, from young scholars – bright young souls such as, I like to think, I once was myself. They naturally assume that since they have worked hard and long in their subjects and attained excellent qualifications, they will now attain a university post.

Would it were so! Alas, even as they finish the grind of their theses, the British university system in which they hope to find a niche is being dismantled about their and our ears. The demolition men are in the universities these days, and all I can write are sad and dusty answers. Indeed, I fear that the following tragic letter is going to serve me on many future occasions:

My dear Dr Messmer,

Thank you so much for your letter of two or three weeks back, written on the excellent notepaper that Porterhouse College so kindly provides its members (oh, I can smell those freshly mown lawns even now!), indicating your remarkable qualifications and inviting me to direct you into a happy lifetime of academic employment. Naturally I would have answered it when it came, three or four weeks back, but I was compelled to attend a conference in the Seychelles that, I fear, dragged on for an interminable length of time. May I congratulate you on the many documents with which you have inundated me. Your twelve-page curriculum vitae reads like a dream, and I am sure your early work in the Boy Scouts will impress everyone who hears of it much as it has impressed me. The offprint of your article in *Diuretics* on 'The Broken Typewriter of Henri Mensonge' had me in a state of readerly ecstasy from start to putative finish; please send me the last three pages sometime, as I cannot wait to see how it all comes out. The two pieces from the *Guardian* on camping in the Algarve show you really know your way around the field, and my wife is trying your *Time Out* recipe for syllabub right this minute. I can recognize scholarly distinction when I see it, and I see it now.

Thus it greatly goes against the grain of my good nature to give you a depressing reply. Yet honesty, they say, is the mark of the truly great scholar, and I am bound by it. Frankly, Messmer, you don't really have a hope in hell. Please understand, Messmer. This has nothing whatsoever to do with your attainments, evidently prodigious, your quality of mind, which, judging from your calligraphy, is meticulous, or your academic dedication, which, if one goes by the many tasks you have performed for worthless journals, must be called undoubted. Oh, would that it were because you were *bad* or *unsuitable* that I am inscribing what can only seem an unhelpful if not negative reply! Alas, good or bad as you may be, it makes little difference. The simple fact is, that like so many of us in the world these days, you have quite the right ambitions and the right qualifications at just the wrong time.

In the happy cloisters of Porterhouse, you could well, I fancy, have missed the fact that our present political masters now regard British universities in much the way that Henry VIII regarded the monasteries. That, you recall, was with less than total favour. After all, they have themselves already attained passable degrees, mostly from Oxbridge, and see no sensible reason why the educational process should continue, when it has so obviously done its work already. The dismemberment of academic life has become a popular national pastime. I cannot explain why; logic would say we need all the intellectual and scientific achievement we can get. But it is true that we have not had the Dark Ages for some time, and it might be interesting to bring them back. So universities are being encouraged to turn themselves into something quite different, like yuppie shopping malls or oil rigs. And my own university, far from looking for new people, is paying distinguished colleagues considerable sums to depart the institution, if not life itself. In fact you are lucky to find anyone here to answer your letter at all, however depressing the reply may be.

Still, I must be positive, and not moan on. After all, what you ask for is advice on how to get appointed – how to apply for university posts, go to interviews, and the like. I think I can be helpful, for I did go through the whole thing myself, quite some time ago, of course. In those days, too, jobs were scarce, though not as scarce as now. So I applied a lot and was interviewed a great deal, perhaps in part because I acquired the unfortunate habit of falling off chairs in a faint when questioned closely. As you say, there must be special techniques to these things. Well, there are, Messmer, depending of course in what country you want the job, and how keen you are to get it. Let us first take the problem of seeking a post in a British university, a system of some complexity which takes quite a lot of explanation.

Here the first step is to persuade a rich, elderly aunt, not hostile to Rupert Murdoch, to take you out a subscription to a learned journal called *The Times Higher Educational Supplement*. This is a glossy trade paper that contains advertisements for nearly all the academic posts that come available; nowadays, for reasons already given, its pages are notably thin. And even the posts on offer – that 'New Blood Appointment in Old Norse', for instance, which must immediately have caught your eye – may not be what they seem. The small print indicates that it is only for three months, while the professor is away recruiting foreign students in Hong Kong, and also probably getting a nice suit made as well. You will also be required to reside within three miles of the Welsh bog in which the university is set, and since the department appears to have no students you will probably spend most of your time painting the house of the Registrar. Yes, it is always wise to read the small print, and also wise to apply for posts in areas vaguely approximating to your own interests – so do not bother with that Chair of Dentistry in Dundee.

Once your prey is identified, you must simply submit your application, in a mere twelve copies. Only an innocent would trust them to the post. Have them delivered by hand by a reliable friend *who is not himself an applicant* and placed firmly into the hands of the departmental secretary – not her friend, her brother, or her babysitter. She is usually the only person in the building who knows where pieces of paper are kept and how to retrieve them for subsequent use. You will know when fortune smiles, for you will then hear that they have, as they say, 'taken up your references'. Frankly, this is one of the most dangerous phases of the procedure. Pick referees who are in and not out of the country, whose attitude towards you is affected neither by envy nor lust for your wife, whose sentences parse and contain only intentional ambiguity, and who do not have young protégés whose cause can be advanced instead of your own.

If this is done correctly, you may then be called for interview. Interviews, I find, are always testing, one reason I suppose why we have them. For these occasions careful preparations should be made to put yourself in the best possible light, or even darkness. A suit is necessary, whether you are male or female, though frankly the answer is obvious, since you are from Porterhouse. Fools will advise you to look smart, but this is dangerous advice. It is never wise to outdress the interviewing committee, who will all evidently have just come fresh from raiding the local Salvation Army shop in their lifelong search for rags and tatters. Never wear ties indicating membership of London clubs, famous regiments, or well-known Oxbridge colleges; every British interviewing committee always contains one raging egalitarian, a specialist on the influence of *Beowulf* on the Miners' Strike of 1984, and he will take offence. On the other hand, other members of the committee will believe there is a direct correlation between white shirts and prodigious intelligence. Of course you cannot please everyone, but for heaven's sake, Messmer, at least try.

As for the correct answers to the questions you will be asked, this is a difficult area. Self-evidently any answer that greatly satisfies one member of a panel will cause great offence to all his or her enemies in the room. The main thing, frankly, is to be friendly and anodyne. For there is one thing that every member of every interviewing committee is looking for, and that is a nice, capable person who will solve the problems of their contentious and chaotic department at a single stroke, answer all the letters, do all the work on the committees, and possibly run the coffee bar as well. In any case, jobs are nearly always won or lost on the very last question, which in fact is not theirs, but yours. That is, the chairman will say: 'Well, now we ought to get on and see the next candidate – we are looking at seventeen people today – but have you any questions you'd like to ask us?'

Be careful, Messmer, very careful. For this is definitely *not* the moment to start wittering on about crèche facilities for your wife, who is looking forward to undertaking some feminist violence locally, or for asking how quickly they will appoint you to a chair, especially if the only one available belongs to the fellow interviewing you. It is certainly not the moment to reveal your hatred of paperwork, or your conviction that all forms of examining are unjust, and should be abolished. It is no time to reveal how much you dislike the existing syllabus, and what you would do to change it – perhaps by concentrating on such badly neglected *magna opera* as *The Swiss Family Robinson*. Indeed it is the time to smile, congratulate the panel on its consideration and civility, to say that nothing would delight you more than to spend your life in their company, and get out of the room quickly, keeping the note of your travelling expenses down to the minimum. That way you just could be lucky, though I doubt it.

But this is simply the British way, and I see that you have, quite rightly, set your sights internationally. Or, as you put it in your letter, you are 'willing to consider America, or indeed any other part of the world'. Well, America is not 'any other part of the world', and though you may be willing to consider it, it remains to be seen whether it is prepared to consider you. It is true that many British academics – especially the ones who have mugged up a few pages of Derrida – have done well there, and it is indeed a safe place of resort for those who wish to escape the violence of the English faculty at Cambridge. However, I should stress that none of the suggestions and rules I have written above apply. Indeed none of the qualities required for getting a post in a British university will stand you in much stead in getting a post in an American one. The British distrust research; the Americans prize it. The British are timid; Americans hustle. The British offer themselves for jobs; Americans go out and find them, just the way they found the West.

In fact, as I understand it, there are three ways to get a post in an

American university. The first is to be so well known they will come right over and headhunt you; you do not, alas, pass on this score, Messmer. The second is to take a list of the entire 25,000-odd American institutions of higher learning and write a long letter to each of them, explaining why they should select you over all other persons. It is tiring, even with a word processor, and I do not give it much hope. The third is to attend the major academic conference in the field we share, you grazing at that end, me at this. I refer to the conference of the Modern Language Association, normally held at Christmas in the high-rise hotels of one of the great American cities. And this, frankly, Messmer, is the best hope you have got, so I should get your application in now.

It will not all be cider and roses. Flying off to a conference in a jumbo jet on Christmas Day can be a lonely business. Your crying loved ones waving from the terminal will not make things any better, and the discovery that all your fellow passengers are historians, political scientists and nuclear physicists all going to *their* professional conferences will probably produce the dismaying feeling that there are far too many of all of us (though, as I say, our government is trying to do something about that). Still, try and remember, Messmer, that you are part of an historic migration or diaspora called the Brain Drain, and that will make you feel better. It is wise at this point to make a note of what subject you are in, and where you are going, or you could easily end up in the wrong hotel in the wrong city and in a quite different field entirely.

I have no doubt, Messmer, that at Porterhouse you have been used to conferences, small and intimate events held over the Niersteiner by a dozen or so like-minded souls. Do not expect the MLA conference to be like that. Remember, it gathers together some 15,000 scholars, every one of them fine-tuned to the latest developments of the newest aspects of the state of the art of our subject, puts them in vertiginous rooms with air-conditioning in the Hiltons and Sheratons of this world, and lets them loose on each other. Before you go you will have received the programme, here called the program. You will assume from this that you will be at an event where the distinguished, grey-haired seniors of the field give papers to one another, engage in the common pursuit of true judgement, develop the field, propose new schools of criticism,

149

initiate new editions of Shakespeare and new scholarly series on literature and gardening, and generally behave in the classic way of professionals everywhere. Messmer, it will not be like that.

There is, it is true, a program, interspersed with the odd lesbian cash bar and the occasional festive night when scholars appear in funny hats singing fraternity and sorority songs and dating chants to each other. But that is the façade. You, I see, have read Thomas Hardy – indeed you have written endlessly on him. You will therefore know about the great rural hiring fairs, quaint, primitive and bestial, that took place on Michaelmas or whenever as the farmers sought their labourers, and the labourers their farmers. Read it again, Messmer, and learn what it is like. For when you arrive, you will check in at the conference desk, put on your lapel badge, and look round the lobby, spying out the scene. You see those young men and women there, standing in their best clothes with big bound books in their hands? Those are the labourers, Messmer, this year's fresh crop of graduate students. The books in their hands are the tools of their trade – their theses, which they have had bound in hand-tooled leather by Swabian craftsmen. They are waiting, like taxis, to be hired, desperately hoping to get stuck in the elevator with some departmental chairman long enough for him to glance at the title page and the abstract, their credentials. It's a cut-throat world, the academy, Messmer.

But play the game, Messmer, play the game. And, if you are lucky, you may get a quick interview in a hotel suite over cans of Michelob and a plane ticket to fly out to a campus or two in the early New Year, just when the really bad weather sets in. The next steps are crucial. Let us, for purposes of illustration, suppose that you have four invitations: to the Squint School of Mining, in Squint, Idaho, which has a freshman program in Mining English; the Thumb Lake State Teachers' College, at Thumb, N.Y., which wants someone to teach feminist linguistics: the Tom Jones University, which wants someone with an English accent to add class to the department; and dear old Traumatic State, in Shock City, North Dakota, which just wants anyone who will live in Shock City, North Dakota. At each one you will be expected to give a lecture to a small but hostile audience – an idea British universities have neglected at their peril, one reason why people who are described as lecturers generally can't.

150

Messmer, be careful. It is all too easy to assume that the lecture is the real test, and that you can now relax at the faculty party afterwards, where the members of the department come and go, talking of Michelangelo, who makes the best pizza in town. No, Messmer, do not think these people have gathered there to give you a good time. They have given up the baseball game that evening for one reason and one reason only, to look you over. Arrive sober, and stay sober, Messmer – especially if this is one of those dry campuses so common in the United States, where Abolition has certainly not been completed yet. For, as soon as you are out of the house, and are stumbling through the woods towards where you thought they said the Faculty Club was, they are out with their notebooks. For the next hour they will be working over your intellectual, moral and aesthetic qualities, your demeanour and charisma, your sociability rating and your bad-breath problem. Also remember that, while you are there for them to inspect you, you had better take the chance to inspect *them*. For these people could be your academic friends, or much more probably enemies, to the end of your life or until they fire you, whichever comes first. Work out their positions, discover their ideologies, explore their enmities, map out their adulteries, and above all find out why they really need you, a Buddhist Leavisite, in the Chaucer field. Get to know your institution, Messmer.

For, since a university in the United States can be one of many different things, it is important for you to find out many different things. Does this department really teach English Literature, or is English a service course for teaching footballers the comma and what to do with it? Is this a liberal college, where everyone has pledged half their salary to help Nicaragua, and where all that sniffing is something other than a bad winter cold passing round the faculty? Or is this a fundamentalist, religious, born-again sort of college, where everyone loves God and the nation He always supports, everybody walks tall, the regents are trying to get Darwin impeached, and you have to have the Dean's permission to speak to a member of a sex other than your own, if they ever let you see any? And, when you wake in the morning at the Faculty Club, do take the chance of a little walk around town. The university may be at the heart of the mugging district, like Yale. On the other hand, if the only sound to be heard is the sound of the rice krispies popping in all the tract houses, that may be it, Messmer, all of it.

Oh, and before you make your final decision, can I suggest that you just glance again at the pages of the professional publication of MLA – which is called, of course, *PMLA (Publications of the Modern Language Association)*. Yes, I know you do all the time, looking up articles on 'The Incest Theme in *The Ancrene Riwle*'; indeed I see from your c.v. that you write most of it yourself. But look *between* the scholarship, at the small and intimate glimpses of daily life in the American departmental lounge that sometimes appear in the news and gossip columns. I mean things like this, from an old issue I have grabbed at random:

> *And you?* [asks one titbit] In the final examination in his course in contemporary British and American literature Jean Ashmead (Haverford) always included passages in Latin, Greek, French, German, Spanish and Russian, critical passages relating to the study of literature. Each student must answer at least one of these questions.

Or this:

> *Ecce, Diogenes.* When Carl Stumpf lectured on the history of philosophy, he told his classes that he would have to omit oriental philosophy because he could not read it in the original.

Or the little glimpses of the softer side, of the world of Vermont cheeses, Hellenic cruises, and slow summery vacations. This, for instance:

> *Did you know?* Gaines Dog Food distributes a list of places where you can stay overnight with your dog (or cat) . . .

My point is simple, Messmer. This is reality you are choosing, Messmer, your life to come. But no doubt you are as pedantic as the next man, and as fond of your dog (or cat) as anyone else. So I wish you well, Messmer, and a happy, tenure-track, brain-drained future. There is only one thing that worries me, though, and that phrase 'the next man' reminds me of it. As your c.v. shows, you have picked some interesting subjects of study, the fruits of a wide-ranging mind; indeed you have done most things right. What you have not picked, Messmer, to be frank, is the right sex. Indeed in the present climate it is unlikely that, without changing it, you will secure an academic appointment anywhere other than in the Islamic world. You have done well, but I fancy as a phallus you have had it, Messmer. So why not forget the whole thing, and, like my own better students, go right into the Stock Exchange. After all, that is one institution these days that *is* doing well, and you won't have to read anything in the original.

With good wishes,
Muriel Utting

(Dictated by Professor B. and signed by his secretary, as he is absent and thought to be in Hong Kong.)

A Professorial Dilemma

Of the various dilemmas that surround the pursuit of a literary and academic life, one is definitely the problem of introductions. I do not mean the difficulty of meeting attractive young women – though in the literary world, unlike the world of music or theatre, these always turn out to be after one's signature rather than one's body. And I am not talking about the problem of sitting up on a stage in front of a large audience, and suddenly realizing that the evening's chairman has misread the entries in *Who's Supposed to Be Who?* and is announcing you as a certain Ray Bradbury. No, I am talking about *Introductions* – you know, those forewords or prefaces that are added to the front of some book by an old friend or a long-dead writer and are designed to give the book two authors instead of one, thus spreading the load a little.

They are a fine publishing wheeze, and they often help to bring back a book that is greatly in need of revival – as, after writing one of these pieces, I am, usually. At the same time they can be touchy matters, especially if you are writing the introduction to a work by a living author, the kind I mostly like to spend my time with. Life-long friendships can founder, enmities start, as some ill-chosen phrase slips off the pen or it becomes apparent that one's admiration is not total, unqualified and euphoric. And even when the writer is someone you admire but is not personally known to you, difficulties can arise – as I found just the other day, when my telephone rang, and I hastened from the bath, where I usually am on these occasions, to answer it.

154

An odd feeling passed over me as a Yorkshire-Irish brogue spoke to me from the other end of the line; for the voice was one I knew well, but the speaker was evidently a total stranger. It took a while for the truth to dawn; I did know the voice well, but not the person. This was because he was a regular radio broadcaster, on a favourite programme which had brought me much solace on Saturday nights when, no one having asked me out to dinner, I sat down before the baked beans in existential despair. *Stop the Week*, as the programme is called, is a prandial affair, where a group of claret-soaked guests gather round the microphone and approximate the manners of an Islington dinner party. No verisimilitude is spared: glasses fall over, there is much talk of Volvos, the Dordogne, *nouvelle cuisine*, AIDS and all of those things that one expects to hear at any good talkfest. Academics are present, and it was one of these − Professor Laurie Taylor − who was addressing me down the telephonic line.

I knew Taylor well in another guise, that of print. He happened to write a column, again much admired by me, in the pages of *The Times Higher Education Supplement (THES* in the trade), which I often consulted checking out the jobs in the business. It was a column of great wit and wisdom, as good in its way as Nelson's, and I enjoyed it enormously. Taylor now told me over the telephone that a publisher wished to collect these pieces, and he now wondered whether I would mind writing, yes, an introduction. It was then that crisis struck. I stammered, blurted, put down the phone. Then, when I recovered my composure (it was under the settee), I sat down and wrote the following letter:

Dear Professor Laurie Taylor,

Please excuse my extraordinary behaviour of this afternoon. It was meant as no discourtesy, either to you or your admirable essays. My strange reaction arises from something entirely different, which I had better explain to you, so that we can both proceed quite carefully thereafter. You may know that I once wrote a novel called *The History Man*, a book set in a British new university, and dealing with the affairs, intellectual and otherwise, of a radical sociologist of the Sixties. I say 'you may know', but I realize that you do indeed, since I have been glancing again at your columns and see it mentioned there as 'a rather over-praised novel' which bears little relation to the truth. Well, we all make misjudgements from time to time; and, in any case, I agree with you that the book is a work of total fiction. As I keep telling my wife, universities are simply not like that, especially in the matter of the availability of female students to members of faculty. Indeed, as I emphasize in the preface to the book, even the year 1972, in which it is set, is a complete fiction.

However, as you may know too, when major works of this kind (and I am sure mature reflection must have convinced you that that is what it is) appear in the world, there is a rush to study and explicate them. Naturally, one hopes these endeavours will concentrate on the work's creative perfection: the irony, the extraordinary paragraphing, the carefully interwoven allusions to the kabbala and the like, the things for which one wishes to be remembered. Alas, among the gathered scholarly throng there will always be some who will attempt to debase matters, by referring to what they call 'reality', which, as we both know, does not exist, except perhaps in Liverpool. People ask what the book is 'about', even though they should know that there is no about about for anything to be about. It has been suggested that my book is an attack on sociology, the new universities, or some such; it has even been said to have influenced government thinking on these matters. I trust not. I should hate to have my ideas influence their thinking, any more than I would want theirs to influence mine.

No, the book is a total work of the imagination. When the British new universities were planned around 1960, you may recall, seven were proposed and six were built. I decided to get to work on the seventh. I employed, as was the custom at the time, a Finnish architect and a Marxist faculty, and built it with words somewhere safely down in the southwest of England, where there are virtually no facilities of this sort with which it might possibly be confused, trusting that the book could not possibly be misread. Little did I know it at the time, but misreading was just becoming the thing in literary studies. Whole departments of it were set up in the United States, and the practice came here too, as it always does. Thus the scholars of my small book became ever more daring, asking all sorts of questions about where the book was set, what it was about, and then – and this is the nub of this letter – *who* it was about. In fact one day a bold graduate student came to me and said that the original Howard Kirk had been at last identified.

Kirk is, of course, the lovable, spirited, sexually engaging and engaged hero who performs the central role, and a good deal else, in the novel. Naturally I was indignant. Shaking the young man by the shoulders, I explained to him that Kirk was simply a creative fiction, a textual actant and narrative prompt, born solely from imaginative processes that lay deep in my own mind. It was no use. Despite my protests, the youth persisted in his nonsense, saying that it was common knowledge that Kirk was based on a certain person. Now we come to my strange behaviour on the telephone. You will notice that when I answered you, I asked the question: 'We've never met, have we?' You confirmed that this was so, and said that one day we should remedy the unfortunate oversight, a view with which I entirely agree. What is more – I am ashamed to say it, but it is true – when I wrote the book I had never even heard of you, though I am delighted to say that that at least has been remedied. Yet I have to tell you that the name my graduate student uttered – when I removed my hands from his throat – was, Professor Taylor, *your own*.

You will see now why I shuddered and shook on the telephone. It is not a natural thing for an author to be telephoned out of the blue by one of his own characters – especially if that person has become the original of one of his fictional inventions without his knowledge, and by quite incomprehensible means. Indeed my reaction to you was nothing less than a major epistemological crisis, of a kind I have sometimes read of in fiction but never experienced in life, which as I say is quite different. It is a crisis we share, Professor Taylor. I do not know you; you do not know I. I have not met you, and by the same token you have not met me. Yet I have invented you, or on the other hand you have been invented as having been invented by me. Thanks to the intervention of that strange Introductions agency that is called Literary Criticism, we are bound together in some strange and unexpected symbiosis: as origin and simulacrum, writer and written. Yet just who has done what to whom it would take Jacques Derrida to explain, and I am told he is too busy.

In short there is a conundrum here, and I fear we must face it. Evidently we are caught up in one of those strange paradoxes of relationship between a so-called fiction and a so-called reality that bedevil all aspects of life in the postmodern world, and indeed keep some of us in royalties as well. There is an old saying that art follows life. I have always believed that the truth is exactly the opposite. Indeed I have evidence of that in my own university, which, when I wrote the book, bore no resemblance whatsoever to *The History Man*. However, attending a departmental meeting just the other day, I realized I had been there already; indeed I had written it once, in my novel. This cannot be because my colleagues had read the book; after all, they are always denying it. It must be that there is some other process at work in the universe, by which it is programmed to produce what has already been invented by its writers. This, I fear, may be what has happened to you, Professor Taylor, and when we do meet I shall not be surprised to find you identical to my imaginary Kirk in every particular, even down to the birthmarks.

And would that were the end of the matter. But, after you telephoned me asking me to write the Introduction to your book, I naturally sat down and read through the columns you had written. They describe, of course, an imaginary university, populated with characters with names like Dr Piercemuller, Professor Lapping, Professor Hannah Mass, and so on. Naturally I had always taken the place for a total fiction, but this time, reading the pieces through, it all suddenly struck me quite differently. Hadn't I, lately *come across* these people? I then recalled that a few months ago a friend of mine at another university had rung me to say that he was on a sub-committee concerned with university cuts: he was Dewhurst Professor of Butchery, so the job suited him ideally. He needed a quick assessment on a certain department that was under threat, and hoped I would do it for him. Naturally the report I sent to him was totally confidential. But in the present circumstances I feel I should divulge it to you. This is what I wrote:

PRIVATE AND HIGHLY CONFIDENTIAL

REPORT ON THE DEPARTMENT OF X AT THE
UNIVERSITY OF Y

I am enclosing my views on the research, teaching and administrative standards, and the general reputation, of the above department. Of course I have not visited it myself, but I have checked it out carefully from the written documentation. This is what I found:

1 Research Attainments. *Perhaps it is a pity that the three books the department submitted as evidence of its research profile were all by one man, Professor Lapping, who also kindly sent us the imaginary timetables he so generously provides for the proceedings of the North Yorkshire Light Railway Society, of which he must be a member. They offer an exciting but alas highly limited view of the research achievement of the department, and I therefore took the trouble to check more widely. It seems there has been some improvement. Dr Prolicks continues to publish in his usual lunatic way, the silence of Dr Turpitz must be regarded as a plus factor, and Professor Freeby's work on the Florentine handbag industry, which required Tuscan residence from him for so long, has – after several warnings – at last appeared in print, from a small Italian press that a lady who may have been his mother assured me is most reputable. It is difficult to read such a book without a knowledge of the language, though many of my colleagues manage it, but it would appear he found the subject loaded with ore, though also quite a lot of small change. Dr Piercemuller's curriculum vitae indicates an active life, especially with the small children, and he has evidently worked hard at home and abroad – indeed anywhere except within the actual precincts of the university, which, with its dark underpasses, must be depressing to anyone.*

So much may be said in favour. But if there is a for there must also be an against, or that has always been my experience. Dr Wenlock has still not completed, never mind published, his behaviourist research, and his complaint that his application for a new rat has been deferred sine die, or until things get better, whichever comes sooner, did not impress me in the least. I fear I am one of those who believe that in entrepreneurial times our colleagues need to get out and fend for themselves; an ambitious, committed man can always find a sponsored rat of his own if he needs one. Still more disturbing is the failure of every Ph.D. candidate in the department to complete research; the excuse that this should be linked to the collapsing marriages of the faculty seems to me absurd. In my own department we yield to absolutely none in this last matter, yet just this year we have gowned at least three of these plodding reprobates; and thank goodness, for the photo-copier is free of them at last.

2. Quality of Teaching and Departmental Administration. *Teaching, of course, is notoriously hard to assess, since none of us can be in every classroom with everyone at once, however hard we try. But the papers suggest many disturbing indications. Surely not every single member of the department needed to attend the Budapest Congress of the Association of Social Scientists this Easter, however many suitcases Professor Lapping chose to take. And surely twenty temporary lectureships for periods of less than three months leads to discontinuity in teaching, however important we may all think it is to ensure that no young person ever acquires anything resembling tenure. On the other hand, it is clear that some very useful economies have been instituted, mainly by gathering together very large numbers of students into one lecture room and then showing them a film. Foreign students have been increased significantly in numbers, and clearly to the benefit of the cuisine in the college refectory.*

Meanwhile faculty size has been substantially reduced – mainly by the departure of Professor Hannah Mass, who has taken early retirement at the age of twenty-seven, and been appointed at a very much higher salary to a very prestigious chair, if not settee, at New York University. But if teaching is hard to assess, one thing we on university committees can surely assess is university committees. Here, judging by the extraordinary mass of agendas, minutes and reports submitted, mainly on the topic of university cuts, things are going well. Evidently there is a good deal less of everything except meetings to make sure there is even less still, and this is surely what we expect of any university today. In this category, though no other, the department may be rated 'excellent'.

3. Summary. *In sum, I find the department quite hard to assess, with quite a lot of this, on the one hand, but a good deal of that on the other. It evidently has some good points, but quite a lot that are bad. However, in the end there can surely be only one way of assessing the quality of a department in another university, and that is by comparing it with the very highest standards, which*

not unnaturally are those set within one's own. On this basis, I fear I cannot say anything positive; after all, it is quite clear that they must be cut long before the sub-committee even starts to think about us. I recommend a judgement both tepid and anodyne, always the best kind, I think. Let us call this department 'average', or perhaps 'typical', and cut it with unbridled severity accordingly.

I hope Laura is well. She seemed in excellent form at Christmas, and Mauritius evidently suited her.

Yours, etc.

Forgive my quoting at such length, but you will now see why. The department about which you write and the department on which I reported are evidently identical. Can it be that you were writing *realism*? Can it be that the department about which you write is the one in which you work and earn your living? If so, I can scarcely bear to think of the consequences of my letter, and its effect on the careers of Piercemuller, Lapping, and the like. It all makes me feel that one of these days we should meet and clear up a few simple matters between ourselves, asking, for example, which if any one of us exists and, if so, under what philosophical circumstances. It would certainly help my mind to clear of the confusion it has felt of late. As for the question of writing an Introduction for you, I should be delighted. After all, I feel I have done so once already. There is one favour you could do in return. Would you mind sending me a photograph of yourself? I'm just starting another novel.

Yours sincerely,

Inspeak:
Your Streetwise Guide to
Linguistics and Structuralism

Not long ago, I was at one of those smart London literary parties where the Perrier flows like wine, delighting the company with an account of a rare, if not unique, interview I had just conducted with Henri Mensonge. Mensonge, as you doubtless know, is probably the greatest French intellectual and philosopher of our day, and doyen of the movement of Structuralism – that radical new idea-system that has transformed intellectual life, upset Cambridge to the marrow, changed – if we had one – our very view of existence, and is now chic talk in every part of the world from Riyadh to Rawalpindi. Mensonge had not been an easy catch. Unlike, say, Jean-Paul Sartre, he is a man very famous for his modesty. Whenever he appears on the television programme *L'Apostrophe* – the French equivalent of *The South Bank Show*, but with more intellectuals – he is always in shadow, his back to the camera, his head in a bin-liner, and he frequently refuses to speak at all. Whereas most French intellectuals live in Paris, he hides in the country. However, I had succeeded in tracking him down to a small *gîte* in the Alpes Maritimes, where I found him living very simply, with just a pig for company, both of them spending their time hunting for truffles, though with no success. And though normally abusive to strangers, and entirely refusing to speak to those who, like myself, were writing books about him, Mensonge had been notably generous to me — giving me quite a lot of his time, rather more of his *marc*, and quantities of his profound modern wisdom.

I was enlarging on all this when I was suddenly accosted by a furious stranger, evidently spoiling for a fight. 'Structuralism, what a goddam waste of time!' he roared at me. 'You goddam intellectuals are all the same, no goddam use at all!' Naturally I expostulated, explaining that Structuralism — the philosophy or science of signs, or semiotics — had *everything* to do with our life today. It was as important to modern thinking as the graphite racket was to modern tennis, and anyone who thought otherwise was a head-in-the-sand obscurantist. If, today, most of us were increasingly doubting whether we were present or absent in the world, if packaging was now replacing content in most areas of existence, if most of us stood looking at the signs outside lavatory doors, totally unsure which was intended for the gender of our choice, this was all largely due to the radical wisdom of the Structuralist philosophers. 'You see what I mean, no goddam use at all!' cried the man, and to be frank a small fracas began. Happily his wife appeared, heaved him into the street, and hefted him into his car — which, as I saw with wry amusement, had furry dice hung over the driver's mirror, a flash saying 'Nerd and Friend' plastered across the windshield, and a sticker declaring 'Windsurfers Do It Standing Up' on his rear bumper. Meanwhile my own spouse appeared, hit me over the head with a copy of the *International Journal of Linguistics*, and intimated that for me too the party was over.

I am not easily provoked, but the moment of mutual incomprehension upset me. As I explained to my wife, as she tied me in with the seat-belt and carried me home for domestic punishment, anyone nowadays who came to a literary party without having boned up on Saussure's *Cours de linguistique générale* and Mensonge's *La Fornication comme acte culturel* fully deserved everyone's contempt. How could he hope to discuss the *nouveau roman* and the *nouvelle vague*, let alone the *nouveau Beaujolais*? Did they not know, even in Cheam or Levittown, that without the Structuralist Revolution there would probably be no word-processing, no bar-coding in supermarkets, no cellular telephones, no Beaubourg, no George

Steiner, possibly none of the essentials of modern life? 'All right, if it's that important, why *don't* more people know about it?' asked my wife, with her usual simple sagacity, before pushing me into the guest-room and locking the door from outside. This gave me a long, lonely night to brood on the question, and I had to grant her point. Why was there such a gap, fracture, or *aporia* between the semioticians who are our modern guides, and the populace at large?

Suddenly – this often happens to me after parties – the answer came in a blinding flash of insight. Why had these people been able to transmit their wisdom only to the very select few – people like myself, in fact? The answer was that, like so many professional people now, they spoke only to *each other*, in a complex professional jargon, or *prolect* – filled, as it happened, with words like *prolect*, and *idiolect* and *sociolect*, and *signifier* and *signified*. These were fine at conferences in Malibu, or when impressing the natives on British Council lecture tours. However, they were of small use to the countless millions who knew they lived in a Structuralist-shaped universe, but could find out little about it.

Evidently someone needed to sit down and write out a popular, useful explanation. But who? Such a person would be rare indeed – someone of prodigious talents who kept company with modern philosophers and linguists, knew their lingo and bizarre rituals, recognized at a glance the difference between a stress and a sibilant, but had his pulse firmly on the finger of the larger world as well. It would be someone with the courage to talk frankly, the clarity of mind to put over difficult ideas in plain ways, the authority to convey the profound importance of the matter, the wisdom to see that this could change many, if not all, lives. Who *did* I know with those qualities? There was only one person; but I was busy. It would mean cancelling all engagements, accepting a month of sleepless nights. No, I could not do it.

However, a few days later my book on Mensonge – called *Mensonge* – appeared. It attracted an enormous postbag, some of it quite conciliatory. Reading through the letters, I realized over again just how necessary the task of explanation had become. The world was full of people seeking help and, thanks to books like mine, they were wisely turning to the new philosophers for their very social survival and their party credibility. They deluged me with hundreds of questions. It was impossible to answer them all separately, but I remembered the notes I had planned. It took longer than I thought, but after six months of sleepless agony the job was done. I was soon to learn my letter of reply was circulating widely, in an underground sort of way, and I gathered it had brought solace to many. Evidently it would be churlish of me not to make it universally available, as follows:

Dear Semiotic Enquirer,

Thank you for your letter, asking me just what use modern semiotics could possibly be to you. You will be fascinated to learn that you are one of hundreds asking me that question. Forgive me, then, if I do not answer you individually. I have tried to reduce the many enquiries I have received to a basic few, and somewhere in what follows I am sure you will find the answer you have been looking for. But do, please, read it carefully, for these comments could undoubtedly change your life, whether for the better or the worse it is up to you, thank goodness, to decide. And if I should at times appear just a little technical, do not be deterred. Wisdom does not always come in simple form. Remember, modern thinking is like everything else in life today . – from word-processing to trying to get money from a recalcitrant bank-dispenser. It all becomes easy, once you have learned the language.

1. *What Is It the Linguists Are Trying To Tell Us?*
This is a good question, a very good question. Briefly, what they've been trying, not too successfully, to tell us is that man is a communicating animal. So is woman, if not more so, and so are all animals. This is why linguists explaining communication often use the example of bee-dancing, which shows that bees constantly communicate with each other by signs, and also give good parties as well. People are much the same; however, thanks to the invention of the pocket dictionary, they often communicate through *speech* or *writing*. This is why we call

human beings language-speaking animals, though this does not apply in parts of Scotland. Human beings are creatures who use complex systems of words and grammars to pass messages to each other, about not parking here, for example. You may have thought this was so obvious it did not need a linguist to explain it, but this is not all. For, by working on the coalface of language activity, linguists have proved many things. For instance, they have shown there are two quite different ways of thinking about language. One is called the Common Sense way, and the other is not.

The Common Sense View of Language tells us we use it to describe the world as it is. Language enables us to know what we mean, mean what we say, and understand everyone else doing the same. Words stick limpet-like to things and not only describe but *are* them. A dog is a dog, except in France, where it becomes a *chien*; but it still remains dog-like, and chases cats up trees, or rather *chats* up *arbres*. Still, with a dictionary and maybe a few francs by way of compensation, we can always sort it all out. For though there are different languages they have names for the same things. English differs from all other languages in having the right names for things and the others have the wrong ones; even so, people are saying the *same* things. I say potato and you say potarto, I say tomato and you say tomarto, but we understand each other, and can even get together in making a very simple salad. We share the same *sort* of language, and therefore a common picture of reality. That is common sense, and this is the Common Sense View of Language.

Naturally, being Common Sense, it is quite wrong. In all the linguistics textbooks there is a buffoon called Ordinary Language Man; he is up the creek by page 17. He is up against the Non-Common-Sense, or Semiotic, View of Language, which takes years to learn and therefore must be right. Derived from Saussure, a great professor at Geneva whose lectures were published posthumously by his students, it says that we cannot describe the world as it is, because it actually isn't. The world is a linguistic invention given the appearance of reality by language. Language is a grid imposed on chaos. We do not speak it; it speaks us. It got here first, before we noticed, and programmed us to learn it. It had no time to give things their right names, just arbitrary signs, which only made sense within a total linguistic system. All

166

linguistic systems are different, being based on different codes. A fish may look fish-like to you, but to a Japanese it looks quite different, probably more like a horse. This is because Japanese do everything from back to front and right to left, and have a completely different code for everything.

This proves that names are not realities, but accidents that got mixed up with things and have never really liked it. You might now wonder why you are reading this, since according to what I have said these words must be totally arbitrary. Do not be dismayed. All we are showing is that language, thanks to modern linguistics, has now lost its innocence. To understand this, think of sex (perhaps you were doing so already?). At the start of the century Freud came along, with new theories of the unconscious which totally destroyed the innocence of sex, along, fortunately, with the guilt of it. Freud proved that *everything* was sex, so making even things like coughing or bicycling far more interesting than previously thought.

This is what is now happening with language. Like sex, it too has now lost its innocence. And now the semioticians have proved that *everything* is a language, including sex itself, actually. The great French semiotician Roland Barthes showed, for instance, that food is a language, and he used to take his students out for delightful dinners where they spent the evening reading plates of steak-and-chips. So he invented the *nouvelle cuisine*, food to interpret rather than eat. In fact everything we display, signal or exchange with is a language – sex, food, money, clothes, sport, wives. Everything is a sign system governed by rates of exchange (a good title for a modern novel, incidentally). I am a language and you are a language, though some of us are better at it than others.

That is how it is now; but let it not reduce us to grim silence. When sex lost its innocence, this did not stop people from having any. It merely discouraged them from pretending they did not know what they were doing when they were doing it, which turned out to be even when they thought they were not. Exactly the same is true of language. Today we all need to recognize that we are signifying adults, engaging in semiotic activity at all times. There is no need to panic; we are here, now, and in it. All I would say, therefore, is what Sigmund Freud said in Old Vienna: 'Lie back please there, and relax. There is someone here who can help you.'

2. *Will I Need To Learn To Talk Again?*

Frankly, yes. For the language and sex problems are similar in another way; both have been around for centuries, but no one quite noticed. From early times, ever since the Tower of Babel, people have known that, if they are to find friends, win lovers, make groups, form nations, or support the home team, they must join together in a distinctive language-group. For a language is the way to *construct the world we want*, by making a grid of meaning that every speaker of it agrees with, and non-speakers do not. Language is a form of in-group that forces everyone else into an out-group. Are you worried by the fact that what one person calls 'democracy', someone else calls 'totalitarianism'? Or that what *we* call 'love', *they* call 'sexual harassment'? Ordinary Language Man probably thinks this means that the same thing can be described in two ways. Once again, the poor fool misses the point. What we are watching is the creation of a *dialect*, a language fiction, a plot for the control of reality which will keep the in in, and the out out.

On this principle, tribes, nations and the Nixon administration were constructed. For this reason children have secret codes, Sloane Rangers and Valley Girls have slang, lovers have pillow-talk, and even birds in trees have their own distinctive gang whistles. This is why theologians have Latin, doctors write secret hieroglyphs on prescription pads, lawyers have laws of tort and sequestration, opera singers sing in what they pretend is called Italian, and British aristocrats talk in distinctive brays quite unlike all other human speech. These people are simply defending the privacy of their space, or the mystery of their calling. In fact, just like the linguists themselves, they have a professional dialect (*prolect*) which made their wisdom seem scarcer and therefore much more expensive. This is why these comments are such an act of courage on my part, since they break open the prolect of probably the most important of modern professions. That is why what I am doing is called by them *vulgarization*, and by me *free speech*.

I have spoken of *dialects*, the in-language of a group, and *prolects*, the in-language of a profession (a prolect is a dialect you get paid for). There are also *ideolects* (not to be confused with idiolects, a different matter entirely), which is an ideological language for the control of reality. Ideolects change historically; this is one way we recognize them. In the

Middle Ages everyone had a theocentric ideolect; in the nineteenth century they acquired a Darwinian ideolect; in the twentieth they took up the Freudian ideolect. In every case they appointed priests – bishops, scientists or psycho-analysts – to maintain the dominant fiction. In 1968 we had the ideolect that the world would be more like itself if we had a radical revolution. Now we have the ideolect that it would be more itself if we played more tennis and stopped smoking. These may be passing fictions – remember all language is a fiction – but they attempt for a time to be the only reality.

Now this is all very interesting, you may say (on the other hand, you may not), but how does it help me in my own confusion? The answer is, quite fundamentally. What I am showing is the basic principle, that language exists not for naming things, but for constructing a fiction and making a trade, preferably in your own interest. This is an essential lesson in the management of the modern world. The point is that it is better to be on the inside rather than the outside, better to be a master of language than a slave. For this reason you need an inside language; a dialect, a prolect and an ideolect. In fact what you need is *inspeak*. The comments that follow will help you.

3. How Can I Learn Inspeak?

This is an excellent question. We live, after all, in a crowded, noisy, polyglot, competitive world, a world which is a real scream. Imagine it as a place of endlessly competing signs, languages, signals and codes, rather like an airport on a holiday weekend when the weather pattern is unfavourable. Signs flash, arrows point here and there, flightboards flutter desperately as they overload with conflicting information, messages over the loudspeakers grow more frantic and more and more languages come at you every minute, until at last you go to the wrong place and watch your plane take off without you. We call this the condition of *redundancy*, where noise exceeds the capacity to assimilate it. The trouble with redundancy is that we now have far too much of it. Today more and more languages are being invented, to let computers speak to each other for example, more and more transmitters are sending more and more messages to more and more stations; noise fills the air, banging on the ozone layer, slipping out into the stratosphere. We have not enough ears to hear it, not enough receivers to listen. This is our postmodern condition.

It was not always so. When history worked more slowly, one language was usually enough for anyone. One learned to prattle at one's mother's (or in matriarchal societies, father's) knee, acquiring enough words – 'food', 'money', and so on – to last a lifetime. If, as usually happened, you stayed in one community, took up one trade or profession, from serf to bishop, remained in one sex, and sustained a more or less continuous identity, one dialect took you from first spoken word to last will and testament. Modern life is different; it is a great boutique, with egos, identities, life-styles and professions hanging in sexy profusion from every pricey peg. Buy, and you can go anywhere, do anything, be anyone, for nothing is fixed and everything on offer, if you have the right credit card. Few of us stay in one linguistic spot from the cradle to the grave. After all, who wants to be a stable personality, a fixed point of reference, a pillar of the community?

So the classic professions have faded, as the lawyers sue the doctors and the doctors kill the lawyers. The rules of status have collapsed, and someone invents a new pecking order every day. No one wants to be an aristocrat, least of all an aristocrat. The bourgeoisie is hated by everyone, especially the bourgeoisie. The working class is a Victorian affectation only pursued by Old Etonians. This is not the Age of Aquarius; it is the age of Proteus. Metamorphosis is the name of the game, and never was it harder to signify what, and with which, and to whom. No wonder our most successful books are books of lists, telling us what is in and what is out, though the books are usually out before they even come in. No wonder our newest folk-heroes are designers, the insider-traders in sign, signal, fashion and chic.

Who can keep up? Never seen Wham, never tried crack? Missed out entirely on abstract-photo-impressionism, never done Glyndebourne? Never worn a leotard, never read Lyotard? Never used Pierre Cardin all-over body-rub, never had your nipples pierced? Never done Lacanian analysis, never tried hang-gliding? Never had an ear-orgasm, never read *Gravity's Rainbow?* Is that what you eat? What's your sign? Never met *Mrs* Samuel Beckett? Never lunched *downstairs* at Langham's? In whole areas of Islington and Camden, Carmel and Marin County, there are people who have bought a wok, found a great hot-bread shop, ragged the walls, swum topless at Eilat, been in Esalen and the Hurlingham, bought a laptop, got a timeshare in the Dutch Antilles, divorced six times and won world traveller status on seven airlines, and who *still* feel there is something missing. They have signified and signified, and still failed, and to tell the truth we are all up the same creek without a really good guidebook. For this is the era of lexical glut, the age of the semiotic scream, and there seems no keeping up with it.

The fact is things move so fast that no sign is stable. Did you know that the European Economic Community not only has a beef mountain and a butter mountain but also a *sign* mountain? (Every document has to be translated into twelve languages, one of them called Bureauspeak.) Everywhere the sign is slipping away from the signifier. Travelling in the United States a few years back, I invented the concept of *Havernization*. It came when I was flying on some new deregulated airline, where crew hours had evidently been long. 'I'm Barbie,' said the stewardess down the wire, as we bellyflopped at O'Hare. 'Thank you for flying this F111 flight of Rambo Air, and havernize . . .' Poor Barbie, she did not know whether it was day or night, morning or evening. It did not matter. We were in America, the modern world, and it was time to havernize.

I havernized that night in the airport hotel, where the menu – which described everything as 'succulent', 'handcarved at table', 'served in a priceless sauce' – was far better to eat than the meal itself. I havernized when the waiter came by and said 'Isn't it wonderful here?' I havernized as I read the questionnaire in my executive suite bedroom, which said 'Your room was so clean and wonderful it was like your own home, right?' and 'Maybe this wasn't the most fantastic experience of your entire life but it came close, right?' Havernization is the great split between signifier and signified – a way of using language not to describe but to replace grim reality. It is everywhere, of course, from Tokyo to Tashkent (where the *glasnost* hotels now have signs saying 'This bug has been sanitized for your protection'). No wonder we have to learn to live in the world of the floating sign, and that is why we need all the help the very best philosophers and semioticians can possibly give us.

171

That is what is here. These remarks are no cheap guide to chic, the sort of thing you might pick up in any magazine or bookstore paperback. They are no flashy New Age philosophy from people who came out of EST and are headed for Acapulco. This is not some easy advice about how to feel okay or improve your intimacy path. This is high-quality, Paris-based advice that draws on the thinking of Descartes, Kant, Hegel and Heidegger, to name only a few of the world-famous philosophers who have helped this project. It has been developed by leading professors from famous universities who are used to travelling widely before jumping to any conclusions. The ideas have come from some of the best in the field, especially out of the discoveries of the great Count Ferdinand de Saussure, star professor at the world-famed Université de Genève, in elegant Switzerland, where Joyce wrote *Ulysses*. And it has been checked and rechecked by the prestigious Vienna Circle of Linguists, who come from the city where the delightful Spanish Riding School is to be found.

Study of these great ideas shows this: in today's polymorphous universe, what we need most is not quite a traditional dialect, prolect, or ideolect. We need something new: a *causolect* (a well-based group of fellow life-stylers to be a member of), a *psycholect* (a good psycho-community we can belong to), and a *medialect* (membership not of one of the old professions but one of the new, yuppie post-professions). These are the real needs of the age of lexical glut, upgraded life-styling and computer-age technology. And if you can just get all this right, then the fifteen-speed bike, the waterfront condominium, the Rossignol skis and the Austrian loden coat you have always wanted could easily be yours.

4. Ought I To Try Chest-Talk?

Why not? Chest-talk is one of the most obvious solutions to the problem of trying to utter, articulate and signify in our noisy times. To understand it, all we need do is look at – or rather *read* – the bodies of all our friends and cronies. It is well known that throughout the ages people have dressed for symbolic purposes; that is why clothes were invented, not just to keep out cold weather. Soldiers dress to show they are terrifying, priests to declare their wisdom and purity, and clothes and ornament have always displayed wealth, status and power. They have asserted authority, expressed membership and announced, and sometimes denied, sexual availability. The female breast was a high-intensity area for semiotic activity, and every dressmaker knew that by shaping and stitching, concealing and revealing, it was possible to stimulate attention and desire while denying direct access. However, until lately, all these were *phatic* signs: they implied meaning, but did not speak it. Written words appeared only on hotel doormen, railway porters and signboard men. Today this has changed.

Now one cannot meet anyone without having to read some message or logo – inscribed across the nipples, stitched across the buttocks, sewn into the fabric, printed across the underwear crotch, or otherwise displayed on any body-surface capacious or else attention-getting enough to earn a hieroglyph. The female mammary region has become frank advertising space, its erotic function gladly leased to any old cause or corporation – JOG FOR JESUS, SURFERS AGAINST AIDS, LESBIANS AGAINST SMOKING. All body space full, the activity has spread to every possession – the car, the skis, the dog. In the dark solitude of multi-storey parking lots, cars sit, their owners departed, glowering at each other, spiky with conflicting messages: LOVE IS ALL, BRING BACK CELIBACY, and so on. We call this phenomenon chest-talk, and it is universal. No wonder book sales decline. It is all we can do to find time to read all the people we meet.

Messages come in all kinds. Some are designer labels. Someone might miss that this was a Gucci tie did it not say *Gucci* on it, or not know this was a Liberty scarf were not *Liberty* sewn in large letters into it (my own scarf, slightly different, reads *Equality*). It seems curious that where manufacturers pay footballers large sums for advertising their products, we pay the manufacturers large sums for doing them just the same favour. Some are more personal, saying I'M SEXY or I'M INTELLECTUAL. Others announce membership of some select sub-group (POSTMEN DO IT TWICE A DAY), utter moral exhortation (SAVE THE PIRANHA FISH), or announce an ideological viewpoint (CASTRATE ALL MEN). But most are, indeed, causolects (BOMB THE CHURCH OF YOUR CHOICE), psycholects (I'M AVAILABLE), or medialects (PRIESTS DO IT AT EVENSONG).

173

Why do we need chest-talk? No doubt, in the age of self-presentation, modesty or labyrinthine dalliance is an anachronism. Semiotic speed is the thing; I have only to meet a girl reading RIOT FOR LESBIANISM to move on further down the bar. It provides a quick conversation without moving the lips, and I have several T-shirts that speak Dutch for me, saving me the pain of ever having to learn that horrendously difficult language. And in an age of quickly changing values the messages can be altered quite rapidly, a decent wardrobe providing semiotic access into almost any group. For it is not the opinion that matters. After all, a SMILE badge always leaves you free to frown. The important thing is to have said I AM I, or rather I AM AN I THAT IS IN WITH THE CROWD THAT LIKES TO SAY I AM LIKE THIS. It is no longer enough to be a self. Just as today we study not the author but the text, so now we study not the person but the sign. After all, we are all competing not just with other people, but with ads for Polaroid and Polo-Mints. Yes, the important thing is to have signified.

5. *Would I Do Better with Head-Talk?*
This rather depends where you live. Head-talk started in steamy old turn-of-the-century Vienna, with dear old Sigmund Freud and the talking cure. However, in a Europe that preferred Marx to Freud and history to the psyche, it had a poor future. Hence it moved to America, which did not have a history, just a series of hang-ups. Head-talk is the story of those who have been hung up, and is easy to spot. Once, when you stopped someone on the street and said, 'How are you?', they replied, quite politely, 'How are you?' Nobody learned anything but everyone felt better. But if, now, you meet someone on the street, ask how they are, and are answered 'Well, I've got these, you know, aggressive feelings towards my, you know, mother, but I'm working through them, and this guy I'm living with this week is being, you know, really, supportive, and I could be coming back into committing relationships and going one-on-one again, and I'm right off junk-food now and into this, you know, really healthy falafel diet, and I'm reading Tolstoy, he must have been a really beautiful person ...' you will know, when you get away, if you ever do, that you have been in the presence of head-talk.

174

Head-talk is over-signification on the mental plane, and is the product of the self-aware age where it meets the Me generation. It is based on the doubtful notion that everyone has a consciousness that is, like the *Titanic*, well worth raising, preferably with everyone we meet. It's the discourse of the tribe who are upfront with their feelings, are getting their acts together, know where their heads are, and are becoming real persons. Head-talk has one great advantage: it is always about someone you love greatly, feel good about, and really want to promote. It also suggests that if you talk so much about your self, you must really have one. As French philosophy shows, this is untrue. The self is an invention of language. In this case it is an expensive language, learned at many a couch-session, encounter-group, hot-tub weekend, and consciousness-raising workshop, where you learned how you stand on Klein versus Lacan, what your orgasmic lexicon is, and how you feel – I mean *really* feel – about the fatty area behind your thighs.

To this day, head-talk remains American, part of the national Feel-good syndrome. It has never quite worked in Britain, which has never taken psychology seriously – one reason why in British hospitals even the agoraphobics waiting for treatment have to wait in groups. Head-talk really needs a healthy, wealthy, laid-back, self-aware society with a psycho-analyst on every street corner willing to take all the major credit cards – somewhere like California, in fact. It is also the product of the Lone Ranger society, where the shrine of life is the Singles Bar and everyone is headed from a fully raised consciousness to a lonely old age. Head-talk is also expensive, the trouble with your head being that once you are in it it is hard to get out again. The lesson is clear. If you are really into head-talk, make it a medialect, not a psycholect. Be a psychiatrist, not a patient. After all, a psycholect can keep you preoccupied for a lifetime, but a medialect is a language you get paid for.

6. *Why Do I Need a Medialect?*

Exactly. Well, let us consider for a moment the changing nature of work. There was a time when almost everyone did some, most of it gross, heavy and bestial. Men went down mines, women dug fields, children scrabbled up chimneys with brushes. But work was an acknowledged good, and those who did none were a burden to others and themselves. Today, though, we live in a post-industrial world. Technology has replaced labour, and leisure replaced industry. We therefore need not work but post-work, a new sort of employment that can programme the technology and service the leisure. The grime and grimness of work is fading, but post-work is not easy. It requires a sophisticated education (even clowns go to clown college these days) and, above all, a high degree of presentation. Post-work is very professional; it also makes everything into a profession. Post-work is normally done in leisure wear, especially Lacoste sports shirts; meanwhile work-clothes – jeans off the farm, for example – are worn for leisure.

Post-work can be anything from software to arbitraging, property development to tennis coaching, but a good deal of it is in the area called the 'media'. 'Media' is a term that once was plural but now is singular, and grows more singular by the day. Like a good fabric from Laura Ashley, it can cover many different kinds of thing. If, for example, you run a Soho strip-joint, keep a street-corner café, stick posters on walls, slip cassettes into a player in the local pub, paint your nails behind the counter of a boutique, or word-process in an office, you are, respectively, a theatre director, a gourmet adviser, a creative layout expert, a disc jockey, a couturier, and a personal assistant. And you 'work' in the 'media'. There are whole segments of modern cities – in London it's Islington – where *everyone* is in the media. Here's Sheila, she's a television researcher (she's out a lot), and this Georgina, she's a publisher's reader (she's in a lot). This is Cheryl, she's in public relations (she's in the Seychelles a lot), and that's Charlene, she's a model (undresses a lot).

'Media', as Sheila, Georgina, Cheryl and Charlene are showing us – and aren't they lovely, let's give them a big hand! – is a world of wide variety and great opportunities. It ranges from art to acting, advertising to photography, promotion to public relations, dance to dress design, management to marketing, window dressing to – especially in Charlene's case – window undressing. And what brings all these people together in one big happy party is the fact that they work in the sign-making or semiotic professions: the kinds of profession that, thanks for the need to add gloss to reality, proliferate in the modern world. If you were wondering where to find a left-handed mug or a designer Band-Aid, someone in media will have thought about it. People in media deal in the semiotic stuff itself – signs, images and words – and so have converted redundancy into something everyone wants to buy. Yes, do learn a medialect. The only trouble is, which?

7. Can You Suggest an Easy Way In?

Yes. Most people start with pop-talk. This is an ideal place for beginners to begin, for the pop scene consists almost entirely *of* beginners. It is a scene of endless opportunities chased by endless opportunists – singers who cannot sing, dancers who cannot lift one foot above the other, lead-guitarists who fall over their leads, keyboard-wizards who have not even passed sorcerer's apprentice. Talent is not important, for this is a system of energy, desire, ego-hunger, hysteria, youthful frustration and stylistic tribalism, where it is the spirit that counts. Happily all this means that pop-talk is very easy to learn. After all, if the average teenager can manage to do it, you certainly can.

Pop-talk falls into three categories. The first is taste-talk, about the kind of music you, well, like. It may seem doubtful that you could like any, but the thing about tastes is that there is no accounting for them. But remember, the choices are crucial. Go for Art Rock or Heavy Metal, C & W, Power Pop or Euro-Pop, and you are choosing not just a loud noise but a total way of life. Your choice will determine everything else – your appearance, food habits, lovers, friends and, most importantly, your enemies, for nothing creates more hostility than modern music, unless it is modern football. Pop music is war by other means, and every style attracts its own supporters. It does not matter that the styles are totally evanescent, and will have gone by next week's charts. They are eternal truths, for this week at least. Since they are in fact evanescent, I cannot be expected to offer detailed advice. But the fanzines are filled with portraits of loutish stylists you can attach your rising star to; and many households employ a full-time teenager, sometimes called a house-yob, just to keep them up with the latest scram.

There is also disco-talk, the tactical jargon of the trade, transmitted by professional gurus known as disc-jockeys, who babble endlessly of waxings and tracks, chart-toppers and up-and-comers. And then there is tech-talk, the language required for discussing the technology of the multifarious equipment you will need to buy to blast the sound of your music into the homes of your neighbours. Again there is a trade press ready to keep you up on the data on tweeters and woofers, stacks and decks, CDs and graphic equalizers, so that you will be able to know your Bang from your Ulufson. But all of this is mere preparation, and not true media-talk. This is the language of the consumer. And just as it is better to be an analyst than an analysand, so it is better to be a performer than a listener, a star than a fan.

Of course many others are of the same opinion, and competition is considerable, but it is not hard to succeed. The important thing is not to pursue harmonic excellence but to pursue a style, preferably one of aggression and outrage. Pop music succeeds in terms of its capacity to draw crowds into venues, and this means orchestrating the general sense of disorientation, victimization and frantic sexual hysteria rampant in modern society. Onstage, you should always convey the impression of being on heat, and an appearance of emaciated persecution is widely acknowledged to possess chic, allure and sexual charisma. Fame will come, eventually, and if you can just keep it going for two weeks you will be a celebrity success. Of course this will involve you in many new responsibilities. You may find you are forced to inject yourself with unpleasant substances, engage in perverse sexual practices, and make endless boring world tours as you strut your stuff from Hamburg to Hollywood, and Australia to Tokyo. You will, incidentally, now have to learn a new language – of gigs and venues, skins and wah-wahs, axe-men and liggers, promo-bashes and payola, roadies and groupies, platinum and gold.

It is all worth it. Once you are a chartbuster, the world is open to you. You will be richer than royalty, more powerful than a political leader, more visible than the Pope, and unlike all the rest you will have no moral responsibilities at all. Yachts in the Aegean, beach houses in Miami, Tudor mansions in Gloucestershire, Rolls-Royces by the handful – all will be yours for the asking. You will have found the ideal modern style, which is being wealthy without getting blamed for it.

You will not let success spoil you, and will remain as trivial as you always were. You will tell everyone that you have never forgotten your lowly origins, that money means nothing to you, that all that matters is your art. None of it will be true (your lowly origins are a dump, money is the only thing that matters to you, and you have no art.) But you will be a hero of the modern world, as long as you play it – and I do not mean the music – right. Yes, it's a pity that to get this far, you have to put up with all that music.

8. *Can't You Fix Me a Career in the Media?*

I thought so. Yes, a lot of people, serious people, people who harbour deep literary ambitions or have seen *All The President's Men* at least twice, long to get into the world of the media. They want to be journalists, publishers, editors, television producers. Thus they hope to become makers of opinion, movers and shakers, formers of taste. They aim to explore the reality of the age, deal with the major events of the world, investigate scandal, reform the Times. Alas, it is not like that. The age has no reality. The Times are owned by Rupert Murdoch, and are not available for reform. Opinion is not made but manipulated. It is not necessary for a scandal to exist in order for the press to be outraged by it. The day of the investigative reporter, pen behind ear, foot in door, has gone. Today's foreign correspondent, ducked down behind the barbed wire, is not abroad but at home, in the bunker of the newspaper office, direct-feeding stories gleaned off the wire first into an opinion and then into a computer.

At one time journalism was an attractive profession. Compared with acting, the work was steady. Compared with Abstract Expressionist painting, it was clean. Compared with music, there was no instrument to learn. Compared with television, there was not much technology to fall over. Compared with novel-writing, one travelled a lot. None of these things is now true. The work is far from steady, and rarely clean. There are many instruments to learn, and plenty of technology to fall over, now that newspapers have plugged their journalists into the computer, or rather the computer into their journalists. The days of hot metal and holding the front page for the great story are done with. Most journalists, either because of the pickets or the data-banks that surround them, never leave the office, except to go to the pub round the corner or on a travel-writing freebie to the Seychelles. And as for the news, there is nothing new about it. Most of it was written long ago, in the form of a grid of words – shock probes and mercy dashes, grabs and gotchas, curbs and AIDS, Dis and Fergies – waiting in the technology for a minor up-date.

So most news can be written without ever leaving the office, news by definition being any event that occurs or is described within earshot of a journalist. Most of it will come to you, for there is no doubt that the world is full of people who will happily call by to betray a friend, leak a national secret, strip to the buff, or reveal the sexual practice of last night's concubine, in return for the satisfaction of seeing the story in print. Of course each paper has its own minor differences in style; thus *The Times* dignifies news by giving people in it their full titles, the *Guardian* complicates it by spelling the names wrongly, and *The Sun* simplifies it by not printing it at all. But the essential point is that the news is not an account of reality. It is a newspaper fiction, and a newspaper is a collage novel computer-fed onto the page by a committee not all of whom have turned up, and then printed on inferior paper so that it can be quickly thrown away.

Even so, journalism still has something of the look of a primitive technology, and this is no doubt why most people who want to go into the media nowadays think of television – where, of course, the collage novel has sound and moving pictures instead of words, and the plot is told seamlessly, twenty-four hours a day, so that it never needs to end at all. Hence it requires far more technologies and far more experts – all of whom, down to the chap who added the footsteps, get credits when the show is momentarily over and the titles roll. There are recce people who find the fiction, writers who script it into existence; there are directors to control it, cameramen to let us see it, soundmen to let us hear it, make-up girls to make sure it is cosmetic, lighting men to make sure it does not get lost in the dark. All of them have their own prolects, a complex language of noddies and neddies, cuts and fades, blondes and redheads, gaffers and props. But the real language of television is the television sign itself, the complex technological process where the invented world is shifted from the studio into the great mental audio-visual centre called the human head.

In short, television is now the great fiction that invents the world. It creates life as we know it – life as an endless flickering sign, a long-running serial of serials in which open-ended fictions like Irangate, the Gulf War, the General Election and the Big Bang are interspersed with talk-shows, game-shows, sit.-coms., and commercial breaks. The complex plot we call life happens sometimes in the studio, sometimes on location where endless crowds of extras wave to get the camera's attention. Life's story is sometimes new and sometimes old, sometimes quite colourful and sometimes entirely black and white. Much of the time it is a very low-budget affair, with a bad plot, inferior casting and the look of having run out of funds well before completion. But it is all the life we have now, and invents the great issues and priorities, the heroes and villains, the tears and laughter of the age.

For the moment at least, television is the sign of the times, and before it we have three choices. Like Ordinary Language Man, we can sit there on the sofa with our pot noodles, taking all we see for the nature of a real reality. Or we can try to join its great cast – waving from the margins in the crowd scenes, clapping away in the studio audiences, teenybopping on the music shows, winning the holiday of a lifetime in some game with what are called real contestants. Of course we must accept that the show is already written, the parts are pre-planned, the director is in charge, and the lines we speak are other people's, if we ever get a line at all. Alternatively, we might just possibly try to be a maker or a star – the writer of the lines, the actor with the right to script changes, the person with a credit when the titles roll and we are up against God's great commercial break – and so seek to be not just a signified, but a signifier.

No doubt this explains why so many people nowadays want to be on, in, or behind the media, why television seems the great good place to be. Just for the moment, it is the powerhouse of the semiotic age. Try for it if you must; I suspect, such is the pace of technology, that its days too are numbered, as the noise of redundancy in the universe grows and grows. Personally, if you are serious about the matter, I am inclined to recommend becoming a linguist. There are an awful lot of them around these days, as I suppose was inevitable, once they proved that everything was actually a language. They seem to be consulted on just about everything, and their prospects have never been brighter. The prolect is hard, but as you see it is possible to understand it. On reflection, that is just about the best possible counsel I can offer. All right, maybe it's not the most fantastic advice of your entire life, but it came close, right?

So do think it over, very carefully, And in the meantime, havernize.

Yours, etc.

The Conference:
A Lay-Person's Guide

Quite a number of the letters I receive consist of invitations to speak at the many conferences, congresses, seminars, festivals, talkfests and general get-togethers that litter all forms of professional life these days. I should not like you to think I am an admirer of these events. I cannot imagine just why it is that people in so many walks of life – computer whiz-kids and car salesmen, dons and dentists, managers and motor mechanics, politicians and pornographers – need to hie off to some distant congress hall, sit down with the colleagues they have just left behind in the office or the bar, listen to lectures, pass resolutions that are of no importance to anyone else and often not to themselves, and generally interrupt the smooth rhythm of their daily lives. After all, why should people risk themselves to the vagaries of first-class air travel, and while away valuable hours in first-class hotels in Venice, Honolulu, or Hong Kong, with their distracting pools and intrusive bar facilities, when they could perfectly well settle their business by telephone from their homes in, say, Scunthorpe or Pittsburgh? It really is quite baffling.

On the other hand, I am not dogmatic on the matter. And it is for that reason, and that reason only, that over recent years I have made something of a point of going to quite a few of these events, in various parts of the world, to see whether I am being fair in objecting so violently to them. Thus I have been, several times, to the great professional conferences held by the American Modern Language Association, at which some 15,000 like-minded scholars complete the Christmas festivities by getting together to read the odd paper to one another and have a few more drinks for the sake of old friendship. I have attended a fair number of international writers' congresses, frequently held for some reason in high midsummer in the mosquito-ridden lakelands of Finland, where world-famous authors gather to deliver resolutions on the need for world peace and higher royalties, and have, of course, a seasonal drink together for the sake of old enmity. I have been to conventions in Hawaii, only to find they did not have any, or at any rate not the ones that restrain most of us back home. I have attended intensive study-sessions at Hakone, a delightful venue half-way up Mount Fuji, in – if I remember the small print of my air ticket correctly – Japan, which I can recommend as an excellent place for those who need a night's shelter while they share opinions on the use of tense in the English novel.

Thus I have shown my open-mindedness and dedication to the advancement not just of my own but other people's subjects. I have broadened my knowledge, along with my girth, kept American Express firmly among the top twenty companies, and made a number of fairly intimate friendships that might not have come my way otherwise, though I see no point in going into that matter here. I have also acquired an entire new subject of study. The subject is Conferences, actually. Naturally I have become very much in demand over the matter, and so I have become rather used to writing letters of this type:

Dear Dr Criminale,

Thank you for your kind letter asking me to speak at your forthcoming conference. You will be happy to know that your reputation as a conference organizer has preceded you, and I am honoured that you should have selected me as your keynote speaker. Only one thing worries me – the fact that you have adopted the unhappy modern convention of asking me to forward my lecture to you *in advance*, for what you call 'purposes of translation'. Friends of mine have suffered badly from this practice, finding that once their lectures had been forwarded, their air tickets were not, and that their paper had actually been read *in absentia* to the audience by the conference chairman. But such is the reputation of your own conference that I am prepared to take the risk. I therefore enclose a copy of my paper, with a duplicate to my lawyer. I must ask you not to release it to anyone – the world press, or any of the other speakers – in advance of the speech itself. It is heady and contentious stuff, and I should not want anyone else to have to handle the intellectual furore it will undoubtedly provoke. The fee is most acceptable, and the '79 will do very nicely. I look forward to seeing you at the airport: you will easily recognize me by the copy of *The Laws of International Copyright* I will be carrying. In answer to your other query, my drink is Scotch and branch water.

Yours, etc.

Enclosure

A CONFERENCE PAPER

1

Ladies and Gentlemen,

Thank you, Mr Chairman, for that most lively and stimulating introduction, which told me a great deal about myself I had never heard before, and will certainly follow up. And thank you, each and every one, for the fine reception – indeed the several fine receptions – you have given me, for the generous warmth with which you have incorporated me into your festivities, and for the sensible choice of a suite with jacuzzi; these things are always a great stimulus to thought, I find. But, above all, may I thank you for the honour you have done me in making me your keynote speaker on this auspicious occasion, the twenty-first meeting of the Standing Conference on Conferences, held – sitting down, fortunately – in the wonderfully chosen surroundings of the Hôtel-des-Bains-et-de-la-Gourmand. A fine conference is always known by its choice of setting, and I think we would all want to say that the hotel has not earned its seven stars in vain [wait for applause].

So to my topic, which I am sure you know far more about than I do.

185

It is, of course, conferences – how did they start, how do we plan them, whom do we invite, and what do we do with ourselves after they are over. It would appear that, like all subjects discussed at conferences, this is a field in which far too little work has been done. This may seem surprising, considering the large numbers of these events held these days. But, as people at conferences often find, one can be so busy having a thing one never has time to consider it abstractly. That is what has happened with the conference. However, it would appear, from such research as I have managed to fit in intervals between these gatherings, there was once a time when people who shared a common profession, trade, interest, or ideological persuasion did *not* attend conferences. When five o'clock came, they apparently thought of nothing more than donning their galoshes, running for the train, and spending the evening or weekend around the domestic hearth, content in the knowledge that they would not see their colleagues and workmates again until they re-entered the office on Monday morning. Likewise, when the holiday season came, a holiday was what people took. They cancelled the newspaper, crowded their families into some capacious vehicle or other, left no forwarding address, and set off for Polperro or Acapulco, eliminating work and their colleagues from their minds entirely. Work, in those bleak days, was not considered a wall-to-wall affair, and a colleague was not acknowledged as friend, peer and competitor – simply as a passing office face, to be forgotten in what were then called 'leisure hours'.

But all this was a long time ago – probably in the twelfth century – and it explains the slow speed of economic advancement in early history. Happily since then things have changed for the better. It is believed that it was in the thirteenth century that the conference wallet was invented, and shortly afterwards a primitive form of the lapel badge, and people started to goon on confyrences. During the Renaissance, the after-dinner speech was developed, and, in the eighteenth-century Enlightenment, the conga line. Conference-going in fact dominated olden times, and many people remembered with delight the Treaty of Utrecht, where the band was excellent and many important resolutions were passed. Nonetheless the early conference was probably a primitive affair, and not all went well. The Diet of Worms, indeed, became a classic example of what can go wrong when organizers concentrate on the agenda but forget to check the restaurant facilities.

However, through the centuries, many useful lessons were learned, and today, as those of you who have been wise enough to gather here know very well, the art of the conference has been refined to a very high degree. The discovery of the slide-projector, of built-in tape-recording facilities, fax machines and the en-suite mini-bar all advanced the process. So, of course, did the invention, by the hotel industry, of group concessionary rates, a means of ensuring that their premises could be filled at all seasons of the year by people of an apparently reasonable demeanour and with reliable expense-account facilities. It is not exactly known when the hoteliers reached this decision – there are hints of some such arrangement in Chaucer's *Canterbury Tales* – but we may be sure that, whenever and wherever they took it, they did it at some conference or other.

Naturally, by one of those happy synergies of which modern life seems full, it appears that the expansion of conference facilities coincided with a growth in the demand for them. I need hardly tell you, ladies and gentlemen, that we live today in an age of unprecedented advance and development; at least that is what I understand change of any kind is now called. There has been an exponential development in the rate of technical change, a remarkable growth of knowledge, or at any rate of information and documentation, and an expansion of corporate activity of every kind. In every field – be it viticulture or venery, bacteriology or bicycling – we all need to keep up with the bottom line of the state of the art of the name of the game. All the professions – and even more their recent successors, the pseudo-professions – grow more complex by the day; if they did not, they would soon fall by the wayside. The age of old-fashioned individualism is over, and we all nowadays need not private relations, but public relations.

No, the fact is that we live today in an age of gregariousness. Modern life and modern commerce, modern thought and modern politics, all require the corporate outlook, a sense of collective endeavour. What, after all, is a profession but a *group* of people, all sharing one common expertise, and the gift for making it seem difficult to outsiders, who are, by definition, the people you do not ask to such occasions. What is a corporation but a *body* of people, who need from time to time to foregather in order to understand how the various parts of the body fit together? Today we depend on corporate morale, work-force motivation, group-goal orientation, managerial leadership. How then should we not only encourage but display, to ourselves and others, that unity of purpose and community of feeling we call our profession, our organization, our field of study, our party, our cause? Happily, brilliant minds, like ourselves, have for many years been working collectively together on a solution to these difficult problems. And, in case I have not made myself entirely clear, especially to those people in the back rows who are calling up their loved ones on cellular telephones, that solution is surely what we here at this conference would undoubtedly call a 'conference'.

2.

There are sometimes people – usually the smaller stockholders – who ask whether conferences are really necessary. The question is laughable, the answer an emphatic yes [wait for applause]. Companies and corporations, causes and organizations, fields of study and political parties that neglected to have them would not last long. So what, then, *is* a conference? Well, briefly, it is, as you well know, a happy arrangement by which people who work together regularly in a particular field or activity manage to take all their holidays together as well. In this respect there is much to be said for it. Certainly it does away with the traditional unpleasantness of being stuck in some vacation hotel or campsite for weeks with one's entire family, or else of having to deal all on one's own with unfriendly barmen or recalcitrant night-club hostesses. It is a way of going off to some sort of resort location while ensuring that one really has someone of like mind to talk to, like a secretary or an office superior. Above all, it is a way of getting away to some pleasant setting for a few days without giving the dangerous appearance of losing interest in one's work.

Let us be quite clear about this. I have used the word 'holiday', but I should not like it to mislead us – still less my wife, who is not alas here, though she is not sure why, and certainly not those who felt so deeply down in their institutional pockets to provide the travel grant that enabled me to attend. It is true that the association between the 'conference' and the 'holiday' is often made, perhaps because conferences are sometimes held – as by chance this one has been – in some holiday-resembling context, perhaps in a particularly attractive foreign city, or else within sight of sea, waves and a tropical bar. But this, as we keep pointing out to people, is simply because that is where the hotels are usually found, and in any case these are generally bracing environments, stimulating to intellectual discourse. Besides, we should not forget that many a major conference has been ruined by careless inattention to detail – a lack of shower-facilities in rooms, plugs for the bath, sufficient relaxation in the evenings, or a sun-drenched coastline where informal discussion may continue – and there is no point in skimping on the background, even though we are all here to be in the foreground.

But let us settle this matter once and for all – especially for my wife and others like her. These environments are *not* chosen in order that those who come and put on their lapel-badges with such good grace can feel they are actually 'on holiday'. Indeed a well-organized conference must *never* give this impression. Well before the event, all participants should receive in elegantly printed form a very full and demanding programme – packed with lectures, plenaries, panels, official addresses by major figures, statements by the president, debates, seminars and colloquia. It is essential for them to have this to show to their spouses and those who are providing sponsorship for their attendance. It is also crucial that they should have something they can read afterwards to remind them what it is they are said to have been doing. No, as I have always been careful to point out, if distant holiday-resembling locations are often used, they are chosen for a clear and well-defined purpose. Careful research proves that it is essential that all participants to a congress should have had to travel a long way, surmount many hurdles of missed flights and lost baggage, and experience linguistic confusion and overcharging by taxi-drivers, if the event is to create the mood that a conference depends upon. We call that mood 'camaraderie'. And I would remind you, if you doubt me, how much better we all feel on these occasions when we learn that some of our group have been left behind at the airport, or stranded in Shannon by an air-traffic

189

controllers' strike. The feeling of gratification we all feel then is the beginning of conference camaraderie.

What I am emphasizing to all of you who are here – and even more to those of you who are not – is that conferences are always a continuation of work by other means. And no better proof of that can be produced than the fact that those who go to them never pay for themselves, but are paid for from company, institutional and, on occasion, governmental funds. I am known as a sceptic in these matters. But I can tell you that, on the basis of all the on-the-spot research I have done, I have never attended any conference where the people who chose to be there did not think the occasion absolutely necessary. This we may call an important finding, though a moment's thought – if you can spare one – will explain just why. A conference gathers to confer. And what it mostly confers is prestige. That prestige is conferred simultaneously on two parties: the funding organization or institution which backed it, and the person who is selected to go to the conference him- or herself (a conference that is only himselves without herselves is, incidentally, generally acknowledged, for some reason, very dull indeed). And these two linked prestiges then confer a third – on the subject, the specialism, the profession, or the obsession to which the proceedings of the conference are, at least ostensibly, devoted.

May I stress the crucial significance of this, and remind you to repeat it to others when you get home. There is no moment more fundamental to any area of commerce or other activity – not the moment when we design the logo, invent the tie, produce the T-shirt, get the headed stationery, start the journal – than the moment when it is clear this organization is of such importance that it needs a conference. At last we can prove that this particular sphere of activity – whether it is selling Fords or climbing mountains, preserving the minnow or arranging flowers – now has enough members, devotees, supporters, or subscribers to be able to charter an aircraft, book a hotel, elect a chairperson, hold a general meeting, pass resolutions and send representatives on to the conferences held by everyone else. How could any profession, or even worse any would-be profession, any corporation, or would-be corporation, any political party, or would-be political party, consider itself successful or dignified if it did not bring itself together in a

190

conference? No, the conference is the greatest accolade any activity or cause can bestow upon itself.

Think of the satisfaction nurtured in all who come when they realize that, for the moment, they belong to a class of beings actually capable of engaging in the activity so proudly explained by the chairman in his opening speech, that is coherent and united enough to pass the draconian resolutions urged on the world at the general meeting, or concerned and committed enough to call public attention to the issues raised by the secretary in the interview with the girl from the local radio station done in the broom cupboard afterwards.

However, while it is clear that a conference dignifies the members of a profession, it does not necessarily follow that the members of a profession have always to dignify a conference. After all, it is an inevitable result of such occasions that, if some come to speak, others must come to listen, that to have great speakers there must be great audiences too. My own views on this matter are not rigid. Lectures are, we know, demanding, some – like this one – more than others. But we should not feel overawed by them, and I do not believe myself that every single item on the programme should always be attended by every single person present. Indeed there is a famous phenomenon known as 'conference drift' – in fact I do believe there were one or two people still hanging around in the bar when I myself started speaking.

I suggest that we should not be too worried by this, however surprising it must seem. The point is that the main function of a conference is not always speaking or being spoken to, important as this is, especially today. There are many ways of skinning the same rabbit. In fact the major function of the conference must always be – and I do not want any misunderstanding about what I mean – the endless pursuit of an *esprit de corps*. The task must be to create an *atmosphere*, the atmosphere of a group of high-minded, serious people devoted to the advancement of their work, the good of society, the needs of the future, the righting of the wrongs of the age. Every conference therefore must find ways of making it clear that in this parlous world there is one group of people who are determined not to stand for whatever it is, who mean to improve things, and transform the ills that surround us everywhere. And we must make it clear how fortunate it is that this group of people just happens to be exactly the one that happens to be gathered together in this hall, or just possibly hovering about in the bar outside. As long as *esprit de corps* has been maintained, that conference can be judged a success.

In fact a really good conference is one where everyone present has been filled with such a feeling of common cause that the very notion of going home again is a disappointment – so that they cannot wait to gather again in the same way next year, preferably in somewhere even more sunny. You will know a good conference by the tears in the hotel corridor, the embraces in the lobby, the warm if perhaps rash promises to write every day. Alas, of course, all this will wear off, and that is why it is important that conferences be repeated very regularly. In fact a good deal more research is needed on conference frequency, and I should like to commend just that project to all of you gathered here today. For, clearly, if we are to advance our subject, face the needs of the world in the future, and put everything that is wrong bang to rights, then some far-sighted, clear-minded, well-trained, excellently organized profes-sional body with incomparable qualifications will have to undertake serious work at once. And I need hardly say to you, here and now, that I know of no better body to undertake this task than we ourselves.

Of course the work will not, as one always feels impelled to point out on these occasions, be easy. There is a mass of data to consider – from, for example, the practice of American political parties, who for some reason hold their presidential nominating conventions only once every four years, to the Lower Huckleberry W.I., which has one every four weeks. I think we would be foolish to come to a rapid assessment, and it certainly cannot be achieved in a plenary session like this. My own recom-mendation is that we should resolve to break ourselves down into a number of sub-conferences, perhaps meeting monthly in a variety of reasonably congenial venues, to discuss the various options. Certainly I would be prepared to chair one or several of these sub-conferences myself. They then might report to a plenary session, perhaps meeting twice a year.

It must be evident that this will take much work and a good deal of time. Hence it seems to me likely that our members will recommend that, for the successful management of this difficult business, our own conferences will need to meet a good deal more frequently than they

have in the past. Indeed one solution to the problems resolved by conferences – maintaining continual *esprit de corps*, perpetual advancement of
the subject, the sustaining of a regular passage of resolutions to make
things better, and the like – could be the establishment of the principle
of the permanent or perpetual conference. But that is only one person's
opinion, and I put it to you all to discuss at your – as I see from the
programme – fairly plentiful leisure.

3.

Now I hope you will feel that all I have said so far proves one thing, and
proves it clearly, and that is that the conference is indeed an inescapable
if not self-perpetuating feature of modern life [wait for applause]. There
is no doubt the conference is here to stay, at least for a day or two. So
let us turn our minds away now from the question of whether
conferences should exist – they do, and they will, at least for the
foreseeable future – to the more challenging matter of how to distinguish among them. For the word 'conference' is a generic term describing many very different kinds of activity. And anyone who has been to
conferences in the past will have learned the hard way that it is always
wise to have some clear idea of just what kind of an affair one is, on these
occasions, getting into.

So, when we speak of conferences, we refer to many different kinds
of phenomena – the conference proper, the congress, the convention,
the course, the colloquium, and so on. It would take a whole conference
of its own to establish the differences among them, and I suggest we
hold that next year. But, briefly, a conference is what you hold when
you wish to give a particular group prestige; a congress is what you have
if you wish to make the prestige international; a convention is what you
have if you want to have a good time as well; a course is what you have
if you want the good time to go on for several weeks; and a colloquium
is if you want to have a good time lasting several weeks with a very
small and select number of people. There are other ways of making the
distinction, such as relative degrees of participation (at conferences the
participants confer; at a congress they dissent; at a convention they
listen; on a course they fall asleep; at a colloquium they do the same but

often in the same bed). To put it another way: a conference is an élite meeting on equal terms; a congress is a group of élites meeting on opposite terms; a convention is a mob meeting on equal terms; a course is an élite instructing a mob; and a colloquium is a group capable of considering all these phenomena.

Indeed so great is the plenitude, so wide the variety these days that it is no wonder that the modern conference-goer, however expert, is likely to feel confused. To see the scale of the problem we are dealing with, let us briefly consider next weekend, when some of you at least are likely to be free. The Jungian Psycho-Analytic Circle is meeting in Vienna. The Vienna Circle is meeting in Zurich. The Prague School is meeting in Budapest, and the Social Democrats have still not decided. The Feminist Dyslexics are meeting in Pirus, or possibly Paris, and the Anarchist Association is coming together or more probably falling apart in Amsterdam. Two rival schools of Joyceans are having conferences, one in Howth and the other in Trieste, and the World Association of Philosophers is flying to Mexico City to discuss whether they will then actually be there or not. The choices are plainly very difficult. But some advice can be given for the less initiated, though I doubt there are many of those here. Not all conferences are in English, though a good many are; and three days of papers given in Hungarian may not be sufficiently compensated for by a one-hour trip on the Danube. Rainfall varies between different parts of the world, and the sun is more probable in some places than others. Discussions of gastro-intestinal medicine can be upsetting to some, though not as upsetting as those practical problems that sometimes occur in the same area at conferences in certain countries.

How, then, does one choose which conference to go to? Some people choose by subject, thus neglecting a far more important question, the kind and the quality of the venue. Expert conference-goers know that conferences are held not only in many different kinds of place, but many different kinds of facility, and that they vary enormously from country to country. My friends, we are sometimes told it is our American cousins who have brought the organization of conferences to a fine art. All honour, or honor, to them for that. It is certainly true that in the United States no field of activity – whether commercial, political, recreational, or sexual – does not have a regular get-together. Convention hotels with admirable facilities exist everywhere for this purpose. Baton-twirlers and girls who burst nude from giant cakes have a regular income. The conference is in, and one knows exactly what to expect: a convention hotel at convention time in a convention town with convention rates.

And here all the best habits of good convention practice will be found. Lapel-badges are handed out promptly on arrival, so that everyone knows at once who he or she is, and can keep a record of the fact throughout the following events. Everyone gets at check-in a conference wallet with the programme, some useful addresses (the local massage parlour or the district chapter of Beautiful People Inc., the truly discreet escort agency, etc.), and a supply of rattles, streamers and paper hats inside. Meal tickets are issued for everything, including the free $100-dollar-a-plate medieval banquet with roast swan and saucy serving wench. The bedrooms are comfortable and all identical, readily explaining why so many people end up in the wrong one before the occasion is over. All this is admirable, but some people find it slightly mechanical. That is why specialized conference-goers often prefer conferences in Europe, where rather different practices prevail.

There are, for example, those who recommend conferences in Britain, where things are very different, though matters are definitely improving. Until lately British conferences were held as a matter of course in derelict nineteenth-century spa towns – classic watering places where little has been done to anything since Jane Austen ceased publication, save that for this special occasion the floral clock has been specially weeded, licensing hours extended to nine-thirty, and lights out put back to ten. The rooms in the Hydro prove usually to be subdivided wardrobes, while the toilet, should you ever happen to find it, is up two floors and at the further end of an unlit corridor. As for the label over the classic Victorian floral watercloset, called 'The Rocket', saying 'This toilet has been sanitized for your protection', this is a feckless gesture to modern hotelkeeping that should not be taken seriously.

But the important thing to remember is that the ideal conference venue is, by definition, never found close to one's own home, or indeed one's own country. Perhaps it is in Norway, but remember those large wooden hotels have a high fire-risk potential, the windows are kept open all the time, as in *The Magic Mountain*, and the ski-run to breakfast does not always suit the older delegates. Perhaps it is in Tunisia, where the belly-dancing adds something unusual to discussion of investment analysis, though the sheep's eyes are not always to everyone's taste. Perhaps it is in Switzerland, which is charmingly Alpine, but where there is an awkward word to look out for and distrust; it is *alkoholfrei*, which, alas, does not mean the drink is free. Many conferences these days are held in universities, to prevent them from sinking economically, and these are usually pleasant environments. But do learn to distinguish between, say, a conference at Ledderford Polytechnic and one at King's College, Cambridge. They are both described as desirable academic venues, but the ambiance is not, to be totally frank, quite the same. A discerning conference-goer is someone who does everything to attend the one but has pressing reasons for not being available to go to the other. And learning the art of selection is an absolute necessity for modern professional survival.

4.

Now, speaking of modern professional survival, I realize – if the clanking of bottles in the bar is any guide, and I usually find it a good one – that I am coming towards the end of my allotted time. I know you will all be burning to get onto the next item of the agenda [wait for applause], and indeed the lunch menu the chairman just handed to me, before he fell asleep, promises many treats in store, all of them with kiwi-fruit. I shall therefore turn, *very* briefly, to the final question you have asked me to address – the question of how to choose the best speakers for your conferences. To be frank, I think I have little to teach you in the matter, since you seem extraordinarily expert at it already, if your choice of myself is any guide. However, it is always useful to lay down a few guidelines, especially since in my experience this is the issue that always creates most anxiety amongst conference planners, especially the more naïve ones. Have we, they fuss for weeks, chosen the right *topic*, the burning issue of the year? Have we chosen the right *name*, someone everyone will think they recognize, even if they have never heard of him? If we ask this eminent Nobel Prize Winner, will he actually turn up – or will he, as with Stockholm, send his wife along to read a few chaotic notes? Will Professor X give of his best, as we all know that on a good day he can? Or will he, as at Aberystwyth last year, tank up to excess in the bar beforehand and throw his lecture away, tell us about his recent trip to India, and then refuse to answer questions? And I do admit that, while today you have been peculiarly fortunate, it is perfectly possible for these matters to go wrong.

I am now going to offer you a few words of sage advice which are not necessarily in my own best interest – I can assure you I have enjoyed myself greatly, or will be doing shortly, and hope to come again – but nonetheless bear the stamp of truth. For the fact of the matter is that – except perhaps on the present occasion – your choice of either topic or speaker makes almost no difference to the quality of a conference what-soever. The choice of listeners is much more important, as will become apparent at your final, round-up, what-shall-we-do-next-time meeting, when, of course, all the women present can be guaranteed to complain that far too few of their sex were invited, and all the men can be guaranteed to agree wholeheartedly with them. The quality and mix of the delegates, the texture and thickness of the printed programmes, the standard of the menus, the supply of towels to the rooms, the choice of the band on the last night, the selection of an ideal venue in an ideal season – these are what will ensure the success of your event. And if you should for some reason locate the event in a Welsh hall of residence run by a strict Baptist warden of grim temperance opinions, strong disciplinary inclinations and a low view of adultery, not even Abraham Lincoln on the platform, giving the Gettysburg Address, is going to save you from ignominy.

The real reason for having speakers is simply to make the programme seem credible – and to those who read it before and after, not those who are there at the time. I have never known a conference fail because the topic was wrong or the speaker inadequate, or just did not manage to arrive. After all, a speaker is usually, though happily not today, a brief and fleeting visitor – someone who drifts in suddenly from the airport or station, speaks to the gathering, possibly hangs around morosely overnight, and then is last seen in the street, waiting hopelessly for the airport taxi the conference secretary has forgotten to order. If he or she has been disappointing, this frequently *adds* to the success of the occasion. For this gives the participants the chance to display their own greater knowledge of the subject, their skill in exposing weak thinking, and it provides the group with a perfect scapegoat – an ideal thing to have at any conference.

Nonetheless this does not mean the speaker should automatically be treated badly, though this has been rule-of-thumb at some conferences I have been to. It is surely common courtesy to greet these people, provide them with a chairman so they do not need to introduce themselves, give them food of much the same quality as one is enjoying oneself, make sure they have shelter for the night, and incorporate them as well as possible into the pleasures of the occasion. I say this with feeling, having learned the art of conference speaking the hard way. My first exposure was addressing an assembled group of librarians on the future of the English novel, an occasion I still consider marred by the fact that I was immediately swathed from head to foot in toilet tissue in the party games that followed after. I also recall the arrangements at a conference on Existentialism in the north of England, where I was billed as the major speaker. In the event, I proved the only one, as the programme given to me on arrival made all too clear (Friday evening: conference assembles, tour of pubs; Saturday morning: boat trip, bar provided; Saturday afternoon: bus trip to Yorkshire moors, bring own bottle; Saturday evening: nightclub with Belly Dancing; Sunday morning, lecture: 'Being and Non-Being in the Early Short Fiction of Samuel Beckett', and so on). Grim as they were, I now regard these experiences as invaluable. After all, they did turn me into a Hardened Conference Speaker.

And, frankly, the Hardened Conference Speaker is the only kind to ask to these occasions. An HCS can speak on anything, and usually does. He may know little about your subject, but it is the ones who do, and take the conference at its face value, who usually ruin these events. An HCS always starts by telling the chairman he would rather not take questions afterwards, but meet everyone informally in the bar and get to know them better. This always creates a good impression. He then tells the audience they know far more about the subject than he does, which not only creates an even better impression but is frequently true too. But he is a virtuoso, gifted in the art of the bland leading the bland. He can also be counted on not to make your organizational errors apparent, as when the talk described by the conference organizer in an ill-written letter as on 'The Furniture of Chile' actually turns out to be on 'The Future of China'. An HCS is someone who can always adjust, as is apparent today – for, thanks to a garbled telephone call, I actually came prepared to talk not on conferences but contraceptives, another subject I know very little about, as my seven children will tell you.

There is one thing an HCS can be counted on to do. That is to finish just a little early, since he knows that it is in the bar and other parts of the hotel and the surrounding town and seaside that the conference does its real work. As I have explained to the chairman, and I am sure he will remember when he wakes, I am happy to entertain questions, or any other form of hospitality you would like to offer me, but in less formal circumstances than this. For I do hope to get to know you all a good deal better – especially now I have seen in the audience a young French lady I met just a week ago at a conference on, as it happens, International Affairs, and with whom I have some unfinished business on exactly that theme I hope to pursue further. So I shall be staying with you for a few more days, and you will have the chance to accost me with any queries, preferably when I am alone, though with luck I may not be. And so, Mr Chairman, may I conclude, without disturbing you, by saying what a pleasure it is, and will be, for me to come here. I thank you again for inviting me, hope I have left you with just enough, and not too much, to think about, and say that I, like all the rest of you, look forward to the prospect of a really exciting congress.

[Wait for applause, smile, depart from platform, collect fee.]

The Nympholept's Tale

Frenzy in the world of scholarship! Evidently the cuts to university budgets are at last taking serious hold, if today's postbag is any guide. It is quite clear that the editors and publishers of the scholarly journals and magazines, the symposia and Festschriften, are finding it hard to find serious academic contributions from the heavily depleted world of scholarship, and are turning in desperation to me. Today, then, *Critical Inquiry* asks me to contribute to their special issue on the subject of 'Gaps'. I do not think I shall bother; it seems much more fun to leave them with one to fill. The publishers of *Spaced Out: The International Journal of SF Studies* ask me to write a short guide to the restaurants of the moon. I know what this is; they have confused me, as people do, with my uncle Ray Bradbury, and I shall not reply, at least not by conventional means. A publisher invites me to contribute a critical essay, 'not more than 12,000 words in length', to a collection of essays on the Scots Lallans poet McMurdie. They need not worry about my going overlength, or indeed to any lengths at all. I have never heard of McMurdie until this minute, and I doubt if anyone else has either.

Then there is an invitation to contribute to a Festschrift on Alexander Pope, to be presented to him on the occasion of his 250th birthday. I do not think I shall bother with that either; I am tired of going to these geriatric literary parties. Why is it that I am always being asked to contribute to volumes on authors for whom I possess less than a total veneration, when there are so many – well, a few anyway – whom I admire within an inch of my life? There is V.N., for example, dear old Uncle Vlad; why does the invitation never come to write on him? Of course it will, sooner or later, probably in the lunchtime mail; and I know just who it will be from. Well, when it does, I shall have my reply all ready, and here it is:

Dear Charles Kinbote,

Up to the old tricks again, I see. Well, I am delighted to see that you have recovered from all the difficulties of the last Shadey enterprise, and are up to compiling another volume. But then you did promise you would assume other guises, turn up on other campuses, and continue to exist: and how right you were! Clearly the Guggenheim Foundation have been extremely if not inordinately generous with you, but then you always were a survivor, Charles. As for the project you now propose to me, I do have to confess that – despite all I know about you, and you have done very well for yourself, haven't you? – I am extremely interested. So, notwithstanding the totally absurd contract you suggest (oh, they were right about you, Charles), and the lien on my widow's property it apparently entails, I entirely agree it is time we all put together a *Festschrift* for the old master. What a pity he will not be there to receive it himself, though with him one cannot, of course, be entirely sure. And you are also right in supposing that I do have some very important scholarly information to divulge about V. In fact this stuff could entirely transform Nabokovian studies – one reason why, though I discovered this information some decades back, I have kept it more or less under my belt until now, never being one to rock the boat. Do make whatever use of it you like; after all, knowing you, Charles, you will anyway. The only thing I would ask is that, when you do, you at least give me the credit of one of your extremely notorious footnotes.

The tale I am about to divulge takes us – appropriately enough to its subject – back through memory and nostalgia to quite another time and a distant place, from which I have long been separated. You will pehaps recall, Charles, that when we last met, on the campus of Wordsmith College, two European exiles who had spent our scholarly maturity in the United States, I was about to pack my files and card indices and return to Britain. The purpose I had in mind was matrimony, which I committed shortly thereafter. In fact I recall sending you an invitation to the ceremony, but you did not reply. I was disappointed at the time, and only later did I realize that this must have been because you were in the very last stages of editing the Shade manuscript. Indeed when I check I see your introduction to *Pale Fire* is dated October 19, 1959 – and I was married exactly two days before, on October 17! What a strange place the world is, and how it all fits together!

Marriage, I have to confess, did not prove an easy business. My wife, rather than running a major industry like US Steel, as I had hoped, preferred to idle about the house, typing my manuscripts. As a result the footloose travelling scholar, constantly hopping the Atlantic, all my possessions in one suitcase, thesis in one hand, novel-in-progress in the other, was forced to find full-time scholarly employment. It was for this reason that I took a post in the extra-mural department of a certain northern university, since that seemed the right sort of place for an outsider and an exile to be. It was pleasant enough for a while, writing by day and teaching by night. But the prospect of a lifetime of travelling nightly over blasted moors and treacherous bogs carrying the message of D. H. Lawrence to small groups huddled together in tiny public libraries did, I confess, begin to pall. It was time to do something desperate, to go – as we say in the trade – 'inside'.

I therefore began looking for a permanent post in an English Department, where my taste for scholarship and sherry could be better satisfied, and I was fortunate to be offered a lectureship in English at Birmingham University, a distinguished foundation always very tolerant of writers, which, as you know, not all universities are. Birmingham was a redbrick or provincial university in the British Midlands, notable for the fact that in the middle of its campus is a vast phallic campanile modelled on that at Siena, though several times larger. I understand it was presented by the university's donor in celebration of his honeymoon, and on the evidence it must have been a prodigious event. Alas, once off campus, the comparison with Siena ceased. Birmingham then was a great industrial city still humming with manufacture, now mostly gone, and the entire district surrounding the university banged and clattered to the endless noise of steel pressing, wire rolling, chocolate making, and the stentorian shouts of union officials as they called the automobile workers out on strike.

Frankly, Charles, I am not a metropolitan spirit. My spiritual home-
land was and is the pastoral landscape of the East Riding of Yorkshire,
which no longer officially exists, of course – a delightful and peaceful
area of pleasant and rolling wolds, rich grain harvests, and various of the
minor peerage. I did not – but such is the fate of us exiles, Charles –
feel entirely at home in Birmingham. Nonetheless I considered it life,
something that, if one was a novelist, one was supposed to know a little
about, and go out into now and again. Or so it had been in the Fifties,
when novels were supposed to be works of grainy realism, all set in
suburban Leicester or working-class Cardiff. Happily, though, this was
all changing – and largely thanks to Uncle Vlad himself, one reason
why he became my literary hero at the time. As you will recall, he said
in his note to *Lolita* that reality was a word that meant nothing except
in quotes. In Birmingham, where the best place for reality was most
certainly in quotes, I was ready to agree.

But, in any case, the entire climate of fiction was changing, and V.
had a great deal to do with it. *Lolita*, you will recall, had had to come
out in 1955 from a less than wholesome Parisian publisher, largely
because the preoccupation of his hero, Humbert Humbert, with pubes-
cent girls – 'nymphets', as he called them – was considered unhealthy
by the publishing scene of the day. As you know, we scholars saw the
book quite differently, as a symbolic expression of our own mythic
experience of migration from a so-called experienced Europe to a so-
called innocent America, and so of the great period love affair with the
United States. Be that as it may – there is always room for dispute in
the realm of criticism, as you from violent experience know all too well
– the book did achieve general circulation by the end of the 1950s,
thanks in part, I fancy, to the improved reputation your work on the
Pale Fire manuscript gave to V.'s achievement. Thus *Lolita* not only
caused universal upheaval in the law courts but in the form of the novel,
making every text into a self-conscious fiction, and encouraging us all
to see the form as an art of language and pure invention which had little
to do with life at all. Like Humbert, I too, trapped in brassy Birmingham, was looking for a world of words, of the elusive imagination, the
symbolic and the unattainable, and this no doubt is why V.'s work
came to matter so much to me.

203

At any rate, at the times when I was not attending to the occasional thought-processes of my students, I took to trying to defeat the heavy reality of the world in different ways. Overwhelmed by the banging of the needle factories, and the sight of eviscerated car-bodies constantly passing by on trucks, I made it my Nabokovian habit to wander the Birmingham backstreets, looking for what I was not quite sure. I haunted curio shops and second-hand bookstores, and one of my favourite places of resort was a great storehouse of a place with the happy name of the Treasure Trove, which happened to lie in suburban Birmingham within easy reach of the university. It was a huddle of rooms and sheds in no perceptible order, and it was kept by a man named Vincent, a snapper-up of unconsidered trifles who had chosen to celebrate his own vocation in verse in his shop window. 'Vincent is a man/ Who goes hunting when he can/He chases goods and catches them/And locks them in his van', this extraordinary verse read. Well, Charles, I need hardly point out to you the impact that made on a neophyte Nabokovian, filled as it so obviously was with strange echoes of the master. It would take a real scholar of the matter like yourself to unravel all the allusions properly – but, for instance, the resemblance between the word 'van' and the name of the hero of *Ada; Or, Ardour*, which of course Nabokov would not publish until 1969, very much later, was so blatant as not to be missed.

You can imagine how all this stirred the scholar in me, and how the place strangely raised the highest expectations in the mind of a young writer who shared with the great butterfly-hunter himself a lasting fancy for the ever-evanescent. Naturally I started spending a good deal of time there, rambling through the dusty goodies. In his travels, Vincent had snapped up a good deal of the stuff of the older Birmingham, all now being demolished as the old Georgian and Victorian mansions gave way to the high-rise megalomania of a Bauhausian city council. His sheds were packed with things that but rarely reached the market – not just the Staffordshire pottery dogs and the gilt-framed sub-Piranesi prints that are the natural stock-in-trade of any passing curio dealer, but true rarities: complete church fonts and rood screens, a stuffed lion and two stuffed bears, one of them captured in rigor mortis while wearing a pair of boxing gloves (it was on offer for twenty-five pounds, and is one of those bargains of a lifetime one always regrets having missed), and so on. There were human skeletons in poor states of repair, a couple of large and very naked stone Joves, a set of military uniforms from the Crimean War, a weighing machine that played 'Nearer My God to Thee', and in general a wealth of exotic goodies that would have made the perfect setting for a novel by Iris Murdoch. Or, even more to the point, by dear old V. himself.

Of course all this was wonderland. But it was natural, Charles, that as a literary scholar with a taste for curiosities, I should spend most of my time in the large and chaotic booksheds at the rear of the establishment, where one could pick up, for sixpence apiece or a shilling for three, an extraordinary array of literary oddities and nothingnesses. I spent much time there, and my house is to this day stacked with the various trophies of this short but rewarding hunting season. To take just a couple of examples, I am the proud possessor of the Pitman Shorthand Edition of *Pickwick Papers*, and a book called *The Top Drawer: Random Reminiscences by One Who Was Born in It*, the reminiscences not of a furniture shop foundling but of a man every inch an aristocrat, which begins pleasingly on the following note: 'From the very beginning of my life I was accustomed to consort with the great and to avoid as far as possible those unfortunate, and usually offensive, persons who constitute the great mass of humanity.'

Every day, then, I used to make my way to the sixpenny shed and examine the fat, damp, ancient volumes that stood on old shelves and in sagging crates, and one day I came on a thick and oldish novel in a deep maroon binding the title of which won my attention. The book was by J. L. Carter, author of *Peggy the Aeronaut* and *The Pilgrimage of Delilah*. Charles, you will hardly believe this – but the title of the book was *Nymphet*! So you will imagine my excitement as I picked up the fat, decidedly middlebrow volume and turned it over. The very word had me in confusion; I had been under the impression that it had been invented by our master himself. Naturally I rushed to the poetic Vincent, tossed him a coin without showing him the title on the spine, and fled out into the street, fearful that some other wandering Nabokovian exile would come along and outbid me. The heady glow of scholarly excitement sent me into a daze, and I looked up after a while to discover I had somehow walked many streets out of my way and become totally lost in the Birmingham jungle.

Fortunately, turning a corner, I was able to see, rising high over the houses and factories, the great phallic campanile of the university; and, recalled to my senses and coming scholarly obligations, I hurried homeward towards it. In the corridor outside my room a few students had been waiting, they said for some time. But I told them I could not be disturbed for a day or two, poured myself a glass of sherry from the decanter I always kept there in case of scholarly crises, and began to work. Occasionally some student or colleague would thrust a head in at the door, but my muttered curses and the sight of my dedicated scholarly visage would send him or her away without a word. Was it truly possible that I had acquired, and was now about to read, the original or precursory version of *Lolita*? Filled with the glow of discovery, I set off in pursuit of nympholepsy.

Charles, it was clear at once that in the Treasure Trove I had troven a treasure. Opening the flyleaf, I discovered that Mr Carter's book had been published in London by the firm of Sampson Low, Marston and Co. Ltd. The book itself was undated, but the firm itself no longer existed in that form. Indeed by the whole look of the thing *Nymphet* had probably come out just after the First World War. (In fact my surmise was out by a few years; later scholarly checking in the British Museum dated it as early as 1915, *before* the Russian Revolution!) Evidently the book predated our master's by more than half a generation! Inspecting further, I discovered it had the appearance of a light romance, and the end-papers were filled with advertisements for books of a similar kind – Jeffery Farnol's *The Chronicles of an Imp*, a tale which proved to bear some relation to the present one, and Mary Taylor Thornton's *When Pan Pipes*, of which it was said: 'In these days when the sex question is so frequently dealt with and enlarged upon in the realms of fiction, it is absolutely refreshing to find a book in which not one questionable incident or word is allowed to appear.'

This, I admit to you, all seemed a little discouraging. And so was the description of the book I was holding that appeared, one might think a little redundantly, amid these same end-papers to the volume. '*Nymphet*', they said, 'is a pretty comedy of sentiment, fresh and invigorating as the sea-breeze that blows over Littleham, the quiet watering place where the scene of the idyll is laid.' On the other hand, there was a faint whiff of promise about it, since nymphet stories, from Poe's *Annabel Lee* to V.'s own, have traditionally been set in part in a 'kingdom by the sea', though I suppose that is not surprising, since nymphs and water have always had much to do with each other. But any hopes raised seemed to be dashed by what followed. 'There are no "problems" in this book', it declared. 'It is a simple love-story, characterised by warm humanity and distinguished by an under-current of gentle humour.' This was intensely disappointing, but, on the other hand, it still failed to explain how the nymphet came into it.

I looked down the page a little further, and found a decidedly anodyne answer:

The gallery of portraits of children who act as goddesses from cars in sentimental comedy is already pretty full, but Nymphet is a welcome addition to it. Few children have been portrayed in fiction who are so little artificial and so true to ordinary life as this delightful little maid of eleven, with her pluck, her quick intuition, her devotion to her sister, and her loyalty to her friend. The author has achieved something of a triumph in the creation of Winnie Filder, the 'Nymphet' of this pretty comedy.

You will not be surprised, then, that my first reaction was one of disappointment. The whole thing seemed to call up a long-gone, simple world of middlebrow books that were designed for reading on long train journeys or in deckchairs on summer beaches. Indeed it was just that sort of summer holiday that the whole book was evidently about. How could it possibly have anything to do with the intricate fictionality of the master?

A lesser scholar might have given up at this point. But, as you know very well, Charles, your true bibliolept is someone who senses the unusual within the usual. And there were just a few teasing features about the tale. For example, I did not fail to note that the plucky,

delightful little maid of eleven fell very neatly inside 'the boundaries –
the mirrory beaches and rosy rocks' of Humbert's own definition of the
nymphet – between, that is, the ages of nine and fourteen. The hero,
on the other hand, was strikingly older, indeed thirty-five. What is
more, he was, interestingly enough, a writer, and one with a quiverful
of credits to his name. He was a novelist who had created a round dozen
romances, amongst them *The Celibate* and *A Man of Earth*, and 'a
successful dramatist with the tender humour, great physical strength,
the vast capacity for love and kindness' that entirely qualified him to
write whatever it was he did happen to write, and do whatever it was
he had to do.

Naturally, Charles, I knew at once what *I* had to do, and I dashed for
the shelf of dictionaries to check on the interesting word 'nymphet'. I
had carelessly assumed the word to be of recent coinage, and possibly an
invention of V. himself. The *Oxford English Dictionary*, Vol. VII, N to
POY, quickly disabused me of my error:

Nymphet (ni'mfet). [f. NYMPH + -ET] A young or little nymph.
1612 DRAYTON *Poly-olb.* xi. Argt. Of the Nymphets sporting there
In Wyrrall and in Delamere. 1616 DRUMM. OF HAWTH. *Poems* 2
Where names shall now make ring The echoes? of whom shall the
nymphets sing? 1855 SINGLETON *Virgil* I. 60. Who could the
nymphets sing?

It was a Renaissance word, and apparently a thoroughly respectable one
too, since Drayton's nymphs who haunted the bosky groves of Cheshire
or wherever seemed, when I glanced at *Poly-Olbion*, to be perfectly decent
girls. But this was not the only view among nymphologists, as I was soon
to discover. Indeed, simply by looking in the adjacent columns, I was
reminded that, despite the eagerness of seventeenth- and eighteenth-
century poets to find dryads in stones and nymphs and nymphets in
running brooks, they could not always be guaranteed to be safe company.

Indeed there was the state of 'nympholepsy', the condition which, of
course, Humbert Humbert considers himself to be in, which is 'a state

of rapture supposed to be inspired in men by nymphs; hence, an ecstasy or frenzy of emotion, esp. that inspired by something unattainable.' After all, nymphs are not the likes of us, but something either sub-divine or demonic, and relationships across these generic lines are, as Humbert keeps telling us, always risky. This term reminded me of another, 'nymphomania', which, of course, does not mean a mania for nymphs. In fact the plain-speaking Collins dictionary defines it as 'a neurotic condition in women in which the symptoms are a compulsion to have sexual intercourse with as many men as possible and an inability to have lasting relationships with them. Compare *satyriasis.*' I did, of course.

But by now I was in an ecstasy or frenzy of emotion of my own, and I began turning the pages of all the works of reference, trying to find out the nature of the nympholeptical contract, and the risks involved. I looked in the American *Webster's Dictionary*, which had another supplementary meaning to 'nymphet': 'a sexually precocious girl, a loose young woman'. I now felt myself in a state of considerable confusion. Had this been put in before or after the publication of *Lolita*, and did it show a popular definition or a change V. had brought to the language? If so, the definition was a little wide of the mark; after all, Lolita's interest for Humbert is not that she is loose, but putatively below the age of sexual awareness and desire, and therefore taboo. In fact for Humbert it is her 'experience' that proves a great disappointment. More significantly, remembering that V. and Humbert were both dedicated butterfly men, it seemed wise to check on other associations: *nymph* and a variety of words from this root are important physical terms in the development of insects and butterflies. This led onwards to even more difficult issues, for I found myself reminded that the term 'nympha' has an anatomical meaning: 'one of the *labia minora.*' I was clearly getting into delicate matters in many a sense.

It therefore seemed important, before I pursued my own fleeting catch any further, to check once more the actual definitions given by Humbert, or V. himself, in the pages of *Lolita*. You will recall that Humbert offers us a very careful as well as lyrical portrait of his own condition or state of desire:

Now I wish to introduce the following idea. Between the age limits of nine and fourteen there occur maidens who, to certain bewitched travellers, twice or many times older than they, reveal their true nature which is not human, but nymphic (that is, demoniac); and these chosen creatures I propose to designate as 'nymphets'.

Humbert is indeed bewitched, and only because of this can he recognize the non-human or nymphic quality in the butterflies he chases. Not all girl-children are potential nymphets, or 'we who are in the know, we lone voyagers, we nympholepts, would have long gone insane'. It requires a special passion to know one, but the girl herself is indeed unaware of her state, and her attraction:

You have to be an artist and a madman, a creature of infinite melancholy, with a bubble of hot poison in your loins and a super-voluptuous flame permanently aglow in your subtle spine . . ., in order to discern at once, by ineffable signs – the slightly feline outline of a cheekbone, the slenderness of a downy limb, and other indices which despair and shame and tears of tenderness forbid me to tabulate – the little deadly demon among the wholesome children; *she* stands unrecognized by them and unconscious herself of her fantastic power.

This then was the state of the nympholept.

It was only now, with my scholarly quiver packed with these useful arrows, that I felt it time to address myself to reading the pages of Mr Carter's 'Comedy of Sentiments for Ever-Serious People'. And a curiously light read it proved, compared with the *Ulysseses* and *Magic Mountains* you and I generally spend our free time devouring. In fact little more than an hour after starting, I was already jumping the final fence. No, the book was not deep, and the plot, such as it was, could be easily summarized. Claude Kempton, the well-known light novelist and dramatist, is caught as we open in a state of melancholy boredom, and is even found recalling his days as an indigent newspaper reporter

210

with an unhealthy nostalgia. His flagging spirits need restoring, and what better for that than a holiday in the seaside resort of Littleham? Seated in the train compartment he reads, with gloomy sneers, an article on love at first sight, always a fatal thing to do in the first chapter of a romantic novel. It hardly needs saying that he has only to look up to encounter 'another pair of eyes – large, clear, hazel eyes, whose long lashes curled back like the petals of some dusky brown flower', which prove to be attached to a girl of about twenty-five who has 'an intangible, spiritual force that attracted him'. In a rapid mood-change, Kempton now perceives ahead of him 'a goodly holiday'. Alas, as he descends from the train he is caught up in some lowlife comedy with various menials, and the eyes disappear into the social forest of Littleham along with 'a pair of twinkling black silk ankles'.

However, by nightfall Kempton has tracked the girl, eyes, ankles and all, down to her hotel and is found mooning passionately outside ('not for an instant did he doubt that they were affinities, soul mates, possibly even lovers in a previous existence'). Next day he is up and about early in order to spy on his beloved in her bathing dress through the telescopes conveniently provided for this purpose on the promenade ('Littleham was a progressive little place, for it not only permitted, but encouraged, mixed bathing'). Then, by some rock-pool, he makes the acquaintance of a girl of eleven who bears a striking resemblance to the owner of the eyes and ankles, and so greatly interests him. And it is now our title comes into play, for he decides to call her 'Nymphet':

'Nymphet?' she said, puckering her brows, 'Why do you call me that? What does it mean?'
'A young nymph,' he said.
'A nymph's a sort of fairy?' she queried. 'Isn't it?' Kempton nodded gravely.
'A very beautiful fairy,' he said . . .

Now of course, Charles, as definitions go, this comes nowhere near the *OED* class, never mind V.'s. But it was certainly enough to keep the true bibliolept reading on with a sense of increasing excitement. It proved well deserved. For at this point a strange confusion now arises: for some reason Kempton concludes that this must be his loved one's daughter. It is hard to see why, since she is eleven and he has estimated his affinity's age at twenty-five. However, Kempton now begins to strike us as a little adrift in matters of sex, while being decidedly interested in the matter. Of course it is possible that he possesses that lack of mathematical ability all too common in authors, who have other skills to offer; it is also possible that he is strangely preoccupied with the ambiguous nature of pubescence. At any rate, he now consoles himself by befriending the tot, although 'in his heart of hearts Kempton knew that he ought to leave Littleham. If only for his own peace of mind, he ought not to see his affinity again. She was Mrs. T. J. Filder. And he was a healthy-minded Englishman.'

Feeling that Kempton's healthy-mindedness was to some degree becoming disputable, I poured myself another sherry at this point and then returned avidly to my reading – to find at once that Kempton, for all his proudly expressed Britannic virtue, is actually unable to resist peering at Mrs Filder through beach-hut doors and following her conspicuously about in the streets, 'for all the world like a tripper trying to "pick up" a flapper!', as he tells himself. But what is even more striking is that he now pursues his beloved by offering more and more affection to Nymphet, whose sublunary name proves to be Winnie Filder, thus seeming to follow the reverse strategy to Humbert Humbert's, who concealed his interest in the nymphet by pursuing her mother. It is clear that by the standards of 1915 this earned him no suspicion at all, despite the fact that the ill-assorted twosome are soon indulging in some very heavy mixed bathing together ('After many efforts he had managed to button that skimpy costume at the shoulder and now he was shyly reconnoitring through the crack of the door. There were such crowds of people – and ladies, too! How things had changed! Well, it was no use being squeamish. So, with a fine recklessness he threw open the door and stepped out').

As is the way with romantic comedy, the early confusions are resolved, and the owner of the hazel eyes indeed proves not to be Nymphet's mother, but her unmarried sister Ruth. Alas, a dance at the

Beach Hotel, where a new trot called the Boston is essayed, brings the lovers into contact only to tear them apart again, for fresh obstacles appear. Not only has an insistent step-mother forced Ruth's engagement to a Captain Branel, but Kempton himself finds he is being hotly pursued by Evelyn Joy, a London actress, a 'tiny five-foot-nothing of femininity' who is 'not called the "elfish, elusive Evelyn" for naught'. She has discerned merit in Kempton's play ('I opened it, quite idly, at the place where Malcolm comes in and finds Janet writing to Geoffrey'), procured its performance, and now, 'a mercurial little creature who changed her lovers as she did her hats', has come to the seaside to claim her reward, and there is no getting free of her.

Finally she approaches Kempton in the sea in the most daring of rigs ('those elaborate sandals, the diaphanous black silk stockings, and the saucy bathing costume of shaded pink'), gets toppled by a wave, and 'swarms up his person until she had her arms tightly round his neck'. By good fortune this attracts the attention of the watching Captain Branel, and the basic plot is as good as over. We still have to enjoy a chase through London that drives Kempton to seek shelter in the flat of a woman xylophone player who holds 'the ladies' endurance record', but, thanks to the matchmaking efforts of Nymphet, who has more than taken to Kempton, the nuptials clearly prefigured in the railway carriage coming down are duly achieved. Thus the two of them, or to be more accurate the three of them, set off into the end-papers and the rather complicated business of living happily if triangularly ever after.

Nymphet indeed proved to be a romantic idyll after all. But if there is one thing we modern critics know, Charles, it is that nothing in literature is ever quite what it seems, or our services would scarcely be needed at all. I had sensed from the start that this story, bonhomous as it appeared, was not lacking in strange overtones, and I realized how right I had been. What was clear was that the fly in the ointment, the nymphet in the woodpile, was Nymphet herself. For at every stage in the story she attracts a good deal more attention, especially from Kempton, than her matchmaking role entirely warrants. For one thing, he is constantly attending to 'slim brown legs', 'slim little arms', 'deep, serious, laughing eyes', 'tender mouth' and 'provocative laugh'. And 'fierce kisses' between them are regularly exchanged, not least when he

213

goes up to the hotel room with Ruth to kiss Nymphet goodnight. 'Oh, you dear big thing!' Nymphet cries, hands stretched out to him. 'You'll have to come and do this every night now.' Not only does she then crush 'his great hands to her slim bosom', but several pages of sweet and sickly nothings are then exchanged, and thereafter they continue through the book on a regular basis.

What is more, even in permissive Littleham – a place geographically rather handy for the summer homes of the Bloomsbury Group, and one they had, in my view, often visited to good or rather bad effect – this does not pass entirely without comment. 'Now, if Winnie were ten years older, I should scent a romance!' cries Winnie's and Ruth's stepmother – whose suspicions might have been even the greater had she troubled to lift down a handy copy of the works of Dr Froit, or even just the *Oxford English Dictionary*, should Littleham have boasted the facility, from the bookshelves. And if Nymphet's enthusiasm for Kempton is frank, it can hardly be called one-sided. In fact for most of the book Kempton is a good deal more delighted with Nymphet than he is with her older sister Ruth, whom, by the standards of literary wooing, he pursues in a strangely desultory fashion, once the fun of spying her ankles through telescopes is over and done with.

But why not, when things are so much more satisfying with Nymphet? 'Why was not Ruth like Nymphet – so soft and gentle and unsophisticated?' we find him complaining from time to time. Given his views it is perhaps not surprising that we find Nymphet and Kempton quite frequently discussing the prospect of matrimony, and generally agreeing that nuptials of that kind would be a decided improvement on marriage with Ruth. As Kempton reflects of Nymphet: 'The very thought of her was refreshing, soothing. What a sweet, womanly way she had! And such gentle, refreshing eyes!' On the other hand, there is the awkward age difference, one of the classic problems in the field. However, there is one thing to be said for marriage to Ruth: it does enable him to remain close to dear old Nymphet.

Thus the fact of the matter is that Winnie not only shows a good many of the tempting and erotic qualities our dear V. associates with the nymphet, but that Kempton is decidedly susceptible. Nymphet is described, in both the classical and the Nabokovian fashion, as a kind of demonic sea-creature, and this is what distinguishes her from all the other children on the beach. Kempton therefore spends much of his time in the sea with her, splashing her with water a good deal and enjoying himself rather more than might be expected. In one water-splashing romp, for instance, the fun goes on 'until at last her simple costume of stockinette clung closely to her': ' "Oh, please!" she cried in surrender. "You've won." '

In short, Winnie seems inclined to be a case of the classic Nabokovian nymphet, and Kempton equally seems to be an ideal example of the Nabokovian nympholept. Thus V.'s Humbert, you will recall, Charles, has the classic fantasy, found in Poe, of sailing off alone with his nymphet to another country in which the old, troubling rules no longer apply. 'A shipwreck. An atoll. Alone with a drowned passenger's shivering child. Darling, this is only a game!' If we cast our eyes onto a chapter called 'In Which Kempton and Nymphet Are Very Happy', our twosome play in the sea with a toy boat, and the inevitable happens. Kempton speaks:

'If only that boat were big enough, or we were small enough, I would make you sail away with me, little Nymphet, away over the edge of the water there, away to a country where there would be no one but you and me.' Nymphet had been busy sailing her boat, but she turned to him with her palms ecstatically pressed together.
'Oh, it would be lovely! No lessons! And we could just live on bananas. I love them ever so much better than meat and things.'
'And we could call our island "Paradise",' he said.

There we have it, surely as clear a case of classic nympholepsy as one could hope to find at a respectable seaside resort in a fairly innocent age. And there, m'lud, I rest my case.

Now clearly there is not a competent modern critic with an eye to his, or more likely these days her, standing in the Deconstructive profession (how *are* you on Derrida, by the way, Charles?) who would take any of Mr Carter's so-called problem-free comedy at its face value. No literature is problem-free these days, or certainly not after the critics have been near it, and there is not one of us who could not demythologize and decon-struct the 'real' point of the story. As these lads and lasses would at once point out, Kempton's real interest is quite clearly with Nymphet, but in the light of contemporary reader response and the dominant bourgeois ideological superstructure it is necessary for him, and more importantly his author, to transfer this to the more adult – though interestingly also the more innocent – Ruth. This not only supports the dominant hegemonic paradigm but also brings a clear narrative and emotional reward. In short, by marrying the older sister, who closely resembles the younger one, Kempton is not only able to acquire a surrogate but adult Nymphet, but improve his access to the actual younger one!

Charles, we have seen this strategy before, by which I mean after. Remember, it is precisely the one V. endows on Humbert in *Lolita*. He marries Mrs Haze, his beloved Lo's mother, in order that she can be both her surrogate and his means of access. In the very first photographs Mrs Haze shows him of her youthful self, he is able to read 'a dim first version of Lolita's outline'. 'I kept telling myself, as I wielded my brand-new, large-as-life wife, that biologically this was the nearest I could get to Lolita', he reflects, though this of course does not stop him from trying to get a good deal nearer still. Admittedly no such con-scious cunning is depicted in Kempton's mind, or even directly hinted at by Mr Carter. But then his business is, after all, problem-free comedy, the year is still 1915, and there is a good half-century of de-mythologization and Dr Froit still to come afterwards, complicating life, literature and for that matter sex for one and all of us. But I do think that we can say that Mr Carter's book is the innocent man's *Lolita* – just as V.'s book is the guilty man's *Nymphet*!

Now naturally I am not suggesting, particularly to a scholar as wise as yourself in these matters, that Carter's novel is the one and only work of fiction to prefigure *Lolita*. Indeed V. wrote one himself, *The Enchanter*, in the years just before the war: 'the first little throb of *Lolita*', he said, and the 'proto-nymphet', says his translator, his son Dmitri. In any case, as only our great master could, V. packed his own book with an intricate web of allusions to various previous treatments so elaborate that it would take a scholar as precise as yourself, Charles,

216

to unlock all the connections. Other scholars have made further comparisons, like our good colleague Mr Leon Edel, who draws our attention to the young Henry James's first endeavour, *Watch and Ward* – a novel which deals, as you know, with a young man who adopts a young girl in order that she can become his wife when she grows up, a story that doubtless in turn has its own considerable debt to Poe, as of course our master did too. Edel, in his preface to James's novel, proffers some very appropriate comments which might refer as well to *Nymphet*, describing the book as having 'a persistent erotic imagery and innocent erotic statement which seems to have been set down with bland unconsciousness on the author's part'. He then directly makes the comparison with *Lolita*, observing that the difference between the two novels is that what James seems to write in innocence Nabokov later explores in 'full awareness of its theme'. James himself was, as we know from *What Maisie Knew*, himself to grow a little wiser as the years rolled by. I fear I have no evidence that the same happened to Mr Carter, but then that hardly upsets the argument.

No, my point about *Nymphet* is, of course, that we can discern in it what V. himself calls, if in a rather different context, 'a dim first version of *Lolita's* outline'. Now evidently, Charles, this raises a very important question. Good scholars that we are, we must therefore wonder whether at some point in his exiled wanderings V. actually *read* Carter's problem-free comedy. Is it just possible that – perhaps when visiting some seaside resort of progressive disposition, as he sat there, possibly watching the bathers through his sunglasses – the great butterfly hunter and curio collector himself actually took down off some shelf of holiday reading Mr Carter's 'comedy of sentiments for ever-serious people'? Is it possible that he read it with tingling spine, and felt some strange electricity pass between its fat pages and his own hungry if ever-elusive muse? There is also another question to consider. Who is Mr J. L. Carter? Could it be that, even as early as 1915, the already cosmopolitan V. was summering in small British resorts writing pseudonymous fiction – and that the 'proto-nymphet' of *The Enchanter* was not the first venture of the kind?

Of course these could well be, as we scholars say, the sorts of question to which we shall never definitely know the answer. If you want my own view, I am inclined to doubt both surmises, though solely on the grounds that when V. was at the seaside of a summer he probably, my instincts tell me, found far more interesting things to do. But these are fascinating questions, and decidedly worth further study. Indeed, Charles, there could well be another year's Guggenheim in it all, wouldn't you say? Naturally you might then come up with negative evidence, but of course that itself would by no means be the end of the matter. For, so advanced and sophisticated has our critical and scholarly profession become – and it is no doubt in part thanks to V.'s own influence that it has done so – that we no longer need such proofs to be able to establish a significant connection between the two books.

We do, after all, have the happy concept of 'intertextuality'. And intertextuality – as you well know, Charles, if you keep up with these things, and I have no doubt you do – proves that all texts are related to all other texts. Indeed not only does it demonstrate the universality of that pattern of allusion, quotation, cross-reference, parody and parallelism which has always kept us scholars in business and in research grants; it also shows philosophically that authors do not write writing at all, but that writing writes authors. So cunning are the ways of intertextuality that we need no evidence to show that V. did actually open the pages of Carter's book, let alone wrote it in the first place, in order to prove that he was influenced by it. Many a book has been a proven influence on a later author without his ever having taken the trouble actually to read it.

Thus the whole question could well remain an elusive and fascinating surmise. In fact I should not be sorry if it did. After all, what V. taught us all – writers and scholars, butterfly hunters and nympholepts, critics and curio dealers, all those of us who like Vincent (and I must say that, now I think of it, that name calls up some Nabokovian source or other) go hunting where we can – is that the important thing is always be ready, net in hand, super-voluptuous flame in your subtle spine, to go chasing what is elusive and obscurely unobtainable. On the other hand, you are the dogged scholar, Charles, and you have trodden paths like this one before. If you should manage to track it all down, do please let me know. After all, there might be a book in it, for one or the other of us, whoever is the smarter.

Yours colleagually,

218